Medical Law in Spain

Medical Law in Spain

Second Edition

Asier Urruela-Mora
Carlos María Romeo-Casabona†
Iñigo de Miguel-Beriain
Emilio José Armaza-Armaza
Sergio Romeo-Malanda
Arantza Libano-Beristain

This book was originally published as a monograph in the International Encyclopaedia of Laws/Medical Law.

Founding Editor: Roger Blanpain
General Editor: Frank Hendrickx
Volume Editor: Herman Nys; Associate Editor: Tom Goffin

Wolters Kluwer

Published by:
Kluwer Law International B.V.
PO Box 316
2400 AH Alphen aan den Rijn
The Netherlands
E-mail: lrs-sales@wolterskluwer.com
Website: www.wolterskluwer.com/en/solutions/kluwerlawinternational

Sold and distributed by:
Wolters Kluwer Legal & Regulatory U.S.
920 Links Avenue
Landisville, PA 17538
United States of America
E-mail: customer.service@wolterskluwer.com

ISBN 978-94-035-4799-2

e-Book: ISBN 978-94-035-4809-8
web-PDF: ISBN 978-94-035-4819-7

This title is available on www.kluwerlawonline.com

The Authors

Asier Urruela-Mora (Bilbao, Spain) graduated in Law and Economics from the University of Deusto (1997), Doctor in Law from the University of the Basque Country (2002, Extraordinary Doctoral Award), Doctor in Medicine from the University of Saragossa (2014) and Expert in Criminology by the National University of Distance Education-UNED (2005).

Former Associate Lecturer of Criminal Law at the University of the Basque Country (2002–2006) and Professor-Tutor of Criminal Law and Criminology of the Associate Centre of the National University of Distance Education-UNED in Bergara (Gipuzkoa). From 2004 to 2006, he was Coordinator of Publications and Research in the Inter-University Chair, BBVA Foundation – Provincial Government of Biscay, in Law and the Human Genome, University of Deusto – University of the Basque Country. Since 2006, he has been Professor of Criminal Law at the University of Saragossa (first as Associate Professor and nowadays as Full Professor). Honorary Professor of the Catholic University of San Agustín de Arequipa (Perú) and of the University José Carlos Mariategui de Moquegua (Perú).

To broaden his education and research, he has carried out several research stays abroad at the Universities of Munich, Dresden, Lüneburg, Münster, Fribourg (all in Germany), Toulouse (France), Coimbra (Portugal), as well as training stays in Salzburg (Austria), having obtained several grants awarded by national and international institutions.

He has participated as a speaker in several national and international Conferences, Workshops and Seminars in Spain, Europe, Africa and Latin America. He has also authored numerous scientific articles and monographs in the fields of Criminal Law, Bioethics and Biolaw.

He is currently Director of the collection of monographs 'Estudios de Derecho Penal y Criminología' by Comares Publishers (Spain) and Independent Expert to the Committees of the Parties of the Council of Europe Convention on the counterfeiting of medical products and similar crimes involving threats to public health (MEDICRIME Convention) and of the Council of Europe Convention against Trafficking in Human Organs.

The Authors

Sergio Romeo-Malanda is Associate Professor of Criminal Law at the Faculty of Legal Sciences, University of Las Palmas de Gran Canaria (Spain). He also teaches biolaw courses at the Faculty of Health Sciences and coordinates the Master's Degree in Bioethics and Biolaw. A former Postdoctoral Research Fellow at the Centre for Law and Genetics (UTAS Faculty of Law, 2006–2008), he currently holds an adjunct associate-professorial appointment with the UTAS Faculty of Law and the Centre for Law and Genetics. He graduated with a Law degree in 1999 from the University of Deusto (Bilbao, Spain), where he also completed a PhD in 2005, focusing on *Genetic Interventions on Human Beings and Criminal Law*. Since then, he has advanced his career at the University of Tasmania (2006–2008) and the University of Las Palmas de Gran Canaria (2008–present). His research has focused on two main areas: criminal law and biomedical/biotechnological law. He has authored numerous scientific articles in these fields. This dual focus has led to a significant body of work exploring the intersection between these disciplines, particularly in areas such as genetics and criminal law, and biomedicine and criminal law. Topics include genetic criminality, DNA evidence in criminal proceedings, genetic inheritance and criminal culpability, medical criminal liability, the crime of abortion, euthanasia, and more. Additionally, his work addresses other critical legal issues, reflecting the highly interdisciplinary and multidisciplinary nature of his research. Notably, he has a keen interest in the legal analysis of problems related to minors in biomedicine and the use of human biological materials, including organ and tissue transplantation, research involving biological materials, and biobanks.

Arantza Libano-Beristain (Bilbao, Spain) graduated in Law and Economics from the University of Deusto, Doctor in Law from the University Autònoma de Barcelona and Master in Sociology of Law from the International Institute for the Sociology of Law in Oñati (Gipuzkoa). Former lecturer at the Faculty of Law of the University of Deusto (Bilbao), she is currently Associate Professor of Procedural Law at the University Autònoma de Barcelona.

She has undertaken research stays at several international institutions, including the Universities of Munich, Münster and Fribourg (all in Germany), Nevada-Reno (USA), Toulouse (France), Coimbra (Portugal), having obtained several grants awarded by national and international institutions. Her research and publications (scientific articles and monographs) have focused on different areas mainly connected with procedural law and biolaw, including criminal proceedings, prosecution of criminal offences, procedural aspects of domestic and gender-based violence, neuroscience and procedural law, genetics and biotechnologies, medical law and criminal procedure and codes of medical ethics.

She has participated as a speaker in several national and international conferences, workshops and seminars in Spain, Europe and Latin America.

Table of Contents

List of Abbreviations

Art.	Article
CC	Código Civil (Civil Code)
CEA	Comité de Ética Asistencial (HealthCare Ethics Committee)
CEC	Comité de Ensayos Clínicos (Clinical Trials Committee)
CEEA	Comité de Ética de Experimentación Animal (Animal Research Ethics Committee)
CEI	Comité de Ética de la Investigación (Research Ethics Committee)
CEIC	Comité de Ética de Investigación Clínica (Clinical Research Ethics Committee)
CEIm	Comité de Ética de la Investigación con medicamentos (Research Ethics Committees with medicines)
CNRHA	Comisión Nacional de Reproducción Humana Asistida (National Assisted Human Reproduction Committee)
DS	Derecho y Salud (Journal)
EU	European Union
GDPR	General Data Protection Regulation
GP	General Practitioner
HLA	Human Leukocyte Antigen
INGESA	Instituto Nacional de Gestión Sanitaria (National Institute of Health Management)
INE	Instituto Nacional de Estadística (National Statistics Institute)
IMSERSO (former INSERSO)	Instituto de Mayores y Servicios Sociales (National Social Services Institute)
INSALUD	Instituto Nacional de la Salud (National Institute of Health)

List of Abbreviations

INSS	Instituto Nacional de la Seguridad Social (National Institute of the Social Security)
IVF	In vitro fertilization
LAP	Ley 41/2002, de 14 de noviembre, básica reguladora de la Autonomía del Paciente y de derechos y obligaciones en materia de información y documentación clínica (Basic law regulating Patient autonomy and the Rights and Obligations regarding clinical information and documentation of 2002)
LEC	Ley 1/2000, de 7 de enero, de Enjuiciamiento Civil (Civil Procedure Law of 2000)
LGS	Ley 14/1986, de 25 de abril, General de Sanidad (General Health Law of 1986)
LIB	Ley 14/2007, de 3 de julio, de Investigación Biomédica (Biomedical Research Law of 2007)
LL	La Ley (Journal)
LO	Ley Orgánica (Organic Law: Law affecting Fundamental rights which needs to be approved by a qualified majority in the Parliament)
LOFCA	Ley Orgánica 8/1980, de 22 de septiembre, de Financiación de las Comunidades Autónomas (Organic Law on the Financing of the Autonomous Communities of 1980)
LOPS	Ley 44/2003, de 21 de noviembre, de Ordenación de las Profesiones Sanitarias (Law on the Regulation of Health Professions of 2003)
MO	Ministerial Order
NHS	National Health System (Spain)
OMC	Organisation of Colleges of Physicians
ONT	Organización Nacional de Trasplantes (National Transplant Organization)
PC	Penal Code (Código Penal: as in latest reform of 2024)
PGD	Preimplantation Genetic Diagnosis
RCA	Root Cause Analysis
RD	Royal Decree
RevDerGenH	Revista de Derecho y Genoma Humano/Law and the Human Genome Review
SAC	Severity Assessment Code
SiNASP	Sistema de Notificación y Aprendizaje para la Seguridad del Paciente (Spanish Patient Safety Reporting and Learning System)

UN	United Nations
UNESCO	United Nations Educational, Scientific and Cultural Organization
VET	Vocational Education and Training
WHO	World Health Organization

List of Abbreviations

Acknowledgement

This monograph has been prepared within the framework of the projects El Derecho Penal ante los retos actuales de la Biomedicina (DERPEBIO) PID2022-136743OB-I00 and Gobernanza de los usos secundarios de datos de salud y genéticos en espacios compartidos (GODAS) PID2022-137140OB-I00 financed by:

> Esta monografía ha sido elaborada en el marco de los proyectos El Derecho Penal ante los retos actuales de la Biomedicina (DERPEBIO) PID2022-136743OB-I00 y Gobernanza de los usos secundarios de datos de salud y genéticos en espacios compartidos (GODAS) PID2022-137140OB-I00 financiado por:

MINISTERIO DE CIENCIA, INNOVACIÓN Y UNIVERSIDADES

UNIÓN EUROPEA
FONDO EUROPEO DE DESARROLLO REGIONAL
"Una manera de hacer Europa"

AGENCIA ESTATAL DE INVESTIGACIÓN

Acknowledgement

G.I.
CISJANT

EUSKO JAURLARITZA
GOBIERNO VASCO
HEZKUNTZA SAILA
DEPARTAMENTO DE EDUCACIÓN

Grupos Consolidados de investigación del Gobierno Vasco IT 1486-22 en Ciencias Criminales ref IT 1541-22 en Ciencias Sociales y Jurídicas aplicadas a las Tecnociencias

General Introduction

§1. The General Background of the Country

I. Geography and Climate

1. Lying at the southwestern end of the European continent and with a total area of 504,782 km^2, which includes the Balearic and Canarian archipelagos, Spain occupies the bulk of the Iberian Peninsula. Of its 5,849 km of peninsular perimeter, 3,904 correspond to the Cantabrian Sea, the Atlantic and the Mediterranean, with the remainder taken up by the country's borders with Portugal (to the West) and France and the Principality of Andorra (to the North). Spain is the second most mountainous country in Europe after Switzerland and is characterized by a combination of mountain ranges and river basins. The country enjoys one of the most benign climates in Europe, with a marked contrast between the predominantly mild climate and even temperatures of the coastal areas and archipelagos and the more continental climate – although temperatures rarely fall to very low levels – inland.

II. Cultural Make-up

2. Even if the country's national language is Spanish, the official status granted to the Catalan, Basque, Galician and Valencian languages in their respective Autonomous Communities has led to a strengthening of the corresponding regional cultures.

3. Spain has no established church of the state, as the Constitution of 1978 abolished the Roman Catholic Church as the official state religion. However, it plays a significant role in Spanish society; according to a Survey of 2024, 58.4% of the population define themselves as Catholic, 3.5% as believers of other religions, 10.1% as agnostics and 26% as non-believers or atheists. Among believers, 48.5% assert they never or almost never go to any religious service; by contrast, 17% attend one or more masses every week.

III. Political and Judicial System

4. The Spanish Constitution of 1978 is the body of legislation which underpins the country's political system. Article 1 stipulates that Spain is a social and democratic state based on the rule of law and also describes the political system as a parliamentary monarchy.

5. The King (or Queen) is the head of state, without legislative powers, and is also commander in chief of the armed forces.

6. The government, or executive branch, is responsible for the country's international and national policies, as well as the state administration. It consists of the president, vice-presidents, ministers and other members stipulated by law. The King proposes a candidate for the presidency of the government after consultation with the leaders of the political groups which gain parliamentary representation in a general election. The candidate put forward must obtain the approval of the Congress of Deputies.

7. Legislative power lies with the Spanish Parliament (Cortes Generales), which comprises two Chambers: the 350-member Congress of Deputies, which represents the Spanish people as a whole, and the 266-member Senate, which represents territories and provinces. Both chambers are chosen by universal suffrage in elections at which all Spaniards over the age of 18 are entitled to vote. Voters choose between candidates in each of the country's fifty-two constituencies (fifty provinces, together with the autonomous cities Ceuta and Melilla, located on northern Africa's coast). Exceptionally, however, some senators are appointed directly by the Autonomous Communities.

The seventeen Autonomous Communities (Andalusia, Aragon, Asturias, Balearic Islands, Basque Country, Canary Islands, Cantabria, Castilla-La Mancha, Castilla y León, Catalonia, Comunidad Valenciana, Extremadura, Galicia, La Rioja, Madrid, Murcia and Navarra) have their own governments and regional parliaments. The extent to which each Community is competent to handle its own affairs depends on the processes provided for in the Constitution and the corresponding Statutes of Autonomy. State and Autonomous Community elections are held every four years.

8. The judicial power is tailored to the State's political structure in accordance with the provisions of the Constitution of 1978 and the subsequent Organic Law on Judicial Power of 1985 (substantially amended in January 2025). The system consists of a Supreme Court (Tribunal Supremo), as well as a National Court (Audiencia Nacional) and a Central Court of Instance (Tribunal Central de Instancia), all of which have jurisdiction over the entire state; High Courts of the Autonomous Communities (Tribunales Superiores de Justicia); Provincial High Courts (Audiencias Provinciales); Courts of Instance (Tribunales de Instancia) with different Sections – which may have provincial jurisdiction or jurisdiction corresponding to a judicial district (partido judicial) – for civil procedures and criminal proceedings, as well as for administrative litigation and labour disputes; and Justice's Courts (Juzgados de Paz) in municipalities where none of the above exist.

9. The Constitutional Court (Tribunal Constitucional) is supreme in matters relating to the interpretation of the Spanish Constitution. The Constitucional Court, whose jurisdiction extends over the entire country, deals with appeals and questions of unconstitutionality concerning laws, regulatory provisions or acts with the force of law. It also handles appeals for constitutional protection in cases involving the violation of fundamental rights and public freedoms (recurso de amparo) and conflicts of competence which arise between the State and Autonomous Communities or between the Autonomous Communities themselves. Its competences are laid down in the Constitution and in the Organic Law of the Constitutional Court (1979). Twelve Magistrates – acting in Plenary, Chambers or Sections – make up the Constitutional Court.

10. Spain's Constitution of 1978 was drawn up with Europe in mind. Chapter III of Title III concerning international treaties provides a flexible system for the conclusion of treaties under which competences derived from the Constitution may be transferred to international organizations or institutions (Article 93). It also provides for the incorporation of such treaties into national legislation (Article 96). Spain joined the European Communities in 1986, although it was not until 1992, following the Maastricht agreements which marked a substantial step forward in the process of European integration, that modifications were made to adapt the Spanish Constitution to European Union (EU) legislation. On the one hand, Article 13 was amended to extend voting rights in local elections to foreign EU residents. On the other hand, in September 2011, Article 135 of the Spanish Constitution on public debt was amended, setting the concept of 'budget stability' in the text and introducing the absolute priority of debt and interest repayment.

IV. Population and Vital Statistics

11. Spain's population as of 1 January 2025 was 49,077,984, from which 24,068,350 were male and 25,009,634 were female (51%). Its population density, at 97/km^2 (251/sq. mile), is lower than that of most Western European countries. With the exception of the capital, Madrid, the most densely populated areas lie around the coast.

According to data released by Spain's National Statistics Institute (Instituto Nacional de Estadística, INE), a total of 322,034 babies were born in Spain in 2024 (1,378 more than in 2023). The figure marks a rise of 0.42% over the previous year and is the first increase recorded in the country in ten years. In terms of births, the report shows that the number of babies born in Spain has fallen 24% since 2014. In terms of deaths, the report reveals that 433,163 people died in Spain in 2023, a 6.7% decline compared to the previous year. That is 9 deaths per 1,000 inhabitants. Infant mortality was 2.6 deaths per 1,000 live births in 2023. Life expectancy rose in 2025 compared to the previous year, going up 0.13 years to 84.2 (the highest on record). In 2022, the average life expectancy for men in Spain was 80.4 (0.2 years higher than in 2021) and 85.7 (0.1 lower than in 2021) for women. Spain's fertility rate (the number of children the average woman will have during her lifetime) is one of the lowest in the world. It was last measured at 1.2 in 2022, according to the World Bank.

Concerning voluntary interruption of pregnancy, the number of abortions being carried out in Spain has since 2021 significantly increased in accordance with the latest official statistics. The latest figures for 2023 show that the number of women who terminated a pregnancy rose in that year by 4.8% compared to the year before. A total of 101,322 women opted for the procedure during 2023 – 4,722 more than the previous year and 12,435 more than in 2021 – under legislation that has been in place since 2010 in Spain and allows access to abortion on demand until the 14th week of pregnancy. The majority of the women who decided to have an abortion in 2023 (23.45%) were aged between 20 and 24. The minority were over 40. There are no specific figures for minors, although the data supplied by the Ministry of Health reveals that of the total number of terminations, 10.79% were performed on women aged '19 and under'.

V. Social and Cultural Values Regarding Health

12. According to the European Health Interview Survey in Spain 2020, the most frequent chronic health problems were high blood pressure (19.03%), high cholesterol (15.29%), osteoarthritis (14.37%), pain in the lumbar spine (13.69%), pain in the cervical spine (11.33%) and allergies (10.80%). For children, figures from Spain's INE indicate that under the age of 15, the most prevalent chronic conditions were allergy (11.6%) and asthma (6.6%) in 2017.

There were 1.61 reported cases of pertussis for every 100,000 inhabitants in 2020, 5.33 cases of mumps, 2.9 cases of measles in 2023, and 0.01 cases of rubella. All of these transmissible diseases are included in the vaccination calendar and have exhibited a downward trend since the 1990s, although mumps have appeared in epidemic waves. Hepatitis A had 2.01 cases per 100,000 inhabitants in 2019 and 0.6 in 2023; however, in 2024, a growth in reported cases of hepatitis A was detected, with a change in the epidemiological pattern. Concerning hepatitis B, during 2019–2023, there was an increase from 1.06 to 1.18, and during 2023, there were 4.76 cases per 100,000 inhabitants in other types of viral hepatitis. During 2012–2022, a significant upward trend has been observed in the estimated incidence per 100,000 inhabitants of gonococcal infection (49.0) and syphilis (17.1). In the decade 2013–2023, the number of new HIV infections has fallen by 27.5%, while AIDS cases have dropped by 39.1%.

According to the Annual Report on the National Health System (NHS) of Spain 2023, the leading causes of mortality were circulatory diseases and cancer, which caused 50% of deaths. With regard to tumours, the types responsible for the highest mortality were trachea/bronchial/lung cancer and colon/rectum cancer. The cancer that caused the most deaths among men was trachea/bronchial/lung cancer, while among women, it was breast cancer. The adjusted suicide rate was 8.8 out of every 100,000 persons (13.3 in men and 4.5 in women), with a slight increase over the preceding years.

As for tobacco use, 19.8% of the population aged 15 and older smoked on a daily basis, and 21.8% of students aged 14 to 18 consumed cannabis in 2022. With respect to alcohol, 1.3% of the population aged 15 and older had engaged in hazardous drinking at some time in 2022 (with 50% more men than women). One out of ten young people aged between 14 and 24 declared binge drinking at least once a month in 2022.

With regard to body weight, 16% of the population aged 18 and over showed obesity.

Spain continues to hold its place as the global leader in the number of organ transplants conducted. The National Transplant Organization (ONT) has reported that in 2024, Spain, once again, broke its own record after carrying out a total of 6,464 transplants. Figures show that the donation rate in 2024 was 52.6 donors per 1 million inhabitants. Spain has been the world leader in organ transplants since 1992. Spain also broke records last year in relation to the number of kidney transplants. A total of 4,049 kidney transplants were carried out in 2024, up almost 10% from the previous year. One striking figure was the number of kidney transplants made from living donors – 398 – which accounts for 9.3% of all kidney transplants that took place in 2024. In 2004, there were just 61 transplants from living donors. The majority of organs (66.2%) came from people who died from strokes. Sixty per cent of all donors were over the age of 60.

§2. General Description of the HealthCare System

I. General Review of the Spanish HealthCare System

13. The precursors of the NHS (Sistema Nacional de Salud) put in place by the General Health Law (Ley General de Sanidad, LGS, of 1986) were the National Providence Institute (Instituto Nacional de Previsión), the National Institute of Health (Instituto Nacional de la Salud, INSALUD) and the National Institute of the Social Security (Instituto Nacional de la Seguridad Social, INSS).[2] Up to the early years of the last century, Public Welfare was a state scheme which catered for the needs of the destitute and the poor. In addition to providing health cover, the scheme also covered other areas of need such as food, education and employment;[3] the advent of epidemiological diseases led to a strengthening of action in the field of public health.[4]

2. *See* M. Beato Espejo, 'El sistema sanitario español: su configuración en la Ley General de Sanidad', in *Revista de Administración Pública*, nº. 119, May–August 1989, p. 385.
3. The first law on Health was passed in 1855. On the basis of physicians' freedom to practice their profession, the law aimed to provide assistance for the poor; the healthcare it included covered collective – as opposed to individual – health only. 1925 saw the passing of Municipal and Provincial Regulations which once again focused on collective health and assistance for the poor. *See* P.P. Mansilla Izquierdo, *Reforma Sanitaria. Fundamentos para un análisis* (Ministerio de Sanidad y Consumo, Madrid 1986), pp. 5–7.
4. The General Public Health Instructions issued in 1904 created a system for the control of epidemiological diseases; similarly, the Regulations of 26 Jul. 1945 governing the fight against infectious diseases, disinfection and protection against insect pests, and the Regulations of 4 Feb. 1958 on the fight

There was, however, a large sector of society which, although not destitute, did not have sufficient means to meet its health needs. Demands were growing for a type of protection to ensure that such people would not be forced into poverty, which was a requirement for Public Welfare eligibility. Particularly vulnerable were workers who, although they found it difficult to make ends meet, were not entitled to Public Welfare given that they were not 'poor'. Others, meanwhile, were better off and could afford to take out private social insurance cover. In this way, independent social insurance gradually became established as a means of providing cover for old age, subsistence, accidents at work, family responsibilities, common illnesses, invalidity, illnesses derived from the exercise of one's profession, etc. Eventually, the State responded to working-class demands and created Compulsory Health Insurance (Seguro Obligatorio de Enfermedad) under a Law passed on 14 December 1942. The scheme provided protection for the least well-off sectors of the population and afforded health assistance for general medical care as well as a variety of outpatient surgery specialities and medicines. National healthcare centres[5] were set up to deal with certain illnesses, whereas other levels of (hospital) healthcare were provided by local corporations and non-profit making institutions such as the Catholic Church and the Red Cross. Subsequent endeavours were made to develop a Social Security system. The first step was the promulgation of Law 193/1963 of 28 December which established the bases of the Social Security system. This law attempted to bring together all existing forms of social insurance and was followed by the Social Security Law of 21 April 1966 (Decree 907/1966) that aimed to provide health assistance for a specific sector of society, i.e., workers. Workers were brought under the system because as paid employees they (together with their employers) helped finance the cost of Social Security services (Revised Text approved by Decree 2065/1974 of 30 May). The scheme forms part of the current NHS, which covers a wide range of beneficiaries.[6]

---

against trachoma, venereal diseases and dermatosis. *See* J. Pemán Gavín, *Derecho a la salud y Administración sanitaria* (Publicaciones del Real Colegio de España, Bologna 1989), p. 119.

5. The 1944 law which established the bases of the NHS marked the first attempt to coordinate existing healthcare networks (those of municipalities and provincial governments organized under the welfare system) and to cater for individual and not just collective health. *See* Mansilla Izquierdo, *Reforma Sanitaria*, *supra*, p. 9.
6. The extension of Social Security cover since 1983 has been based on the labour status of the beneficiary. Cover was thus extended to the unemployed and unemployed members of their families (Law 31/1984 of 2 August), self-employed persons and their families (Royal Decree 43/1984 of 4 January), dependants under the age of 26 (Royal Decree 1377/1984 of 4 July), emigrants and their children (Royal Decree 916/1986) and persons over 26 who are unemployed and live with the direct beneficiary (Royal Decree 1682/1987 of 30 December). On 31 Dec. 1989, 38,433,425 people – 96.14% of the total population of Spain – were entitled to healthcare cover, according to a report on healthcare institutions by the Ministry of Health and Consumer Affairs. Cover was further extended under Royal Decree 1088/1989 of 8 September to those with insufficient incomes, which brought many elderly persons and those on the edges of society into the system. The 'health cover for all' process was completed by Social Security Law 26/1990 of 20 December, which partly reformed the Revised Text and created non-contributory pensions for retired people and invalids. Under this system pension entitlement is extended to persons over 65 resident in Spain, who have not paid social security contributions and do not have sufficient income.

   In 2023, according to the Ministry of Health, 96.6% of the population (46,700,000) relied on the NHS, while 3.4% were covered through private entities arranged by the civil servants' mutual funds.

The healthcare system underwent gradual transformation until the State decided to include the Social Security system as yet another of its functions. The system was granted its own normative provisions and it began to move away from the 'labour' criterion on which entitlement to health assistance was previously founded.[7]

14. A new stage was reached with the passing of the Spanish Constitution of 1978, which recognizes the right to health protection in Article 43.1. Entitlement covers all Spaniards as well as foreigners resident in Spain;[8] Article 41 of the Constitution also stipulates that 'the public authorities shall maintain a public Social Security system for all citizens, to guarantee sufficient social assistance and services ...' One can deduce from this that the Social Security system has become totally 'decoupled' from worker status, given that it has to cater for all Spaniards, which has obvious repercussions on the manner in which the system is financed. Under this constitutional principle, the authorities are obliged to implement and safeguard health protection; health thus is given the status of a *public service* in accordance with the provisions of Article 43.2 of the Constitution.[9] A reflection of this can be seen in the univerzalisation of Social Security assistance, which resulted from the creation of a system of non-contributory pensions.

The basic principles on which the NHS is founded are those set out in the LGS, which was drawn up to enforce the mandate of Article 43.2 of the Constitution.[10] The public bodies responsible for health protection are the State Administration, Autonomous Communities and local corporations. The NHS comprises all the Health Services of the State Administration and those of the Autonomous Communities. Decentralization, which is a requirement set out in the Constitution and in the Statutes of the Autonomous Communities, is a fundamental principle which determines to a large degree the way in which health services are provided. These services are brought under the wing of the Autonomous Communities, while the State is essentially charged with powers of management and coordination. The State is competent as regards basic concepts of care, general coordination and top-level inspection, aspects which aim to maintain unity in the field of health and to achieve basic equality among citizens as regards their health. Executive-type services are the

7. *See* A. Palomar Olmeda, 'Las normas jurídicas de Seguridad Social y las normas jurídico-administrativas', in *Revista de Administración Pública*, nº. 126, September–December 1991, p. 412.
8. For an analysis of proposals for the reform of the healthcare system made during the period 1977–1982, *see* F.J. Elola Somoza, *Crisis y reforma de la asistencia sanitaria pública en España (1983–1990)* (Fondo de Investigaciones Sanitarias de la Seguridad Social, Madrid 1991), pp. 71 ff.
9. Article 43.2 of the Constitution states that 'the authorities shall organise and safeguard public health through the taking of preventive measures and the provision of the necessary facilities and services. In this respect, the law shall determine the rights and duties of all concerned'. In the opinion of J.M. Rodríguez Pastrana, *El servicio público de la Sanidad: el marco constitutional* (Civitas, Madrid 1984), pp. 31 ff., 'what is inferred from the Constitution is, therefore, a *Public Health Service*, which should not be confused with a monopolised National Health Service ... The basic idea of the National Health Service is, to a certain extent, the socialisation of health management, which is placed in public hands ... However, in a Public Health Service, although the State is ultimately responsible for all public and private health-care activities, it does not reserve for itself the exclusive management of said activities ...' Elsewhere, Art. 3.2 of the LGS states that public healthcare assistance shall extend to the entire population.
10. Article 7 of the LGS states that healthcare services shall be organized and shall function in accordance with the principles of efficiency, promptness, economy and flexibility.

responsibility of the Autonomous Communities, which also exercise normative powers where the State has not reserved these for itself in relation to health. Local corporations participate in the management and control of Health Areas.

II. Regulation of the HealthCare System

15. A new legal framework to govern health was needed as the 1944 Law, which established the basis of the National Health Service, had become obsolete and out of touch with society's needs and health requirements. The LGS, under which the current NHS was created, gave specific form to the healthcare principles and objectives which had been mapped out previously in the Constitution. In doing so, it did away with the models of public healthcare action which had prevailed in the nineteenth and early twentieth centuries and which concentrated on collective as opposed to individual assistance. Today's priorities include health promotion, prevention of illnesses and diseases and health education. The system, which covers mental health also, caters for the entire population, including those not covered by Social Security and persons without means of subsistence (Article 3 of the LGS).

Management of the health services has been progressively transferred to all Autonomous Communities, while some continue to be operated by the National Institute of Health Management (Instituto Nacional de Gestión Sanitaria, INGESA) part of the Ministry of Health. The activity of these services is harmonized by the Interterritorial Council of the Spanish National Health System (Consejo Interterritorial del Sistema Nacional de Salud de España), in order to bring cohesion to the system and to guarantee the rights of citizens throughout Spain.

Article 46 of the LGS establishes the fundamental characteristics of the NHS:

i. Extension of services to the entire population.
ii. Adequate organization to provide comprehensive healthcare, including promotion of health, prevention of disease, treatment and rehabilitation.
iii. Coordination and, as needed, integration of all public health resources into a single system.
iv. Financing of the obligations derived from this Law will be met by resources of public administrations, contributions and fees for the provision of certain services.
v. The provision of comprehensive healthcare, seeking high standards which are properly evaluated and controlled.

16. The protection of *public health*, particularly aspects of prevention, is a primary concern of the Spanish State, as reflected in the passing of Organic Law 3/1986 of 14 April on Special Public Health Measures, which empowers health authorities to adopt certain measures in cases or situations of emergency or need. The measures cover examinations, treatment, hospitalization or control when there exist reasonable grounds to assume that the health of the population may be at risk (Article 2). It also enables the Administration to temporarily centralise supplies of medicines or health products where problems of supply exist, in order to ensure efficient distribution (Article 4). Furthermore, in addition to authorizing preventive action – with the corresponding curtailment of citizens' freedoms – the law also empowers the Administration to control the sick or persons who have been in contact with them and their environment in cases where public health has already been affected (Article 3). The legal protection of collective is present also in the Criminal Law, which penalizes a series of conducts deemed to be dangerous to the health of the public;[11] in addition to all the above, there exists a wide range of administrative regulations governing aspects relating to health protection.

17. The *individual health* of citizens is a public health priority of the State, both in terms of prevention and assistance. State care is a constitutional obligation and an area in which significant progress has been achieved, particularly as regards the care provided by the Social Security system. The univeralization of individual protection, which has entailed partial abandonment of the former mode of financing the system through contributions, means that public healthcare is now available to all citizens.

The LGS allows citizens to choose their primary care General Practitioner (GP) in their Health Area; it provides for the creation of an integrated network of public hospitals and the association of private general hospitals to the NHS when required. It also provides for the right to freely practise a healthcare profession and for freedom of enterprise in the health sector, in accordance with the provisions laid down in the Constitution.

18. The structure of the model of assistance is thus conceived as a whole, which comprises activities to enhance and promote health, prevention, curative assistance and rehabilitation. Health services are *structured* in such a way as to facilitate user proximity and a form of decentralized management which allows for public participation. Each Autonomous Community has its own Health Service, which includes all the centres, services and establishments in that Community. The cornerstones of these Services are the Health Areas, which are generally designed to cater for populations of between 200,000 and 250,000 and which provide all the services available under the health system. For smoother running, Health Areas are divided into Basic Health Zones for primary healthcare. The Zones' Health Centres and General Hospitals, in addition to providing assistance, also play a role in promoting health, preventing illness and disease and in teaching and research, all in accordance with the programmes which each Health Area draws up as complementary activities to those undertaken by the primary care network. To this end, the basic organization of the system centres nowadays[12] on the NHS (Sistema Nacional de Salud) – which is managed by the Social Security System – with health services organized as follows:

11. *See* Arts 359–378 of the Spanish Criminal Code. Among conducts deemed to constitute an offence are the unauthorized manufacture and selling of substances which are dangerous to health, breaches of regulations governing trade in such substances, the illegal dispensing of drugs and medicines, the alteration of medicinal substances, or fraud concerning food products and illegal drug trafficking.
12. Previous to the NHS (Sistema Nacional de Salud) there was, until 2002, in Spain the National Institute of Health (Instituto Nacional de la Salud, INSALUD).

1. On the territorial level, the health system comprises essentially Health Areas (Áreas de Salud), divided in turn into Basic Health Zones (Zonas Básicas de Salud), as the unit for a primary healthcare team.
2. As regards assistance, the following levels exist:
   a. *Primary Care*. It is a basic level of patient care that guarantees the comprehensiveness and continuity of care throughout the patient's life, acting as manager and coordinator of cases and flow regulator.[13] Primary care includes health promotion, health education, prevention of illness, healthcare, maintenance and recuperation of health, as well as physical rehabilitation and social work. Primary healthcare includes service provided either on-demand, scheduled, or urgently, both in the clinic as well as in the patient's home. The Health Centres are staffed by GPs, paediatricians, nurses, social workers and administrative personnel. The staff carry out their work in the Centre itself and in the patient's home and may be called to deal with emergencies. Health education is also undertaken by Centres.
   b. *Specialist Care*.[14] Hospitals, which are better equipped both in terms of staff and facilities, are the cornerstones of specialist care. They also act as centres for teaching and research and carry out their own health promotion and prevention activities in accordance with Health Area programmes.

Medical assistance comprises General Medicine, as well as Specialist and Emergency Medicine services which are provided in health centres, on an inpatient basis or in the patient's home. Users covered by Social Security receive such services free of charge and do not have to pay anything in addition to their normal contributions.

Pharmaceutical assistance covers pharmaceutical specialities, items and accessories as well as prescriptions issued by doctors under the Social Security system. These are completely free of charge in certain cases (OAPs and their dependants, persons with disabilities, individuals who have sustained accidents at work, etc.). In other circumstances, users pay different rates (10, 30, 40, 50 or 60%) of the retail price of the drug or medicine, except for some of a special nature. The fee is paid directly to the dispensing chemists.[15]

In addition, promotion and prevention work is carried out in the field of primary healthcare via the Health Centres. In some cases, such action is targeted specifically on, for example, family planning, mental health and maternity care (Family Planning Units and Centres, Mental Health and Psycho-prophylaxis Units).

19. General HealthCare Coordination is the means by which minimum common goals for prevention, protection, perception and assistance are determined. To

13. Article 12 of Law 16/2003 of 28 May, on Cohesion and Quality of the National Health System.
14. *See* Art. 13 of Law 16/2003 of 28 May, on Cohesion and Quality of the National Health System.
15. Users may also be entitled to other services, such as payment for drugs or medicines not available in Spain, for fixed and orthopaedic surgical appliances of a permanent or temporary nature, invalid vehicles, use of ordinary means of transportation (ambulances) for patients who require them frequently to follow treatment such as dialysis, radiotherapy, rehabilitation, etc.

this end, a number of competences are granted for coordination purposes and support is available from the Interterritorial Council of the National Health System, a body chaired by the Minister for Health and also consisting of the Members of each Autonomous Community in charge of Health. Coordination is also achieved by means of the Integrated Health Programme (Plan Integrado de Salud) which is of paramount importance in ensuring that health services function efficiently. This integrated programme brings together State and Autonomous Community programmes as well as any joint plans drawn up to enable both sides to carry out their respective healthcare functions.[16] Coordination at the State level is also achieved through agreements concluded by the State and the Autonomous Communities and any joint action which they may agree to undertake.

20. In general, health services are organized on the basis of direct public management, that is, through publicly-owned centres staffed by personnel who are subject to Public Law statutes.[17] However, provision is also made for the use of private forms of management of health services; this means that privately-owned centres may provide assistance on behalf of the healthcare system. The public network is thus complemented through association agreements reached with private centres or through the linking of private hospitals to the public system.

In order to exercise its functions,[18] the State relies on the administrative machinery of the Ministry of Health. All healthcare centres and services come under the Autonomous Communities,[19] with the exception of the Instituto de Salud Carlos III, an independent institution belonging to the State Administration, set up to provide technical and scientific support to State and Autonomous Communities Health Services.

The State Health Administration is charged with assessing the suitability of medicines and other health products and articles and is also responsible for authorizing their use and controlling the quality of such products.

The LGS lays down certain minimum principles to be followed by the Autonomous Communities in the organization of their Health Services, although it does not interfere with competences granted to them under their respective statutes. Each

16. Article 64 of Law 16/2003 of 28 May, on Cohesion and Quality of the National Health System.
17. Prior to 1978, the Social Security system was managed by the National Providence Institute (Instituto Nacional de Previsión), which was dissolved under Royal Decree 36/1978 of 16 November. Its functions were taken over by, among other bodies, the management institutions of the Social Security system: the National Institute of the Social Security (INSS), which handles payments of benefits under the system; the National Social Services Institute (INSERSO today IMSERSO – Instituto de Mayores y Servicios Sociales) which manages complementary social services (for the elderly and persons with disabilities), and the INSALUD, which managed and administered the system's healthcare services.
18. Under Art. 149.1.17 of the Constitution, the State is exclusively competent to draw up 'the basic legislation and establish the economic regime of the Social Security system, although services may be provided by the Autonomous Communities'. Under Art. 149.1.16, it is solely responsible for 'external health. The bases and overall coordination of health. Legislation governing pharmaceutical products'.
19. Under numbers 20 and 21 of Art. 148.1 of the Spanish Constitution, and in accordance with the terms laid down in their Statutes, Autonomous Communities may take on competences in relation to social assistance and health and hygiene.

Community delimits its Health Areas, which, in addition to an Area Board and Manager, must also include an Area Health Council, a collegiate body for consultation and monitoring of public health management in which the public participates (citizens, trade unions). In exercising their competences, the Autonomous Communities must allow for democratic participation by all interested parties, including representatives of unions and employers' organizations. Each Community draws up its own Health Plan which contains all the actions necessary to help accomplish the goals set for its healthcare centres. The plan also regulates the organization, functions and allocation of material and staff.

III. Financing of the HealthCare

21. The Law on Cohesion and Quality of 2003[20] establishes that the financing of the Spanish health system is the responsibility of the autonomous communities in conformity with the accords of transfer and the current system of autonomic financing, notwithstanding the existence of a third party liable to pay. Sufficient financing of services is determined by the resources assigned to the autonomous communities in conformity to what in the laws of autonomic financing is established. Inclusion of a new service in the catalogue of services of the NHS is accompanied by an economic memo that contains the positive or negative financial impact it is expected to imply. This memo is brought up to the Council of Fiscal and Finance Policy (Consejo de Política Fiscal y Financiera) for analysis and approval as to whether to proceed.

The LGS advocates a tightened belt approach to solve the problem of the large health service deficit caused by increased expenditure and squandering of resources.[21] Obviously, if the goals of the new health system were to be attained, an increase in spending was necessary to enable care to be extended to the entire population. The planning and fixing of the major principles of the system were crucially important, as were the search for sources of financing and the distribution and management of financial resources.[22] Prior to 1986, restrictive health budgets were the order of the day; however, the gradual widening of the system of social security assistance to cover the entire population required more spending on public health and, therefore, increased funding for the sector.[23]

20. Article 10.
21. *See* Elola Somoza, *Crisis y reforma de asistencia sanitaria pública en España*, *supra*, p. 109.
22. Article 81 of the LGS states that '*the generalisation of the right to health protection and assistance, which entails bringing public health assistance and services into line, shall be accomplished by allocating financial resources which take into account both the size of the population in need of assistance in each Autonomous Community and also investments in health which need to be undertaken to correct health-care inequalities between territories, in accordance with Article 12*'.
23. Increased expenditure was caused not merely by the extension of healthcare to the entire population but also by the need to cater for mental health, the organization and structure of the National Health System, research and the Instituto de Salud Carlos III. *See* Elola Somoza, *Crisis y reforma de la asistencia sanitaria pública en España*, *supra*, p. 113. Elola Somoza argues that '*the increase in health expenditure produced by the LGS was clearly underestimated*. This, combined with the aforementioned ambiguity and the absence of specific commitments in the Law, lends support to the theory that *the LGS lacked sufficient policy backing to enable it to carry out its proposals. To a certain*

The system is financed by social security contributions paid by employees and employers, transfers of State funds, fees charged for certain services and contributions made by the Autonomous Communities and local corporations.

Financial functions in the field of healthcare are exercised by the State. The funds which it transfers to the Autonomous Communities depend on the size of the population to be covered. In addition, the Communities receive financing for their healthcare centres from the Social Security budget, although they also contribute their own funds and raise money by charging for health services provided to third parties.

Apart from this basic funding mechanism, the State may at its discretion use other complementary forms to correct imbalances between regions. It may draw up its own action plans, including those for investment, and may provide partial or total financing of Autonomous Communities health programmes or contribute to the financing of joint programmes drawn up between the State and one or all of the Communities.

22. *Reducing financial costs.* The costs of healthcare supported by the Public Health System have increased constantly, and today are among the highest economic burdens to which public finances are faced. Some measures have been taken to reduce these costs to keep the system sustainable while preventing any inequality based on economic or territorial situation of citizens.[24] We will mention the most important measures taken for medicines and other diagnostic or therapeutical treatments:

1. *Medicines.* The *encouragement in the market of generic drugs*, as they are cheaper, since they become free of patent rights, and the copayment of the prescribed medicine by patients themselves.[25] Generic medicines, which have been produced based on efficacy and safety data of innovator medicines and following the exclusivity period, ensure lower-cost medicines availability. When a generic medicine is bioequivalent to the innovator medicine, it is considered to have the same therapeutic effect. Therefore, in this goal of sustainability, the measures incorporated in the legislation on medicines are intended to eliminate obstacles to a greater presence of these drugs on the market. According to Article 87 of *Royal Legislative Decree* 1/2015, health authorities will encourage the prescription of medicines identified in the medical receipt by their active principle. In cases where the professional prescriber indicated in the receipt simply an active principle, the pharmaceutical will dispense the medicine at the lowest price.

---

extent, it served rather to lay out a final scenario which successive reforms should aim towards, insofar as sufficient resources could be allocated in future to implement them'.

24. Article 91 of Royal Legislative Decree 1/2015, of 24 July, which approves the refunded text of the Law on guarantees and rational use of medicines and health products.
25. N. Laguna-Goya et al., 'Legislación sobre autorización de genéricos', in *Farmacia Hospitalaria*, Vol. 30, Nr. 6, 2006, pp. 379–384.

The *copayment of the prescribed medicines* by patients themselves is a legally established general practice.[26] The question is whether still a surplus (co)payment as it was decided by some Autonomous Communities (one euro extra for each medicine) is lawful or not. The authorities of the State (Central Government) claimed to the Constitutional Court against these decisions as exceeding the constitutional competences accorded to the Autonomous Communities. In its Sentences 71/2014, of 8 May 2014, and 85/2014, of 29 May 2014, the Spanish Constitutional Court upheld the appeals lodged by the Government against the implementation in Catalonian and Madrid Autonomous Communities of the 'Euro per prescription' system. The Constitutional Court pointed out that on the matter of public health, as opposed to other shared competences between the State and Autonomous Communities, 'the economic sustainability structure is part of basic State competences'. The Organic Law 8/1980, 22 September, on Financing of Autonomous Communities (Ley Orgánica 8/1980, de 22 de septiembre, de Financiación de las Comunidades Autónomas, LOFCA) states, furthermore, that 'the State will guarantee throughout Spanish territory a minimum level of the fundamental public services under its competence',[27] to include public health. The Constitutional Court recalls that the NHS is but one and that its financing depends on the Fundamental Public Services Guarantee Fund, specific social funds used to 'ensure that each Autonomous Community receives the same resources per inhabitant necessary to finance fundamental public services essential to the Welfare State'. Therefore, the judgment states, given that public health is a basic competence of the State, that there can be no 'imposition of a rate as the one being reviewed, which alters, at an extra cost for the beneficiaries, the cost of participation in the system established' in the Law.

2. *Reviewing the common services portfolio* of the NHS. In order to prevent arbitrariness and unequal provisions of medical care services for all citizens (including lawful foreign residents), the Spanish NHS has regulated which of these provisions should be included. More specifically, the aim of establishing this common portfolio is to ensure the protection of health, equity and accessibility to adequate healthcare to which all citizens have right regardless of their residence. The portfolio of common services of the NHS sets out the techniques, technologies or procedures that currently cover that system. This regulation is intended to define, ensure and establish the procedure of updating the provisions that currently are being offered by the Public Health System to citizens.[28]

Health authorities have perceived that it is necessary to control the very high costs of healthcare provisions and that for this aim, a clarification and reduction of

26. *See* Art. 101 of Royal Legislative Decree 1/2015.
27. Article 15 Uno.
28. *See* Royal Decree 1030/2006, of 15 September, for establishing the common services portfolio of the National Health Service and the procedure for updating (Real Decreto 1030/2006, de 15 de septiembre, por el que se establece la cartera de servicios comunes del Sistema Nacional de Salud y el procedimiento para su actualización).

the common services portfolio is needed. This is the reason why government measures have established the reorganization of the sector to enhance sustainability, improve management efficiency, achieve greater territorial coordination and reduce spending and defaulting for providers of the public health system, among others.[29]

§3. Medical Law

I. Definitions and Functions of Medical Law

23. Medical Law is not clearly circumscribed in the Spanish legal system and is often confused with Health Law, Legal Medicine and – in the past – Medical Deontology; currently there is also some overlapping with Bioethics.[30] Strictly speaking, Health Law embraces the legal system of health in its entirety, particularly the public health system, public health actions and citizens' relations with the healthcare system (Derecho Sanitario). Legal Medicine is the part of medicine which is used as an auxiliary instrument in the administration of justice. Bioethics (as well as Biolaw) is an interdisciplinary approach to life and health-related conflicts.

Medical Law can thus be defined initially as *the parts of the Law which concern with Medicine, that is, the medical profession and, by extension, other health or health-related professions.* Medical Law refers to the professional relations of physicians (and other similar professionals) with the system of healthcare, with (public and private) healthcare users and patients, and other health professionals. However, in view of the constant widening of the scope of actions affecting health, nowadays, Medical Law includes *the legal implications of the application to human beings of the so-called Biomedical Sciences*, that is, not just medicine but also biology (e.g., genetics), biochemistry, biophysics, biotechnology, etc. To a certain degree, it also takes in the specific legal aspects of the use by health professionals of certain technologies, such as computers (bioinformatics). A problem currently exists with regard to the delimitation of Bioethics, due in particular to the influence exerted on the concept by the Americans, who understand Bioethics as comprising not just the ethical aspects (applied ethics) of the biomedical sciences but also philosophical, sociological and legal considerations as well. Both Bioethics and (Bio)Medical Law study the biomedical sciences and how they affect human beings, although they do so from different perspectives: the former from the ethical viewpoint and the latter from the legal standpoint. However, it is now accepted that Bioethics, in the broad sense of the term, may constitute a focal point for the multidisciplinary study of the implications of the biomedical sciences for human beings. It should be stressed nonetheless that these sciences are independent and autonomous disciplines.

Medical Law as such is not taught officially in Spanish universities, although it does figure occasionally in postgraduate courses (i.e., Masters in Biolaw, Medical

---

29. Royal Decree-law 16/2012, of 20 April, on urgent measures to ensure the sustainability of the National Health System and improve the quality and safety of their services (Real Decreto-ley 16/2012, de 20 de abril, de medidas urgentes para garantizar la sostenibilidad del Sistema Nacional de Salud y mejorar la calidad y seguridad de sus prestaciones).
30. *See* C.M. Romeo Casabona, *El médico y el Derecho Penal, vol. II, 1* (Rubinzal Culzoni, Santa Fe 2011), p. 17.

Law or Bioethics) or as a short matter in graduate studies in Medical and Law Schools. In the case of Schools of Medicine, most curricula have tended to include Bioethics, due partly to the confusion referred to just now and partly because it is probably considered that teachers of Bioethics will not necessarily require previous training in the subject (an opinion which, if that is indeed the case, would be misguided).

In any case, it has to be accepted that (Bio-)Medical Law today is an autonomous discipline which is of crucial theoretical and practical importance given its potential effects on society.

II. Sources of Medical Law

24. Specific Medical Law sources in Spain have developed considerably over the years, especially over the last four decades. As will become clear in the following pages, a number of Laws in Spain address medical issues: the 1979 Law on the Removal and Transplantation of Organs, the LGS of 1986, as examples of the oldest and the Law on Biomedical Research of 2007 as the youngest most relevant.

Other Laws have been updated or are completely new: the 2002 Law on patient's autonomy and on rights and duties related to information and clinical records, the 2006 Law on Techniques of Human Assisted Reproduction, the Law on guarantees and the rational use of medicines, the 2010 Law on reproductive health (voluntary interruption of pregnancy, modified in 2023), and others.

These issues are taken up further in Royal Decrees, which cover other aspects also, such as blood donation, organs and tissues for therapeutic purposes, biobanks and human samples for research purposes, clinical trials, and Ministerial Orders (MOs). Although still rather scarce in this field, court rulings have enhanced their quantity and quality (argumentations) and can also constitute substantive sources of Medical Law and provide important (although not legally binding for third parties) points of reference.

25. As regards non-specific sources, mention should be made first and foremost of the Spanish Constitution of 1978, which sets out fundamental rights which may be affected by medical practice: the right to life and to physical and moral integrity (Article 15), the right to ideological freedom (Article 16), the right to freedom (Article 17), the right to privacy (Article 18), etc. The Constitution also enshrines the principle of non-discrimination (Article 14) and refers to the dignity of the human person and the free development of personhood (Article 10.1). In addition to the above, there are numerous provisions in both criminal and civil law which are applicable to the practice of medicine, particularly as regards liability in respect of malpractice and personal data protection.

On the international level, special reference should be made to the human rights Conventions subscribed and ratified by Spain, which, as a result, now form part of domestic law (Article 96 of the Constitution) and are of help in the interpretation of the fundamental rights laid down in the Constitution. Of particular interest in this regard is the Universal Declaration of Human Rights, which is mentioned expressly in the Constitution (Article 10.2). Other examples include the European Convention for the Protection of Human Rights and Fundamental Freedoms (1950) and the International Covenant on Civil and Political Rights (1966).

Over the last decades, International Law has developed specific legal instruments, binding or not binding, in matters directly related to biomedical activities of which Spain is a part: Council of Europe Convention on Human Rights and Biomedicine (1997) and its Additional Protocols;[31] United Nations Educational, Scientific and Cultural Organization's (UNESCO's) Declarations on the Human Genome and Human Rights (1997), on Human Genetic Data (2003), on Bioethics and Human Rights (2005).[32]

31. The Oviedo Convention was signed by the Kingdom of Spain on 4 Apr. 1997 and ratified on 1 Sep. 1999 (in force since 1 Jan. 2000). Concerning Additional Protocols Spain has signed and ratified the one referred to the Prohibition of Cloning Human Beings (Paris, 12 Jan. 1998; in force in Spain since 1 Mar. 2001) and the one concerning Transplantation of Organs and Tissues of Human Origin (Strasbourg, 24 Jan. 2002; in force in Spain since 1 Apr. 2015).
32. Concerning the UN Declaration on Human Cloning (8 Mar. 2005), Spain voted against it.

Part I. The Medical Profession

Chapter 1. Access to the Medical Profession

§1. Healthcare Education

26. From a general viewpoint, Spanish law incorporates the freedom of professional practice in Articles 35.1 and 36 of the Constitution. The first of these Articles includes, in general, the right of every citizen 'to the free choice of profession', right which not has to be confused with the right to engage in any professional activity. Meanwhile, Article 36 of the Constitution states that the peculiarities of the exercise of each profession must be regulated by specific laws. In this sense, it is up to the lawmaker to decide when a profession requires an Official Degree to be exercised, if there are other kinds of requirements for such purpose, as well as the definition of the minimum content of the activities included in said profession.

27. Spanish legal literature maintains that until 2003, there was an unsatisfactory regime of the peculiarities and requirements for the exercise of the health professions. Until then, it had only regulated the legal system of professions related to dentistry and other oral health-related professionals.[33] Finally, such deficiency would be corrected with the entry into force of Law 44/2003 of 21 November on the Regulation of Health Professions. Said norm states that the exercise of a health profession (both in private and in public sector[34]) requires the possession of the pertinent Official Degree that expressly authorizes the holder to exercise his profession.

28. Our legal system states that 'Graduated Health Professions' are those whose undergraduate or specialized training is specifically and primarily aimed to provide applicants with the knowledge, skills and attitudes for healthcare and are organized in Professional Associations officially recognized by the Public Authorities. Taking into account the type of University Degree, Spanish law classifies such professions into two groups:

---

33. Aspects developed, in a generic way, in the Law 10/1986 of 17 March, governing dentists and other oral health professionals.
34. Are similar the regulations governing the legal relationship that links health professionals with the public administration. Consult the Art. 30.5.b) of the Law 55/2003, of 16 December, on the Framework Statute for Health Services Staff.

1. Health Professions of Bachelor level: Are those professions whose practice is authorized by the degrees of Bachelor of Medicine, Pharmacy, Dentistry and Veterinary Medicine, and the Official Degrees of Specialist in Health Sciences (these latter could be obtained by the Bachelors in Psychology, Chemistry, Biology, Biochemistry and other University Bachelors).[35] However, Law 44/2003 also states that when necessary[36] and by a regulation having the force of Law, it would be possible to formally declare the character of 'Graduated Health Professions' of an activity not included in the previous list.
2. Health Professions of Diploma level: Are those professions whose practice is authorized by the Degrees of Diploma in Nursing, Physiotherapy, Occupational Therapy, Podiatry, Optics and Optometry, Speech Therapy and Human Nutrition and Dietetics, as well as the Official Degrees of Specialist in Health Sciences for those Diplomas specified in the Title II of the Law 44/2003.

29. It is important to remark that in Spain, they are not considered 'Health Professions' the Vocational Education and Training (VET) Qualifications (or equivalent Qualifications) linked to the family of health professions, even if they are of Medium[37] or Superior[38] Level. This type of VET Qualifications confers to its holder the consideration of 'Technician' or 'Superior Technician', respectively, and does not authorize him to exercise a health profession but to perform their duties under the supervision and with respect for the competence of Health Professionals.

§2. Education of Health Professionals

30. Regulation of the healthcare profession in Spain is currently in line with the guidelines laid down by the EU Law, particularly the regulations designed to harmonize conditions and requirements for entry to and specialization in medical studies throughout a community, which is highly sensitive to the importance that the profession holds for society.[39] Would-be students of medicine at university must pass compulsory aptitude tests designed to examine whether they are properly prepared for such studies. They are held annually in universities and may be taken by Spaniards resident abroad and foreigners who attest to having followed a suitable course of study abroad. Once they have successfully taken these tests, candidates cannot then be asked to take further entrance exams, although faculties may limit

35. *See* Arts 6.3 and 19.1 of the Law 44/2003, of 21 November, on the Regulation of Health Professions.
36. Due to the characteristics of the activity, to improve the efficiency of health services or to adapt the healthcare structure to the scientific and technological progress.
37. Some of these VET Qualifications are: Technician in Auxiliary Nursing Care and Pharmacy.
38. Some of these VET Qualifications are: Superior Technician in Pathologic Anatomy and Cytology, in Dietetics, in Health Documentation, in Oral Hygiene, in Imaging for Diagnostic, in Clinic Diagnostic Laboratory, in Ortho Prosthetic, in Dental Prosthesis, in Radiotherapy, in Environmental Health and in Audio Prosthesis.
39. A good reflection of this is Council Decision 75/364/EEC of 16 Jun. 1975 to set up an Advisory Committee entrusted with the principal task of assuring a comparatively high level of training of physicians (including specialists) within the European Community (Art. 1).

the number of places on offer, in which case those who obtain the highest marks in the university entrance exam will be admitted.[40]

31. In Spain, the basic medical training leads to obtain the Official University 'Qualification of Bachelor' of Medicine, established by Royal Decree 1417/1990 of 26 October, or to obtain the 'Qualification of Graduate' established in accordance with the provisions contained in the Order ECI/332/2008 of 13 February, under the terms of the Agreement of Council of Ministers of 14 December 2007.[41] Persons who have either of these two Qualifications can be considered 'Graduated Health Professionals'. The degrees themselves are valid throughout the country, although each faculty is at liberty to organize and plan its own syllabus leading to the award. Syllabuses are designed primarily to ensure that doctors trained in faculties of medicine gradually acquire sufficient clinical experience and expertise. The aforementioned Royal Decree[42] stipulates that training must provide students with:

1. an adequate knowledge of the sciences which form the basis of medicine and a sound understanding of scientific principles, including the measurement of biological functions, evaluation of scientifically proven facts and data analysis;
2. an adequate knowledge of the structure, functions and behaviour of human beings, healthy and otherwise, as well as of the relationships between states of health and man's physical and social environment;
3. an adequate knowledge of clinical subjects and practice in order to provide students with a coherent view of mental and physical illnesses, the preventive aspects of medicine, diagnosis and therapeutics, and human reproduction;
4. adequate and appropriately supervised clinical experience in hospitals.

Training focuses on the preventive, diagnostic and therapeutic aspects of medicine, with the help of clinical experience acquired in hospitals. Agreements reached between the public administrations and universities and health institutions in which university training is provided guarantee the practical teaching of medicine (universities have at least one teaching and research hospital).[43]

The Royal Decree guidelines state that medical studies shall be split into two cycles, each lasting three years. Each cycle must offer a minimum of 250 course credits (a credit is the equivalent of ten hours of theory or practical instruction), with

40. Under Art. 26.1 of the University Reform Law (Organic Law 11/1983 of 25 August), it is up to the government to establish selection procedures for admittance to University centres. RD 1005/1991 of 14 June was drawn up to fulfil this aim; Art. 5.1 endorses the observations made in the text.
41. Decision of 17 Dec. 2007, of the Secretary of State for Universities and Research, which publishes the Agreement of the Council of Ministers of 14 Dec. 2007, which establishes the conditions to which the curricula leading to degrees that enable the exercise of the regulated profession of Physician must be adapted (B.O.E. of 21 Dec. 2007).
42. *See also* Art. 23.1 of the Council Directive 93/16/EEC of 5 Apr. 1993.
43. Article 104 of the LGS (Law 14/1986 of 25 April) states that all care structures of the health system must be made available for the continuous postgraduate teaching of professionals. RD 1558/1986 of 28 June sets out the general bases of the system of agreements between universities and healthcare institutions. Among other things, such agreements aim to assure clinical training for undergraduate and postgraduate medical students.

a weekly teaching load of between twenty and thirty hours, including practicals. The amount of theoretical content shall not exceed fifteen hours per week.

Although each faculty can plan its own courses leading to the degree in medicine, there are certain compulsory core subjects which must be included in medical studies in all Spanish universities to ensure that the qualifications awarded are consistent and uniform.[44]

Royal Decree 99/2011, of 28 January, which regulates official doctoral studies, regulates the third cycle of university studies and the awarding of PhDs in medicine. Postgraduate students wishing to obtain this degree must successfully submit a doctoral thesis giving evidence of original research work.

32. Dentistry has been part and parcel of medical studies since the beginning of the century. It was made a specialist subject (Stomatology) by a Decree of 7 July 1944. However, the scarcity of dental health specialists, the criteria in force in neighbouring countries and in particular Community directives,[45] and also the need to avoid possible discrimination between specialists trained in Spain and the rest of the EU made it necessary to create the specific profession of Dentistry. This came about through Law 10/1986 of 17 March, governing dentists and other dental health professionals, and Royal Decree 970/1986 of 11 April (subsequently modified by RD 1418/1990 of 26 October) which develops this law and creates the official qualification of Degree in Dentistry, which entitles the holder to practise the profession and thus firmly establishes dentistry as a separate academic discipline.

Thus, dentistry is granted its own syllabus, which is broken down into theoretical, practical and clinical teaching. Training aims to provide dentists with the necessary competence to prevent, diagnose and treat abnormalities and diseases of the teeth, mouth, jaws and tissues. However, in this field of health, the highest level of specialization continues to be stomatology and maxillofacial surgery.[46]

33. Finally, it is important to remark that the regulation of the training and educational action in the field of health professions is based on the following guiding principles:[47]

1. The permanent collaboration between the agencies of the competent public Administrations in matters of education and health.
2. The agreement between universities and teaching centres of vocational training and the institutions and health centres, to ensure the practical teaching of lessons that require it.
3. The disposition of the whole structure of the health system to be used in undergraduate, specialized and continuous teaching of professionals.

44. *See* Annex to RD 1417/1990 of 26 October.
45. *See* Directives 78/686/EEC, 78/687/EEC and 78/688/EEC of 25 Jul. 1978 and 81/1057/EEC of 14 Dec. 1981.
46. The Order of 9 Sep. 1988 regulates access to specialist training in Stomatology and defines training and the awarding of the qualification following completion of the curriculum, in accordance with Community Directive 75/363.
47. All af them are included into the Art. 12 of the Law 44/2003 of 21 November.

4. The consideration of the health centres and services, also, as centres of scientific research and training of professionals, as long as the conditions suitable for those purposes are fulfilled.
5. The permanent review of teaching methodology and lessons in the health field in order to achieve a better adaptation of the professional knowledge to the scientific and technical evolution and to the health needs of the population.
6. The permanent updating of knowledge, through continuous education, of health professionals, as a right and a duty for them. For this aim, health institutions and centres will facilitate the realization of continuous training activities.
7. The establishment, development and updating of methodologies for the evaluation of knowledge acquired by professionals and of the functioning of the own training system.

§3. Licensing of Physicians

I. General Practitioners

34. In Spain, since the University Law of 1943, the legislation has determined that the degree of Licenciado en Medicina qualifies for the practice of medicine in any field or specialty, provided that it is not practised as a specialist. In order to practice the medical profession as a specialist doctor and to occupy a public or private job as a specialist, it is necessary to have the corresponding medical specialty qualification.

In fact, it was already in the 1990s when Directive 86/457/EEC, of 15 September, ruled that as of 1995, the exercise of the functions of GP in the framework of a public social security system should be subordinated to the possession of specific training in general medicine.[48] This was imposed in Spain by Royal Decree 853/1993, of 4 June 1993, on the NHS. Today, this medical speciality is ruled by Law 44/2003, dated 21 November 2003, concerning the organization of health professions, and its training cycle is specified in Order PJC/798/2024, of 26 July, which approves and publishes the training programme for the specialty of Family and Community Medicine, the evaluation criteria for specialists in training and the accreditation requirements for the Multiprofessional Teaching Units of Family and Community Care.

According to the current regulatory framework, in short, the objective of the current degree in Medicine is to provide the so-called 'basic medical training'; the training that all medical graduates must acquire regardless of their future orientation. However, in order to perform the functions of a GP in the framework of the public Social Security system, specific training is required, which is provided by the specialty in Family and Community Medicine.

48. *See* J. Carreras, 'Diseño de nuevos planes de estudios en el contexto del Espacio Europeo de Educación Superior (II): Perfil profesional del graduado en Medicina', in *Educación Médica*, 11(3), 2008, pp. 113–123.

The situation of MESTOs (medical specialists without an official family medicine degree) has been particularly complex in the Spanish system. These are doctors who finished their career before the EU made it mandatory to have at least two years of specialized training or a certification of their functions as a GP and were unable to meet this requirement through the MIR because the supply of places was insufficient. However, the healthcare needs of the health system meant that they were hired in hospitals and health centres where they had already been practising for decades.

In order to regulate their situation, in 1998, it was established that professionals who had been family physicians for at least five years, accumulated 300 hours of training related to the specialty and passed a competency assessment test would also acquire the title. The measure allowed some 10,000 practitioners to obtain a degree through this route in recent years, but at least a thousand more were not yet specialists in 2024. Finally, this situation has led to the approval of Royal Decree 1137/2024, which amends 1753/1998 on exceptional access to the title of specialist in Family and Community Medicine (MFyC). This regulation will allow access for professionals who have not yet obtained their specialist degree through a single aptitude test organized by the Ministry of Health. This consists of a questionnaire with alternative answers, with or without associated images. Half of the maximum score must be achieved to obtain the qualification of 'apt' and, therefore, the title.

35. Concern for the continuous training of physicians was evident at the EU level, as reflected in the adoption of Council Directive 85/547/EEC of 15 September 1986, which provided for specific and essentially practical training in general medicine lasting two years on a full or part-time basis. Practitioners' continuous training has not been overlooked in Spain, and at the present day, Law 44/2003 of 21 November, on the Regulation of Health Professions, establishes a set of detailed provisions on this matter. Article 33.1 of the aforementioned Law establishes that Continuing Training is the active and permanent teaching and learning process to which health professionals are entitled and obliged, which starts at the end of undergraduate or specialized studies, and that is intended to update and improve the knowledge, skills and attitudes of health professionals taking into account the scientific and technological development, as well as the social and health system demands and needs. In any case, we should note that Continuing Training has been presented in the aforementioned Article 12f) of Law 44/2003, as one of the guiding principles of the training and teaching action in the field of health professions and that has been configured from two dimensions: as a right and as an obligation. This implies that, on the one hand, the employer must provide such training, and on the other, the health professional must attend and participate in such training. In addition, we must remark that, in order to ensure the achievement of the objectives of Continuous Training, Law 44/2003 has created the Commission on Continuing Training of Health Professions. Such commission is a body composed of representatives of the Interterritorial Council of the National Health System, Professional

Organizations, Universities, and the National Council of Specialties in Health Sciences and of Scientific Societies. Some of the functions of this Commission are:[49]

1. The detection, analysis, study and assessment of the needs of professionals and the health system in the field of continuous training, according to the proposals of the competent bodies of the autonomous communities, scientific societies and, where appropriate, professional organizations represented in the Professional Advisory Commission.
2. The proposal for the adoption of programmes or for the development of activities and actions of continuous training of priority and common character for the entire health system.
3. The proposal for the adoption of appropriate measures to plan, coordinate and harmonize the activities of the various actors in the field of continuous training of health professionals.
4. The study, report and proposal for the establishment of procedures, criteria and requirements for accreditation of centres and activities of continuous training.
5. The study, report and proposal for the establishment of procedures, criteria and requirements for the accreditation and the advanced accreditation of professionals in a specific functional area of a profession or specialty, following the development of the accredited continuous training activities.

II. Medical Specialists

36. Specialist medical training was not regulated in Spain initially. Previously, the degree in medicine and surgery authorized the holder to engage in any medical activity, specialist or otherwise, and status as a specialist was obtained through constant practice by qualified physicians who performed specialist activities in health institutions or physicians who had followed a specialist training course at postgraduate level and also those who were actually practising as specialists.[50] This rather chaotic situation came to an end with the promulgation on 20 July 1955 of a Law governing the teaching and practice of, and qualifications needed for, specialist branches of medicine (the law was developed further by the Decree of 23 December 1957). This law created the official degree of Specialist Physician, awarded by the State to graduates in medicine on completion of the appropriate specialist studies and prescribed periods of practical work. These courses were offered in university departments with chairs in the relevant subject or in Ministry of Education-approved specialist institutes or schools and clinics managed by university professors. In all cases, an examination had to be taken at the end of the specialist training.

At the same time, alongside the system created by the 1955 law, and in response to the ever-growing need for specialist doctors, a special system was being put in

49. *See* Art. 34.4 Law 44/2003.
50. *See* J.M. Rodríguez Pastrana, 'Régimen Jurídico de las especialidades médicas', in *Revista de Administración Pública*, nº. 116, 1988, pp. 158 f.

place in Social Security institutions.[51] This training system was no longer tied directly to universities, and candidates (interns and resident doctors) were linked to Social Security by virtue of an employer-employee relationship, as opposed to the teacher-student relationship which operated in universities. Access to this type of training was limited by a *numerus clausus* mechanism and candidates were chosen on the basis of merit and their performance in an examination. On completion of the training, successful candidates were not awarded a degree (Specialist Physician) but rather a certificate attesting to the type of specialist training received.

Subsequently, it was decided to adopt a single specialist training system, which was taken out of university hands. The first step in this direction was the passing of Royal Decree 2015/1978 of 15 July, which regulated the awarding of qualifications in specialist branches of medicine,[52] although this was later derogated by RD 127/1984 of 11 January,[53] which regulated specialist training and the awarding of the degree of Specialist Physician. The determination of health specialties was made through RD 183/2008, of 8 February 2008, which determines and classifies the specialties in Health Sciences and develops certain aspects of the specialized health training system. The transversal training of specialties in Health Sciences, in turn, has been regulated by Royal Decree 589/2022, of 19 July which regulates the transversal training of specialties in Health Sciences, the procedure and criteria for the proposal of a new title of specialist in Health Sciences or diploma of specific training area, and the revision of those established, and the access and training of the areas of specific training; and establishes the rules applicable to the annual tests for access to training positions in specialties in Health Sciences.

At the present moment, access to specialist status is, in general, regulated by Law 44/2003, dated 21 November 2003, concerning the organization of health professions, whose Article 22.1 determines that it will be based on an annual national call for applications (MIR system). The 'system of residence' is conceived as the appropriate procedure for the training in all specialties in health sciences of the bachelor or other university degrees that allow access to them. In this sense, even those specialties that until now did not have a residence system must be removed or modified within five years. This system consist in a programmed and remunerated clinical practice that progressively allows the professional to assume responsibilities while the supervision of his/her activities is reduced.[54] It is important to note that in order to participate in the system of residence (specialized training), the applicant must successfully pass an annual and national selection process. In this respect, the new regulation represents a significant change concerning this selection process, given that the test that applicants must pass is not a simple knowledge test anymore. Such process is composed of a test or a group of tests that aims to evaluate the theoretical

51. *See* MO of 28 Jul. 1971 on Internists and Resident Physicians and MO of 9 Dec. 1977, which regulates postgraduate training in Social Security institutions.
52. The MO of 11 Feb. 1981 establishes equivalences for specialist branches already in existence prior to the passing of RD 2015/1978, of 15 July and, in order to respect acquired rights, sets up a transitory system for the awarding of specialist qualifications to cater for those who had commenced their training before 1 Jan. 1980.
53. Derogatory Provision Number 1 also derogates the Law of 20 Jul. 1955.
54. Article 20.3 of the Law 44/2003 establishes the criteria governing the training through the system of residence.

and practical knowledge, the clinical and communication skills, as well as the academic and professional merits of the applicants.

The number of vacancies available for this training system is set by the so-called Commission on Human Resources of the National Health System, with the previous reports of the National Council of Specialties in Health Sciences and of the Ministry of Education, Culture and Sport, taking into account the proposals made by the Autonomous Communities, the needs of specialists of health system and the available budget. The system for awarding all the positions offered in the annual call is carried out according to the decreasing order of the score obtained by each applicant in a test, with the peculiarities established with respect to the positions in privately-owned centres.[55]

37. Residents undergo a theoretical and practical training that implies a personal and progressive participation of the specialist in training in the activity and responsibilities of the specialty in question. On the basis of the Law on the Regulation of Health Professions of 2003 (LOPS), it is possible to group the specialties in Health Sciences with core training criteria, with a minimum common training of two years. The 'core', 'trunk' or 'backbone' training could be defined as the common formative period of a group of specialties in Health Sciences that is based on the acquisition of clinical competences shared by all the specialties that make up the 'trunk' (formed by two or more specialties), and with a minimum duration of two years. With this new system, specialized training comprises two periods: The backbone formative period, in which common competences to all trunk specialties are acquired, and the specific training period, in which the resident will be trained in each specialized skill. It is important to remark that the Government must establish which degree/qualification is required in order to access each speciality. The 'Areas of Specific Training' are created, as an upper cycle after specialization, within one or more specialties in Health Sciences and based on specific programmes and in competence assessment tests.[56] The Certificate of Specific Area of Training (issued by the Ministry of Health, Social Services and Equality) have official character and national validity. This Certificate entitles its holder to use the title of 'specialist in a particular area of specific training', but it is not a requirement to obtain a job (as it is the official qualification of specialist). However, it can be valued as a merit to access a highly specialized work in public or private centres or establishments.

In any case, the LOPS establishes that the training of specialists will take place by the residency system in accredited centres (Article 20.2 LOPS), training that will meet the following criteria (Article 20.3 LOPS):

55. *See* A. Urruela Mora/A. Libano Beristain, 'Lección 16. La ordenación de las profesiones sanitarias. Las agresiones a los profesionales sanitarios', in C.M. Romeo Casabona/P. Nicolás Jiménez/S. Romeo Malanda (Dirs), *Manual de Bioderecho* (2ª edición, Dykinson, Madrid 2025), pp. 435 ff. https://bioderecho.eu/manual-bioderecho/

56. This definition must be explained in the context of the RD-Law 16/2012, of 20 April, concerning urgent measures to ensure the sustainability of the National Health System and to improve the quality and safety of its services.

a. Residents will carry out the training programme of the specialty on a full-time basis. Residency training will be incompatible with any other professional activity. It will also be incompatible with any training activity, provided that it is carried out within the working day of the resident's special employment relationship.
b. The duration of the residency shall be established in the training programme of the specialty and shall be indicated in accordance with the provisions, if any, of the Community regulations.
c. The professional activity of the residents will be planned by the management bodies together with the teaching commissions of the centres in such a way that it is fully integrated into the ordinary, continuous and emergency operation of the health centre.
d. The residents should develop, in a programmed and supervised manner, the activities foreseen in the programme, progressively assuming, as they advance in their training, the activities and responsibilities of the autonomous practice of the specialty.
e. The activities of the residents, which must appear in the Resident's Book, will be subject to the evaluations determined by regulation. In any case, there will be annual evaluations and a final evaluation at the end of the training period.
f. During the residency, a special labour relationship will be established between the health service or the centre and the specialist in training. The Government, taking into account the specific characteristics of the training activity and the healthcare activity carried out in the health centres, and in accordance with the criteria contained in this chapter and in the first additional provision of this law, will regulate the special employment relationship of residency.

The training programmes of the specialties in Health Sciences should specify the qualitative and quantitative objectives and the professional competencies to be fulfilled by the candidate for the degree during each of the annual courses into which the training programme is divided (Article 21.1 LOPS).

Lastly, it should be stressed that any physician who wishes to call himself a specialist and engage in specialist practice must hold the degree of Specialist Physician. Furthermore, the degree is a compulsory requirement for positions in public and private specialist units and institutions (Article 1 of RD 127/84).

§4. Manpower Planning. Freedom of Establishment

38. As was stated earlier, the NHS devised by the Spanish Constitution is based on the setting up of a public health service. In the words of Rodríguez Pastrana,[57] this merely means that 'thenceforth the State possesses a legal instrument which allows it to intervene to regulate and control activities. However, in no way is it prejudged that management of the system will be the exclusive prerogative of the State or will be achieved through a state monopoly, directly or indirectly, or that it will

57. Rodríguez Pastrana, *El servicio público de la sanidad: el marco constitucional*, *supra*, p. 31.

coexist alongside private initiative, albeit one which would come under the system's specific regime'. Article 36 of the Constitution provides that 'the law shall regulate specific aspects of the legal regime of Professional Associations and the exercise of professions requiring qualifications … ', although it also acknowledges the freedom to choose one's profession (Article 35.1) and freedom of enterprise in the health sector (Article 38). Moreover, Articles 88 and 89 and ff. of the LGS recognize both the right to freely practise a health profession and freedom of enterprise, in accordance with constitutional provisions. In short, freedom to engage in professional practice must be guaranteed, although room is made for limitations imposed by constitutional requirements, which aim to protect users of medical services by ensuring that the providers of such services are properly trained.

39. It was stated above that the medical profession is one which requires a professional qualification and is regulated by law. A person may call himself a physician only if he has obtained a degree in Medicine, on completion of a university course. In the case of physicians who have obtained a degree, a special prodecure must be carried out in order to validate it. The Ministry of Education is in charge of recognizing medical degrees obtained in the EU/EEA (for EU foreigners) and of homologating and validating medical degrees obtained outside the EU/EEA (non-Community foreigners). The homologation grants the foreign degree, from the date on which it is granted and the corresponding credential is issued, the same effects as the Spanish degree or academic degree, with which it is homologated throughout the national territory.[58]

40. However, the holding of the degree in itself is not enough to commence practice. Article 35 of the Statutes of the Organisation of Colleges of Physicians (OMC) makes registration a compulsory requirement for anyone wishing to practise medicine of any form in both public and private centres.[59] The OMC, which comprises all physicians in professional practice of any kind, either as independent doctors or in the employment of central or local administration, Autonomous Communities, and all public or private entities,[60] requires members to comply with a

---

58. *See* M. Salmerón Salto/M. Pernas Martínez, 'Régimen Jurídico de los títulos de medicina en España. El reconocimiento de los títulos universitarios en el marco del Derecho Comunitario: homologaciones y convalidaciones', in L. Parejo Alfonso/A. Palomar Olmeda (Coord.), *Manual jurídico de la profesión médica* (Dykinson, Madrid 1998), pp. 151 ff.
59. H. Losada González, 'Ordenación de la profesión médica mediante la Organización Médica Colegial', in L. Parejo Alfonso/A. Palomar Olmeda (Coord.), *Manual jurídico de la profesión médica* (Dykinson, Madrid 1998), pp. 481 ff.
60. Constitutional Court doctrine (particularly ruling 89/1989) endorses the view that compulsory registration with the College is constitutional, even for physicians employed by the Administration. It is not incompatible with freedom of association since, according to ruling 131/1989, of 19 July, which deals specifically with the issue, 'although the professional services are provided under the public service regime or are dependent on a public organisation, the profession of physician is still being exercised, albeit with a compulsory registration requirement imposed by the legislature and the corresponding statutory provisions ... at the end of the day, this circumstance does not modify in any way whatsoever the nature of the activity, which continues to serve the same users. Although it is true that the requirement does involve a restriction on freedom of association, in that a physician is not free *not* to register, it is justified in the light of the general interest at stake in the professional practice of medicine: professional discipline, ethical rules, the good faith of third persons, all of

series of obligations (membership fees, national health insurance, etc.) and to adhere to certain rules of discipline.[61] Specialists must hold the appropriate specialist qualification, regardless of whether they work in the public or private sector.[62]

41. Freedom of enterprise must also be assured in the health sector, and this enables public and private healthcare to coexist in the sector. The acceptance of the premise that health, under the Spanish Constitution, is a public service necessarily implies that the public administrations are empowered to regulate and control private sector health activities also. However, this cannot be taken to mean that the Administration is the sole body entrusted with healthcare management. The LGS – which provides for private health services also – presupposes direct management of public health services, although, at the same time, it contemplates two basic avenues of indirect management, namely, agreements concluded with approved hospitals and other forms of association.

Agreements of this type enable the public administrations to harness outside resources to provide health services. In doing so, they can guarantee assistance and at the same time ensure that the approved centres do not themselves put in place complementary services which would undermine the optimal use of public resources. In concluding agreements with private centres, public administrations must give priority to non-profit making entities, as long as they are competitive with other centres in terms of efficiency, quality and cost (Article 90.2 of the LGS). In all cases, the Administration will carry out the role of inspectorate with regard to health, administrative and economic aspects in relation to each patient (Article 94.2 of the LGS).

Private hospitals which are linked to the public sector are virtually placed on an equal footing with their publicly-owned counterparts. As Pemán Gavín[63] has pointed out, linking 'brings them under the wing of the public system and helps make their activities better known'. The centres and establishments in question, as well as their services, remain in private hands, although the public administration is responsible for inspections (Articles 66 and 94.1 of the LGS).

42. The exercise of non-nationals' freedom of establishment and freedom to provide services in Spain is regulated by Royal Decree 1837/2008, of 8 November, which regulates the recognition of diplomas, certificates and other medical and specialist qualifications issued in the States members of the EU. The provisions were

---

which must be protected in conjunction with the constitutional values and rights of health, health care and the lives and physical integrity of the population'.

61. The Statutes of the General Council of Colleges were passed by Royal Decree 300/2016, of 22 July, approving the Statutes of the General Council of Colleges of Physicians. Professional practice denotes the provision of medical services of all types, even where the physician does not practise privately or where he does not have his own facilities (Art. 35.2 of the Statutes).

62. Article 13 of the LGS empowers the government to adopt regulations to prevent illegal practice and malpractice, even though both are covered by Penal Code provisions (*see* other sections of this book) and administrative sanctions govern professional practice by unregistered physicians and aiding and abetting malpractice (Art. 40.1 and Art. 44 ss b) and m) respectively of the OMC Statutes).

63. Pemán Gavín, *Derecho a la salud y Administración Sanitaria*, *supra*, p. 213.

drawn up in response to the need to incorporate various EC directives on the subject into Spanish legislation.[64] Also, we must remark that the RD 459/2010, of 16 April, regulates the conditions for recognizing professional effects to the foreign qualifications of Specialist in Health Sciences obtained in a country which is not a member of the EU.

---

64. *See* Directive 2005/36/EC of the European Parliament and of the Council of 7 Sep. 2005, Directive 2006/100/EC of the Council of 20 Nov. 2006, concerning the recognition of professional qualifications, as well as certain aspects of the exercise of the legal profession and Directive 2013/55/EU of the European Parliament and of the Council of 20 Nov. 2013 amending Directive 2005/36/EC on the recognition of professional qualifications and Regulation (EU) No. 1024/2012 on administrative cooperation through the Internal Market Information System ('the IMI Regulation').

Chapter 2. Illegal Practice of Medicine

43. In the previous chapter, we described the procedure for access to the medical profession. To recap briefly, it is necessary first to have completed university studies leading to obtain the Qualification of 'Bachelor' or the Qualification of 'Graduate' in Medicine, which is awarded by Faculties of Medicine; it is also compulsory to register with the College of Physicians (Colegio Oficial de Médicos) in the intended area of practice:[65] furthermore, specialists must hold the appropriate diplomas accrediting that they have completed the relevant studies and practical work enabling them to call themselves specialists and seek employment as such in all private or public centres;[66] this means that although all graduates in medicine may practice any branch of medicine, no one may use the title of specialist (or take up such a position) unless he holds that appropriate qualification. The profession may be practised only when the above-mentioned legal requirements have been met. All the above make up the exclusive rights of professional practice, which is conferred on physicians in view of the high degree of qualification required and the subsequent penal protection afforded to the profession to prevent practice by nonmembers or non-qualified practitioners.

Illegal practice can indeed constitute an offence of encroachment and is punished by Spain's Penal Code (Article 403, governing the offence of usurpation of functions): '*1. Any person who practices a profession without holding the corresponding academic qualification, issued or recognised in Spain according to the current law, shall be liable to a fine between twelve and twenty four months. If the professional activity requires an official qualification that certifies the necessary training and that legally authorize to its bearer for its exercise, a fine between six and twelve months will be imposed to any person who practices such activity without holding the aforementioned qualification. 2. A prison sentence of six months to two years shall be imposed if concurs any of the following circumstances: a) When the offender, in addition, publicly confers himself the quality of professional certified by the alluded qualification. b) When the offender executes the acts described in the preceding paragraph in a local or establishment open to the public in which the provision of services of that profession is announced*'. It is generally held[67] that persons who commit such an offence harm various interests which have repercussions on society as a whole. The most important of these is the requirement concerning academic qualifications as a means of ensuring correct professional practice; the

65. RD 1018/1980, of 19 May, governing the Statutes of the OMC and the General Council of Colleges of Physicians, stipulates in Art. 35 that it is compulsory for physicians to register with the College in order to practice any form of medicine, including where the physician does not practise privately or does not have his own surgery.
66. *See* Arts 1 and 3 of the RD 183/2008, of 8 February, which determine and classify the specialties in Health Sciences and certain aspects of specialized health training system are developed.
67. J. Montero García-Andrade, 'Comentario al Artículo 403', in A. Roma Valdés (Dir.), *Código penal comentado. Comentarios tras las Leyes Orgánicas 1/2015 y 2/2015, de 30 de marzo* (Bosch, Barcelona 2015), pp. 653 ff.; P. Lloria García, 'Intrusismo', in C.M. Romeo Casabona (Dir.), *Enciclopedia de Bioderecho y Bioética, Tomo II* (Comares, Granada 2011), pp. 1018–1020; G. Rodríguez Mourullo, 'El delito de intrusismo', in *Revista General de Legislación y Jurisprudencia*, 1969, pp. 235 ff.; D.M. Luzón Peña, 'Problemas del intrusismo en el Derecho penal', in *La Ley*, 1985, pp. 1257 ff.; A. Serrano Gómez, 'El intrusismo en la Odontología', in *Actualidad Penal*, 1988, p. 1067.

State endorses the validity of these qualifications in that it, and it alone, is empowered to award them. On a second level lies the collective interest of the profession concerned, which must ensure that professional practice is limited exclusively to those who can provide the necessary guarantees in the form of the recognized qualification. This exclusive right of practice also means that users (in this case, patients) will receive the services of a qualified professional, although it should be said that an unauthorized person who has provided satisfactory services and has cured the patient's illness will still nevertheless have committed an offence.

44. For an offence to exist, the following requirements must be fulfilled:

1. An offence is committed only where the profession – such as medicine – which is practised illegally requires an academic qualification (notwithstanding the fact that the Penal Code refers to an 'official' qualification, which is a much broader term).[68] Alternatively, the qualification may be one which is recognized in Spain according to the current law, which affects particular physicians or specialists (both Spanish and non-Spanish) who have obtained their professional qualifications abroad.
2. The offender must perform actions proper to the profession of physician as stipulated in the regulations governing medical practice (*see* Chapter 1 of this Part). No encroachment takes place where a patient treats himself or is aided by a relative under the guidance of a physician. This is an important point given the increasing frequency with which patients, particularly the chronically ill, treat themselves at home (diabetics who administer their own insulin injections, patients with terminal renal insufficiency who receive dialysis in their own home, patients with respiratory problems who give themselves oxygen, etc.). The offence does not exist either in the case of charlatans (quacks) as long as they do not undertake operations or administer products (e.g., prescribe drugs) which may only be given by physicians.[69] This does not mean, however, that such persons are exonerated from liability in respect of possible injuries they might cause to their patients or where the latter's condition seriously worsens as a result of being prevented from seeking the assistance of a qualified practitioner. The charging of a fee is not an indispensable requirement of illegal practice,[70] although exceptionally, any such charge may mean that the impersonator is guilty of fraud (e.g., if he deceives the patient by leading him to believe in the treatment, when in fact it will not cure him at all or has little bearing on the nature of the problem being treated).

---

68. Lloria García, 'Intrusismo', *supra*, p. 1020; D.M. Luzon Peña, 'El título académico oficial en el delito de intrusismo', in *La Ley*, 1989, pp. 497 ff. Ruling of Supreme Court (2nd Chamber), 6 Jun. 1989 (for a ruling in the opposite sense, i.e., not putting official qualification on an equal footing with an academic one, *see* Ruling of Supreme Court (2nd Chamber), 13 May 1989).
69. The Supreme Court has on occasions punished such acts (where medicines have been prescribed: Ruling (2nd Chamber) of 18 Oct. 1978; and also in the case of a person who ran a Natural Medicine Surgery using the professional title of Dr in Naturopathy and Diet Counsellor: Ruling (2nd Chamber) of 23 Jan. 1984).
70. *See* Ruling of Supreme Court, Second Criminal Chamber, Judgment 1045/2011 of 14 Oct. 2011, Rec. 10365/2011.

3. There is debate as to whether one single action of the type mentioned above is in itself sufficient to constitute an offence or whether several are required. Although it is widely held that one single action suffices (except where the very nature of the profession or its regulations requires something more habitual),[71] we are of the opinion that professional practice in general is characterized by repetition with various persons, and thus the activity deemed to constitute illegal practice must comprise several acts, at least in the case of medicine. Habitualness or repeated actions of the type mentioned above shall give rise to one offence only.
4. Encroachment may only be committed intentionally and thus it cannot stem from negligence, although this does not rule out a legal appraisal of the conduct of someone who mistakenly believes that he can carry out professional acts without the appropriate qualifications.

45. Any person who practices illegally in this way and, in addition, publicly confers himself the quality of professional certified by the alluded qualification shall be guilty of a more serious offence (Article 403, paragraph 2.a of the Penal Code). For this aggravated offence to exist, it is not sufficient for the offender to pass himself off as a qualified practitioner in the presence of one or more patients, but rather – and in addition to actions of encroachment – he must also make others believe that he holds the status in question. It is important to note that the same punishment will be imposed when the offender executes the acts in a local or establishment open to the public in which the provision of services of that profession is announced (Article 403, paragraph 2.b of the Penal Code).

46. The offence of encroachment may be concurrent with other offences: if, during the course of unlawful practice, harm is caused to a patient's health or life because the treatment is inadequate due to the offender's lack of professional training, the person may be liable also for an offence of recklessness leading to homicide or bodily injury;[72] or of forgery of documents (academic or degree certificates);[73] and also, as has been mentioned above, in exceptional circumstances fraud.

47. A physician who fails to register with the College of Physicians, that is, a qualified practitioner who practises without first having registered with the appropriate association or body, where such a requirement is mandatory, shall be guilty of an administrative misconduct (minor administrative offence) and liable to a fine according to the RD 1018/1980, of 19 May, governing the Statutes of the OMC and the General Council of Colleges of Physicians.[74]

---

71. Lloria García, 'Intrusismo', *supra*, p. 1023; Rodríguez Mourullo, 'El delito de intrusismo', *supra*, pp. 259 ff.; Supreme Court Rulings (2nd Chamber) of 1 Dec. 1970 and 19 Jun. 1990.
72. Ruling of the Barcelona Provincial Court of 6 Feb. 1990, by which a nurse was found guilty of professional recklessness, although she was cleared of charges of illegal practice.
73. Supreme Court Ruling 934/2006 of 29 Sep. 2006.
74. *See* Art. 40.

48. Spanish courts have had to deal frequently with cases of illegal medical practice and have used the full weight of this criminal offence to punish such acts, whether by professionals of lower rank (nurses, for example)[75] who have impersonated physicians, or by persons who have no connections whatsoever with the healthcare professions.[76] Dentistry has traditionally been the field to suffer most from encroachment. Although case law includes clear examples which constitute illegal practice of dentistry, such as when a dental technician undertakes implants or other activities proper to a qualified dentist,[77] or where such practices are undertaken by members of the nursing profession,[78] we would question the conviction of a graduate in medicine who does not hold the appropriate qualification required for dental practice, merely because he has habitually practised the speciality although without passing himself off as, or attributing to himself the status of, a qualified dentist, which is the only offence that is expressly prohibited, as was stated above.[79] The Supreme Court (2nd Chamber) ruled that an offence is committed by a medical graduate who, although not holding a qualification in dentistry, engages in habitual practice, but *not* when he does so occasionally and in special circumstances which justify his action, depending on the specific case.[80]

Other healthcare professions, such as nursing,[81] have fallen foul of illegal practice by persons who do not have the necessary training or qualifications.

To sum up, illegal practice (called literally impersonation or encroachment in Spanish) is an offence which may be committed not only by laypersons or by persons with no connections whatsoever with the profession but also by health professionals whose qualifications are insufficient to entitle them to perform such activities. It may even be committed by physicians who do not hold the relevant specialist qualification.[82]

---

75. Ruling of Supreme Court (2nd Chamber) of 8 Mar. 1968, Ruling of the Provincial Court of Burgos, Criminal, 16 Feb. 2010.
76. The aforementioned rulings of the Supreme Court of 18 Oct. 1978 and 23 Jan. 1984. Also Ruling of the Provincial Court of Cantabria, Criminal, of 4 Oct. 2016; Provincial Court of Asturias, s. 8 (Criminal), 13 Sep. 2017.
77. Rulings of Supreme Court (2nd Chamber) of 26 Feb. 1981, 25 Sep. 1987, 11 Apr. 1989, 29 Jun. 1991; Lérida Provincial Court Ruling of 3 Feb. 1990. Law of 17 Mar. 1986, which regulates dental health professions, list the competences of dental technicians as the design, elaboration, making and repair of dental apparatus using products, materials and techniques as indicated and prescribed by dentists. (Article 1.2).
78. Rulings of Supreme Court (2nd Chamber) of 8 Mar. 1968, 18 Oct. 1969; (3rd Chamber) 11 Oct. 1991 (competence to hire a nurse to take blood and carry out analytical tests on council premises).
79. The view is shared by Serrano Gómez, 'El intrusismo en la Odontología', *supra*, p. 1068.
80. Ruling of Supreme Court (2nd Chamber) of 13 Jun. 1990 (although the verdict was that an offence had been committed, the accused was cleared because in the court's opinion, he had unwittingly committed an unavoidable error due to the incorrect legal guidance given by the College of Physicians on a somewhat 'grey' issue (to use the Court's expression)); Ruling of 12 Mar. 1990 (dismissing possible error on the part of the physician), 21 Jun. 1991. A previous ruling, using different arguments, had been given by the Supreme Court (2nd Chamber) on 18 Oct. 1969.
81. For example, in Ruling of Supreme Court (2nd Chamber) of 28 Mar. 1980.
82. C.M. Romeo Casabona, *El Médico ante el Derecho* (Serv. Public. del Ministerio de Sanidad y Consumo, Madrid 1985, 3d. repr. 1990), p. 5; I. Navarro Frías, 'Delitos de falsedades', in C.M. Romeo Casabona et al. (Coords), *Derecho Penal. Parte Especial* (3ª ed. Comares, Granada, 2023), pp. 754–755.

Chapter 3. Control over the Practice of Medicine

§1. The Order of Physicians

I. Legal Framework and General Competences

49. In view of the importance of medicine in the community and the complex nature of medical services, the Administration has sought to reserve medical professional activity for those who are highly qualified both technically and scientifically.[83] Elsewhere we have discussed the fact that the position of physician or specialist can only be attained on completion of the relevant degree course in General Medicine or in the specialist field. The State has the exclusive right to issue such degree certificates, thus providing a guarantee that holders are qualified to provide medical services. However, the medical profession makes a further demand: it is not enough to simply guarantee that those who are admitted to the profession are properly qualified; it is also essential to ensure that medical practitioners perform their duties in accordance with the shared interests of the profession, thus establishing a kind of self-imposed control of the medical profession. The Spanish Constitution reflects this in its recognition of the value of professional associations for such purposes, stating in Article 36 that 'the law shall regulate the peculiarities of the legal regime of the Professional Colleges and the exercise of the qualified professions. The internal structure and functioning of the Colleges shall be democratic'.[84] The Professional Colleges Law of 1974 ('Ley 2/1974, sobre Colegios Profesionales'), which is the basic corpus of regulations in this respect, had to be revised to bring it into line with constitutional provisions, particularly with regard to the democratic processes required of Colleges.[85] Legal exercise of the medical profession is subject to prior membership in a College.[86] Membership is compulsory,[87] as it is in other professional fields, and although this is the subject of no small

---

83. *See* Romeo Casabona, *El médico ante el Derecho*, p. 5: 'Medicine has extended its scope considerably and at the same time has at its disposal a wide range of increasingly efficient and sophisticated procedures and techniques. This situation in turn makes it essential that doctors possess a body of knowledge and technical skill that is also constantly expanding. As a result, a greater degree of specialization, with the accompanying depth of knowledge of this narrower field, is demanded ... Trough this radical process Medicine has become a complex and interdependent activity.'
84. This is perhaps the constitutional provision of greatest relevance to professional colleges, although reference to professional organizations is also made in Arts 52 and 26. Article 52 sets out that 'the law shall regulate professional organisations that defend their own economic interests. Their internal structure and procedures must be democratic'. And in Art. 26: 'Honorary tribunals are prohibited in the area of civil administration and professional organisations.'
85. This was accomplished through Law 74/1978 of 26 December.
86. Following a certain amount of doubt in the past as to whether membership of a college should be compulsory or not, clause 34 of the Law which established the bases of the National Health Service (1944) stated that it was indeed compulsory for physicians. *See* Art. 35.1 of the RD 1018/1980 of 19 May, which passed the General Statutes of the OMC, in relation to Art. 3.2 of Law 2/1974, of 13 February, on Professional Colleges. Failure to comply with this obligation may be viewed as constituting illegal practice and give rise to criminal liability.
87. Aside from the obligation to register with a College, and with the appropriate social security scheme, there is also a right to join a College if one holds the necessary degree and meets all the other conditions (Art. 3.1 of the Professional Colleges Law). The right to join a medical college cannot be

amount of controversy in a wide range of professions, it provides a guarantee for the public and relieves them of the responsibility of establishing whether or not the person performing a medical act does indeed hold the appropriate qualifications for professional practice. Furthermore, it provides an efficient means for members to defend their professional interests against inappropriate, unethical and illegal practices.

50. From the organizational point of view, aside from the above-mentioned law on professional bodies, medical practice is regulated by the Statutes governing the OMC and the General Council of Colleges of Physicians, as passed by Royal Decree 1018/1980, of 19 March, which repealed the previous Regulations dating back to 1 April 1967. Nowadays, the in-force regulation of the Statutes Governing the General Council of Colleges of Physicians is the one set up by Royal Decree 300/2016, of 22 July (which repealed RD 757/2006, that previously repealed in this specific point the RD 1018/1980 of 19 March). The system is made up of the provincial Colleges of Physicians, Regional Councils of Colleges of Physicians (Consejos Autonómicos de Colegios de Médicos) and the General Council of Colleges of Physicians, which constitute the organs of representation and the governing body of the OMC. These bodies are corporations which are governed by public law and endowed with their own legal personality and full capacity to achieve their aims.[88]

51. The *OMC* brings together all physicians who carry out professional activity of any type, whether independently or in the service of the Public Administration or private institutions. It is the sole representative body of the medical profession, with exclusive responsibility for the regulation of medical practice within its area of jurisdiction and the defence of professional interests (Article 1.4 of the General Statutes of the OMC). The fundamental aims of the OMC, according to Article 3 General Statutes of the OMC, are as follows:

1. The regulation, within its jurisdiction, of medical practice; exclusive representation of physicians and the defence of the professional interests of its members, without prejudice to the powers and responsibilities of the Public Administration in respect of physicians who are public servants.
2. The safeguarding and observance of the deontological and ethical principles of the medical profession, as well as its dignity and prestige, through the drawing up and application of the relevant codes of practice.
3. The promotion, by all available means, of the continuing scientific, educational, economic and social development of members through the organization and maintenance of all kinds of educational institutions and the taking of all appropriate measures to ensure adequate social protection for members.

---

denied – except in those cases established by the General Statutes of the OMC (Art. 38) – which means that the right to practice a profession is guaranteed (Art. 35 of the Constitution).

88. *See* Art. 1 of the General Statutes of the OMC and Art. 1 of the Professional Colleges Law.

4. Cooperation with the public authorities in the provision of healthcare services, to which all Spanish citizens are entitled, and of the most efficient, just and equitable regulation of healthcare services and medical practice, as stipulated by the Professional Colleges Law.

52. The provincial *Colleges of Physicians* are the key element in the organization of medical practice.[89] Article 4.3 of the Professional Colleges Law (Ley 2/1974, de 13 de febrero, sobre Colegios Profesionales) prohibits the creation of any other college for the same profession within the limits of the territory concerned. Even so, each College may divide its provincial territories into districts, headed by a district council elected by the members in the area to perform the executive functions delegated by the College Board (Article 29 of the General Statutes of the OMC). Among the powers and duties of the Colleges of Physicians, apart from those specifically stipulated in their individual statutes, are the following (Article 34 of the General Statutes of the OMC):

1. Responsibility for the representation of physicians before provincial authorities and institutions.
2. The defence of the rights and prestige of the members they represent, or any other member, if they are subjected to harassment, injury, lack of consideration or disregard in professional matters, so long as any such situation occurs within the province. The College is also responsible for reporting instances of illegal practice piracy.
3. The keeping of a list of members, a register of professional qualifications and a list of medical districts in the province. They are also responsible for the gathering of statistics necessary for the carrying out of studies, projects and proposals concerning medical practice.
4. The application of the rules of ethics governing medical practice.
5. The taking of disciplinary action in cases of unfair competition, breaches of ethics and abuse of professional status as a physician. Colleges are also responsible for the implementation of disciplinary measures.
6. The study of the financial relationship between physicians and their clients and, where appropriate, the power to discipline members whose actions might undermine the dignity of the profession in this respect.
7. Regulation of the minimum fees for private practice. Colleges shall also express an opinion in fee-setting procedures and shall defend the interests of the medical profession before the Administration, Institutions, Courts, Organizations and private individuals in accordance with the current provisions.
8. Responsibility for the collection of professional fees and charges.
9. Cooperation with the public authorities in the formulation of healthcare policy and planning and implementation thereof, as well as participation in all matters relating to health promotion and healthcare.

---

89. There are also Colleges in Ceuta and Melilla, to wich the Statutes of the OMC apply. Their jurisdiction is limited to the respective municipal areas.

10. The development and implementation of general and scientific educational programmes to complement those envisaged under the Plan drawn up by the General Council.
11. The development and administration of services and institutions to ensure adequate social security cover and other forms of professional cover for members.
12. Raise the revenues needed to fund these institutions.
13. Encourage public or private bodies to provide to the collegiate (medical practitioners) for their professional practice a minimum of material and personnel necessary to perform quality medicine.[90]

Each College must have an Ethics, Medical Law and Authorisations Committee. Furthermore, professional interests are most efficiently served by the setting up within the Colleges of specific Sections that bring together members working in the same professional area and with the same professional concerns. These Sections are responsible for matters relating to the specialist field concerned and for presenting studies and proposals to the college bodies. A certain number of sections are obligatory,[91] although others may be created in the interests of the college concerned and in accordance with its statutes.

The governing bodies of the Colleges are the Board and the General Assembly of Members. The Board consists of a Plenary and a Standing Committee. Among other powers and responsibilities, it can take disciplinary action within its area of jurisdiction. For its part, the General Assembly is the College's highest representative body at provincial level[92] and comprises the total membership of the college. The Board is accountable to the General Assembly.

The financial running of the Colleges is independent of the General Council. They are autonomous in terms of the management and administration of their financial affairs. Each provincial college draws up an annual budget that has to be approved by the Assembly. College funds come from initial registration fees, the ordinary and extraordinary membership fees paid by members,[93] and a percentage of fees charged for the issuing of certificates, official stamps, official forms, medical assessments, etc.

---

90. *See* Arts 33 and 34 of the General Statutes of the OMC.
91. Article 27 of the General Statutes of the OMC stipulates that the following sections are obligatory: Head Physicians, Rural Medicine, Hospital Physicians, Social Security Outpatients' Physicians, Physicians in group practices, Physicians in private practice, Recent graduates (those who have graduated in the last five years and/or are still following a course of training) and Retired Physicians.
92. Agreements adopted by the General Assembly are binding on all college members. Nevertheless, in Colleges with more than 500 members, or where specific provision has been made in the statutes of the College concerned, and in all cases where there are more than 2,000 members, the Assembly may delegate its functions to an Assembly of Delegates elected by personal vote in a secret ballot of all members.
93. In addition to the registration fee payable on joining, members must pay monthly subscriptions, the minimum level of which is set by the General Council. These amounts may be increased by the individual Colleges subject to approval by the General Assembly (Arts 50, 51 and 52 of the General Statutes of the OMC).

53. Regional Councils of Colleges of Physicians (Consejos Autonómicos de Colegios de Médicos), which occupy a middle ground between the Colleges themselves and the General Council, are designed to coordinate and represent the Provincial Colleges and are governed by their own statutes. Responsibility for representation falls obligatorily on one of the presidents of the Colleges making up the Regional Council.[94]

54. The General Council of Colleges of Physicians is the body that brings together, coordinates and represents all the provincial Colleges of Physicians in Spain. It is composed of the General Assembly,[95] a Plenary and a Standing Committee, as well as an advisory body (Deontology, Medical Law and Authorisation Committee).[96] The Council is charged with the representation and defence of the legitimate aspirations of the medical profession, ethical guidance and control of professional practice, social, cultural and professional development and the promotion of the right to health. Among its most important functions are the drafting of the General Statutes of the Colleges, the passing of internal college regulations, the taking of disciplinary action against members of College Boards and of the Council itself, the drawing up of binding ethical rules to govern the medical profession and the application and interpretation of such rules with a view to full and consistent compliance. The Council also handles and resolves appeals against Colleges presented by members, and sets minimum charges for private practice, etc.[97]

55. The democratic structure and workings of professional bodies imposed by the Constitution are reflected in the extensive regulations governing voting procedures for the election of office bearers, length of period of office and the causes of dismissal, conditions of eligibility and candidacies. The OMC also has disciplinary regulations applicable to members who commit any of the offences set out in the Statutes, be they minor, serious or highly serious, as well as the corresponding penalties, which may take the form of a private reprimand, an official warning, temporary suspension from practice or expulsion from the College (Articles 63–68 of the General Statutes of the OMC). Notwithstanding Article 63.2 of the General Statutes of the OMC, which states that disciplinary responsibility is not to be understood as exempting members from liability of any other type that they might incur, the doctrine of the Constitutional Court with regard to breaches of the *non bis in idem* principle should be taken into account.

56. The fact that all practising physicians must register with a College does not preclude freedom of association in the context of a trade union organization. Although the trade union movement is not normally associated with this kind of

94. The Regional Councils of Colleges of Physicians have as their jurisdiction the Autonomous Communities.
95. The General Assembly is the highest organ of government of the Council and is made up of the presidents of all the official Colleges of Physicians, as well as national representatives of the obligatory Sections and other persons (president of the Council, Vice-president, general secretary, etc.).
96. Article 29 of the RD 300/2016, of 22 July.
97. *See* the more extensive provisions of Art. 2 of RD 300/2016, of 22 July.

profession (or rather, it has not been associated with it historically), recently, doctors have become extremely active in trade union relations as a result, chiefly because they more and more are gradually moving from what was traditionally independent practice towards salaried or civil service positions. Physicians' demands are therefore falling more within the realm of labour relations than the general framework of medical practice. We will not go into a detailed discussion of the ideological principles of each association but will merely make passing reference to the trade unions which currently cater for physicians: CESM (Confederación Estatal Sindicatos Médicos), CCOO (Comisiones Obreras), UGT (Unión General de Trabajadores) and CSIF-Sanidad (Central Sindical Independiente y de Funcionarios-Sector Sanidad).

II. Professional Duties Towards Colleagues

57. The notions of 'fraternity' and 'loyalty' describe well the way in which members should conduct themselves towards colleagues, both in the exercise of the profession and in other areas. This involves not only the expectation that they will bring prestige and dignity to the profession but that they will treat with respect those who receive medical treatment, i.e., patients. Patients should not be subjected to doctors casting aspersions on the morals or scientific abilities of a colleague in order to (for example) attract the latter's clients. A special ethical principle prevents a doctor from suffering moral, professional or economic harm as a result of the activities of a colleague. Legal and ethical endorsement for the manner in which physicians should behave towards one another can be found in the Professional Colleges Law, the OMC Statutes and also in the Code of Medical Deontology (2022).[98]

58. Among the functions attributed to them under the Professional Colleges Law, colleges must 'achieve harmony and cooperation among members and prevent unfair competition' (Article 5k). This is undoubtedly the physician's chief duty towards colleagues, since unfair competition, for example, does not only imply unfairly taking a patient from a colleague or depriving him of the resultant earnings or prestige but also poses a threat to the patients' dignity and health. The General Statutes of the OMC (RD 1018/1980) oblige members to 'maintain the utmost *loyalty* in relations with the College and fellow members by notifying the College of knowledge of any ill-treatment or abuse suffered by a colleague in the exercise of his/her profession'.[99] What underlies this precept is the notion of *solidarity* and

98. In this way, apart from the relevant legal regulations, traditionally physicians have drawn up their own codes and regulations for ethical professional practice. In the Code of Medical Ethics, the issue of professional conduct towards colleagues has not been overlooked. Chapter 11 of the Code of 2022 devotes Arts 46 to 51 to relationships between physicians and other patients.

99. This meaning is conveyed in Art. 46.1 of the Code of Medical Deontology (2022), which reads as follows: 'Physicians should treat each other with loyalty, respect and deference regardless of the professional or hierarchical relationship between them. Fellowship among physicians is a primary duty and only the rights of patients take precedence over it.' Article 48.2 also states that 'Physicians must report to the competent authorities, if applicable, and to their College of Physicians, alleged breaches

mutual support that must govern the actions of physicians with regard to their peers.[100]

Duties are also laid down in connection with self-protection of the profession and of medical ethics in relation to activities of members that might encourage illegal practice by third parties. Therefore, one of the functions of professional colleges is to 'adopt whatever measures are necessary to prevent illegal practice' (Article 5.l of the Professional Colleges Law). Similarly, the General Statutes of the OMC, for the same reasons, prohibit members from 'tolerating or abetting a person who does not hold a degree in medicine and who attempts to practice the profession' (Article 44b) and also 'allowing their surgeries to be used by persons who, while they may be graduates in medicine, have not registered with the appropriate College of Physicians' (Article 44m).

Other ethical duties apply to medical care and scientific matters. The Code of Medical Deontology (2022) states that 'professional disagreements of opinion and action among physicians should be resolved in their own professional or collegial setting' (Article 46.4 Code of Medical Deontology). In this regard, Colleges of Physicians may also 'intervene to achieve agreement or arbitration on questions of a professional nature that may arise between members'.[101]

III. Disciplinary Competences

59. Once again, we must begin by turning to the Constitution and in particular Article 36, which states that 'The Law shall regulate specific aspects of the legal regime of professional bodies and the practice of professions for which a qualification is required. The internal structure and the functioning of such bodies must be democratic.'

60. This constitutional formula led to the drafting of the Code of Medical Ethics, endorsed by the Ministry of Health and Social Security on 23 April 1979, which put an end to the vacuum created by the reorganization of professional bodies in 1967, when the ethical rules governing the medical profession in Spain contained in the annex to the 1945 Statute were derogated.[102]

In 1990, a new Code of Medical Ethics and Deontology was unveiled. This Code, tailored to take account of the reports submitted by the Ethics Committee of the OMC and the European Medical Guide, consisted of forty-four articles and one further concluding article.

---

by their colleagues of the rules of medical ethics or professional practice. This duty does not imply an infringement of the proper fellowship among physicians. Anonymity in such communications should be permitted if appropriate.'

100. The Code of Medical Deontology expresses it thus in Art. 51.2: 'If a physician becomes aware that another colleague is being subjected to any form of harassment and/or coercion in his or her professional practice, he or she should report this to the head of the department, the management of the centre, the College of Physicians or the judicial authorities, as appropriate.'
101. Article 5.m) of the Professional Colleges Law.
102. C. Segura/L. Martínez Calcerrada, *Derecho Médico 1* (Tecnos, Madrid 1986), p. 59.

The process of adapting the Code to the new demands of the medical profession continued with the adoption of a new Code of Medical Deontology in 2011. Among the main contributions of the code of deontology of 2011, the following ones should be emphasized: safety, respect, humanism, and responsible and ethical behaviour by the professional on the basis of a changing social reality. It stood, therefore, as the main guarantor on the hand of the Colleges of Physicians of increased competition and better performance by the medical professionals.

Finally, in 2022, the presently in-force Code of Medical Deontology was unveiled. Divided into twenty-six Chapters and ninety-three articles one additional disposition and five final disposition, it laid down, among other aspects, the general principles which should guide professional practice (Chapter II), physician-patient relations, information and consent (Chapter III), medical history and documentation (Chapter IV), quality of medical care (Chapter V), the doctor's responsibility (Chapter VI), professional secrecy (Chapter VII), concientious objection (Chapter VIII), medical care at the end of life (Chapter IX), patient safety (Chapter X), relations between physicians and with other health professionals (Chapter XI), duties with the College of Physicians (Chapter XII), work in health institutions (Chapter XIII), organ, tissue and blood transplantation (Chapter XIV), sexuality and human reproduction (Chapter XV), genetic tests (Chapter XVI), biomedical research on human beings (Chapter XVII), attention to violence, torture, harassment and restrictions on people's freedom (Chapter XVIII), sports doping (Chapter XIX), medical expertizes and witnesses (Chapter XX), training and teaching (Chapter XXI), professional publications (Chapter XXII), telemedicine and information and communication technologies (ICTs) (Chapter XXIII), artificial intelligence and health databases (Chapter XXIV), medical advertising (Chapter XXV), economy and fees (Chapter XXVI).[103]

61. Mention should also be made of the General Statutes of the OMC (Organización Médica Colegial) approved by Royal Decree 1018/80, of 19 May 1980. The General Statutes of the General Council of Colleges of Physicians were set up by Royal Decree 300/2016, of 22 July.

Article 3 of the General Statutes of the former (RD 1018/1980) states that the Organization's fundamental goals are to:

2. Safeguard and observe the ethical and social principles of the medical profession, as well as its dignity and prestige. To that end it shall draw up and apply the appropriate Codes.
4. Collaborate with the authorities in giving effect to the right of all Spaniards to protection of their health and to the most efficient, just and fair regulation possible of health care and the practice of medicine, as well as to all the rights contained in the Law governing Professional Associations.

103. *See* A. Libano Beristain, 'Reflexiones críticas en torno al valor normativo de los Códigos deontológicos (en particular, vigentes en la esfera sanitaria) así como algunas consideraciones acerca de la competencia objetiva en este ámbito', in *Justicia: revista de derecho procesal*, nº. 2, 2016, pp. 301 ff.

Article 31 RD 1018/1980 lists among the General Council's general powers the exercise of the functions set out in the Council's own rules and regulations in relation to the aims attributed to it under Article 3 of the Statutes and the Professional Colleges Law. Specific competences are outlined in Article 32:

> 1. Ethics: supervision of professional practice. Control over professional publicity of media information with reference to the profession, which might prove harmful to public health or to the legitimate interests, traditional prestige and dignity of the medical profession.

The General Statutes also provide for the setting up within the General Council of a Central Committee on Ethics, Medical Law and Authorisations to advise the Council on all matters relating to its sphere of competence, to report on appeals lodged with the Council against decisions of Colleges on such matters and to handle all correspondence with the Administration on the above issues.

Articles 33 and 34 RD 1018/1980 set out the competences of the provincial Colleges, which are charged with the application of ethical rules governing medical practice (Article 34d); it is their job also to ensure that registered members comply with their professional ethical and legal obligations (Article 34e), to take disciplinary action against members who engage in unfair competition, or who breach ethical rules or abuse their position as practitioners (Article 34f), to study the financial relationship between physicians and their clients and, where appropriate, take disciplinary action against members whose actions may undermine the prestige of the profession in this respect (Article 34h).

Title VIII of the General Statutes of the OMC deals specifically with Rules of Discipline, the general principles of which are given in Article 63:

1. Members shall be liable to disciplinary action in the cases and circumstances set forth in the present Statutes.
2. The rules of discipline contained in the present Statutes do not exempt members from liability of any other type which they may incur.
3. Disciplinary measures may only be taken after the setting up of an enquiry to examine the case in question and in accordance with the procedure laid down in the present chapter. However, in cases involving minor infringements and following a hearing of the member concerned, action may be taken without a specific enquiry.
4. The power to impose disciplinary measures lies with the Boards of the Colleges of Physicians. However, the appraisal and punishment of breaches of discipline committed by Board members shall be entrusted to the Assembly of College Presidents.
5. Any disciplinary action agreed upon shall be enforced with immediate effect, although decisions may be appealed. However, where enforcement might lead to irreparable or virtually irreparable harm, the body concerned may of its own initiative or at the request of the party concerned suspend the action against which the appeal has been lodged.

6. Colleges shall notify immediately the General Council of all disciplinary action taken in respect of serious or highly serious offences, and shall forward an extract of the file of enquiry. The General Council shall keep a register of action taken.

Breaches of discipline are described in Article 64 RD 1018/1980 and are classified as minor, less serious, serious and highly serious:

1. Minor misdemeanours:
   a. Non-compliance with regulations governing College documentation or documents which must be processed by the College.
   b. Failure to inform the College of changes affecting professional status, etc., which must be recorded in the member's personal record.
   c. Failure to heed College requirements or to submit reports when so requested by the College.
2. Less serious offences:
   a. Failure to provide a certificate or information where provision does not entail risk to the patient.
   b. Passing oneself off as having a qualification or competence when this is not the case.
   c. Failure to submit contracts for College's approval.
   d. Manifest abuse in billing for services or charging a fee below the minimum stipulated fee.
   e. Persisting in the commission of minor misdemeanours during a period of one year after being disciplined for such offences.
3. Serious offences:
   a. Deliberate and rebellious lack of discipline towards College's governing bodies and, in general, serious disrespect towards the latter.
   b. Acts and omissions which undermine the morals, decorum, dignity, prestige and honour of the profession or which entail disrespect towards members.
   c. Serious intentional or negligent breaches of professional secrecy resulting in harm to third persons.
   d. Non-compliance with rules governing the restricted use of drugs and the exploitation of drug addiction for personal gain.
   e. The issuing of reports or certificates known to be false.
   f. Persisting in the commission of less serious offences during a period of one year after being disciplined for such offences.
4. Highly serious offences:
   a. All conducts constituting offences of intent, within the field of the profession.
   b. Intentional violation of professional secrecy.
   c. Attacks on the dignity of persons in the course of professional practice.
   d. Malicious or intentional neglect of patients.
   e. Persisting in the commission of serious offences during a period of one year after being disciplined for such offences.

The article also adds that '*failure to comply with the duties set out in Article 43 of the present Statutes, violation of any of the prohibitions laid down in Article 44 or non-compliance with the rules contained in the Code of Ethics, which are not covered by numbers (1), (2), (3) and (4) above, shall be adjudged in the light of the similarity of the offence with those listed above. In all cases, the Ethics Committee shall be heard before any disciplinary action is taken*'.

Still, on matters of discipline, Article 65 RD 1018/1980 states as follows:

1. The following measures may be taken in respect of disciplinary offences covered by the previous article:
   a. Private caution.
   b. Official caution.
   c. Temporary suspension from professional practice.
   d. Expulsion from the College of Physicians.
2. Minor misdemeanours shall give rise to a private caution by agreement of the Board.
3. Official warnings shall be given in respect of less serious offences.
4. Serious offences shall be punishable by temporary suspension from practice for a period not exceeding one year.
5. Highly serious offences shall be punishable by temporary suspension from practice for a period of between one and two years.
6. Any member who is expelled from a College shall be barred from registering with another unless expressly authorized by the General Council. This punishment is applicable only where a member persists in the commission of highly serious offences. The decision to expel a member shall be taken by the Plenary Meeting of the Board, at which at least two-thirds of Board members must be in attendance. At least half of those in attendance must vote in favour of expulsion.
7. In taking disciplinary action, Colleges shall assess the responsibility of the accused in relation to the nature of the offence committed, as well as the importance of the offence committed and any other factors which might alter said responsibility. Where more than one punishment is laid down for each offence, the College is empowered to take the action it feels to be most appropriate.
8. Highly serious offences which affect the general interest may be reported in College's publications.

Article 66 RD 1018/1980 governing the expiry of disciplinary liability reads as follows:

1. Disciplinary liability shall expire:
   a. On the death of the accused.
   b. When the member complies with the disciplinary action taken.
   c. On prescription of the offence(s).
   d. On prescription of the disciplinary action or by agreement of the College concerned, which shall be ratified by the General Council.

2. Details of disciplinary action which are placed on the member's record shall be deleted provided that, once the member has complied with the action taken, he conducts himself properly for a period of three months (minor misdemeanours), six months (less serious offences), two years (serious offences) or five years (highly serious offences).
3. Offences shall be prescribed one year after they are committed if no enquiry has been opened, except for offences which constitute a felony, in which case prescription shall be the same as that laid down for the felony, if greater than one year.

Authority to handle matters of discipline is regulated by Article 67 RD 1018/1980, which states that 'minor misdemeanours shall be dealt with by the President of the College of Physicians, by agreement of the Board and in accordance with the provisions of Article 63.3'.

Other offences shall be dealt with by the Board, following the holding of a disciplinary enquiry and in accordance with the procedure described in the next article.

Where the disciplinary matter relates to an offence committed by a member of another Provincial College, the enquiry shall be undertaken in full by the College in whose territory the alleged offence took place. Any action taken shall be notified to the member's College through the General Council.

Disciplinary matters involving Board and General Council members shall be handled by the latter.

Lastly, Article 68 RD 1018/1980 regulates disciplinary procedure as follows:

1. The procedure shall be initiated automatically or at the request of a party, by agreement of the competent body, either of its own initiative or following denunciation.
2. On learning of an alleged offence, the Board of the College is empowered to conduct a confidential investigation prior to taking the decision to undertake an official enquiry. Alternatively, on the basis of the information available to it, it may choose to take no further action and order that no disciplinary measures be taken or impose one of the punishments applicable to minor misdemeanours.
3. Once it has chosen to proceed, the body may take any interim measures it deems appropriate to ensure the proper implementation of its eventual decision. No interim measures may be taken which might cause irreparable harm to those concerned or which involve a violation of rights protected by law.
4. On ordering an enquiry, the Board shall appoint a person to act as the 'instructing judge' from among its members or from among the College's ordinary members. The person appointed must have more years of service than the person facing the disciplinary action or, alternatively, must have at least ten years of professional practice. Acceptance of the appointment is compulsory, unless the appointee has good reason not to do so or his/her appointment is challenged before the Board by the member facing the action. The Board may

appoint a Secretary or authorize the instructing judge to designate one from among the members of the College.

5. The only reasons which may justify non-acceptance of or challenge to an appointment are consanguinity up to the fourth degree or affinity to the second, close friendship, clear enmity or personal interest in the matter.
6. In order that they may be challenged, the appointments of the instructing judge and secretary shall be notified to the person against whom the proceedings have been instigated. The latter may exercise his/her right to contest the appointments within a period of eight days following receipt of notification.
7. The person against whom proceedings have been instigated may appoint a member to defend him or to serve as arbiter. He shall be notified of this possibility and shall be given ten days in which to notify the Board of the name of the person he chooses to appoint and also that said person is willing to act in such a capacity. The appointee shall be present in all the enquiries undertaken by the instructing judge and may propose that other lines of investigation be explored on behalf of the defendant.

   The person facing the disciplinary action may also have his/her counsel accompany him during all proceedings.
8. The instructing judge is empowered to request any background information deemed necessary and to order any enquiries and other actions which might help clarify the circumstances under examination or which might help determine whether or not these merit disciplinary measures.
9. In addition to taking the appropriate statements, the instructing judge shall provide the accused with a written list of accusations, indicating clearly the alleged offences with which he is being charged. The accused shall be given a non-extendable period of eight days following receipt of the notification in which to answer the charges and furnish any proof he may wish. On receipt of this answer or on expiry of the eight-day limit, the instructing judge shall admit or reject the proof offered and order any action which he considers to be of help in clarifying the circumstances.
10. On completion of his/her enquiries and no later than four months after the opening of proceedings, the instructing judge shall propose a solution to the case. A copy of this proposal shall be provided to the accused, who shall have eight days following the date of receipt in which to study the contents and adduce further arguments in writing.
11. All the above proceedings shall be notified to the College Board, which, on receipt of the arguments presented by the accused or once the time limit for the presentation of any such arguments has lapsed, shall take a decision on the case during the first session held thereafter. The Board shall hear the opinion of the College's legal adviser (if one exists) or the Ethics, Medical Law and Authorisations Committee and shall notify the accused of the full text of its final decision.
12. The Board may choose to send the file back to the instructing judge and request further enquiries not pursued at the time but which are crucial to the final decision. In such cases, prior to sending the file back for further enquiries, the Board shall inform the accused of its decision so that he may, within

eight days, present any arguments he considers appropriate. This period is not to be counted as the period for the presentation of further arguments referred to above.

13. Any decision marking the end of the disciplinary enquiry shall be grounded on specific motives. No circumstances other than those which served to draw up the list of accusations or the proposed solution shall be admitted, although said circumstances may well be appraised differently.
14. The accused may lodge an appeal to the General Council against the final decision within fifteen days. All appeals shall be submitted to the College, which shall forward the disciplinary file and its own report within three days to the Council.
15. The defendant may appeal against the decision of the General Council to the Court for Administrative Disputes.[104]

62. The problem may arise when more than one disciplinary body becomes involved. A case of this nature was dealt with by the Supreme Court (4th Chamber) with its ruling of 24 January 1989 (rapporteur magistrate Bruguera Manté). On 27 January 1983, following a disciplinary case concerning a physician charged with a serious offence, the Standing Committee of the General Council of Physicians suspended the accused from practice for a period of nine months. The decision was confirmed by the (as it was then) Territorial Court on 14 May, following an appeal by the accused. However, the Supreme Court allowed the appeal on the following grounds:

> It is inadmissible that, while a criminal procedure is being followed with regard to the very same events which gave rise to the disciplinary action, the case should have been proceeded with and resolved without first waiting for the ruling of the Criminal Court (...). However, it is true that in cases such as this, which involve a relationship of subjection or a special kind of supremacy between the physician and his/her professional association, the power to handle disciplinary matters may be different to and independent of criminal responsibility (...), and different types of corrections may even coexist in the criminal and disciplinary order without violating the principle of exclusion of the same sanction for a single act ('non bis in idem').

However, the ruling also states that 'the necessary subordination of disciplinary powers to the jurisdiction of the criminal courts when a criminal procedure is being followed with regard to the same event means that the disciplinary proceedings may not be proceeded with, opened or concluded while the criminal enquiry continues'.

---

104. Through assimilation to the Administration's powers in matters of discipline. With regard to the appropriateness of this avenue in terms of the Administration's disciplinary powers, which we shall examine further on in relation to medical employees of the Social Security system, *see* Supreme Court Rulings of 11 Feb. 1985, 16 Jun. and 21 Oct. 1986, and 4 Apr. 1988.

63. Separate mention should be made of the disciplinary powers of the Administration with regard to staff of the Social Security system. The Framework Statute provided for in Article 84 of the LGS (Law 14/1986) came into existence with Law 55/2003, of 16 December.

It goes without saying that these rules and regulations apply only to employees of the Social Security system in accordance with statutory provisions.

Disciplinary offences and actions are dealt with in Chapter XII Law 55/2003. Article 71 sets out the basic principles of the Administration's disciplinary authority: principles of typicity, efficacity and proportionality in the whole public health system and the proceeding is subjected to the principles of immediacy, procedural economy and full respect of the corresponding rights and guarantees. In any case, and on the basis of the administrative decentralization existing in Spain (where each Autonomous Community has its own regional health service), the disciplinary authority corresponds to the health service in which the person concerned is serving at the time of commission of the misdemeanour or offence.

Offences are classified in Article 72:

1. Highly serious offences. Article 72.2 establishes a set of twenty-two highly serious offences (letters 72.2.a to 72.2.u), including, among others:
   - Failure to comply with due respect to the Spanish Constitution or with the respective Statute of Autonomy when exerting his/her functions (Article 72.2.a).
   - The breach of the due reservation with respect to data relating to the Centre or institution or to the personal privacy of users and to information related to their processes and stays in institutions or healthcare facilities (Article 72.2.c).
   - Abandoning one's place of work (Article 72.2.d).
   - The notorious breach of duties or of the rules governing the functioning of the services (Article 72.2.f).
   - Failure to comply with the essential services established in case of strike (Article 72.2.j).
   - The requirement of any type of compensation for services provided to the users of public health services (Article 72.2.q).
2. Serious offences. Article 72.3 establishes a set of fourteen highly serious offences (letters 72.3.a to 72.3.n), including, among others:
   - The lack of obedience due to the superiors (Article 72.3.a).
   - Abuse of authority in the exercise of their functions (Article 72.3.b).
   - Breach of duties or the rules governing the functioning of the services when not integrating a highly serious offence (Article 72.3.c).
   - The serious disregard for superiors, peers, subordinates, or users (Article 72.3.d).
   - Sexual harassment, when the active subject of harassment with his conduct creates an intimidating, hostile or humiliating work environment for the person who is the subject of the same (Article 72.3.e).

- Any damage or deterioration in facilities, equipment, instruments or documents, when they occur by non-exclusable reckless (Article 72.3.f).
- The lack of professional performance that affects the normal functioning of the services when not integrating a highly serious offence (Article 72.3.g).

3. Minor misdemeanours. Article 72.4 establishes a set of seven highly serious offences (letters 72.4.a to 72.4.g), including, among others:
   - Unjustified non-compliance with working hours, when not integrating a serious offence (Article 72.4.a).
   - Unjustified absence when not integrating a serious offence (Article 72.4.b).
   - The incorrectness with superiors, peers, subordinates, or users (Article 72.4.c).
   - Neglect or dereliction of their duties when not affecting users, Administration, or health services (Article 72.4.d).
   - Neglect in the fulfilment of the express provisions on safety and health (Article 72.4.e).
   - Breach of its duties or obligations, when not integrating a serious or highly serious offence (Article 72.4.f).
   - The cover-up, consent or aiding with any act to the commission of serious offences (Article 72.4.g).

According to Article 72.5, the Autonomous Communities may, by norms with the status of law, establish other offences in addition to the ones established in the previous sections.

The next Article (73) sets out the punishments applicable to the above offences:

a. Separation from service. This sanction shall entail the loss of the status of statutory staff and only be imposed for the commission of highly serious offences.
b. Forced relocation with change of locality, without right to compensation and with temporary prohibition of participating in mobility procedures for returning to the locality for a maximum of four years. This punishment may be imposed only as a result of highly serious offences.
c. Suspension of functions. When this sanction is imposed for highly serious offences, it may not exceed six years or be less than two years. If it is imposed for serious offences, it shall not exceed two years. If suspension does not exceed six months, the person concerned will not lose his/her professional destination.
d. Forced relocation to another institution or centre without change of locality, with temporary ban, up to a maximum of two years for participating in mobility procedures for returning to the centre of origin. This punishment may be imposed only as a result of serious offences.
e. Warning that will always be in writing and shall only be imposed for minor misdemeanours.

§2. Professional Liability

I. General Aspects

64. The medical profession has become increasingly regulated in recent years.[105] As discussed in Chapters 1 and 2, this regulatory process stems from the need to define the scope of medical practice in light of legal provisions governing professions that require academic qualifications, as stipulated in Article 36 of the Spanish Constitution. It can also be explained by the significant role that medical practice plays in society, which demands thorough regulation not only to protect patients from malpractice and hold physicians accountable for their actions but also to provide clear guidelines for professionals facing uncertainty about their roles.[106] Additionally, regulation helps guide decision-making in complex ethical situations, such as organ transplants, euthanasia, and abortion.[107] At all times, regulation must remain focused on its ultimate objective: establishing a clear legal framework for an increasingly complex medical profession, enabling physicians to perform their duties with confidence and security.

Some have regarded this increased regulation of medical practice as a means for patients or their next-of-kin to take legal action against healthcare providers in cases where treatment fails to achieve the expected curative results. Conversely, others see it as a legal safeguard for physicians, protecting their diligent and responsible actions even when a patient's health is not restored as fully as hoped.

There is certainly some truth to this perspective, which is why it would be one-sided to assume that the regulation of medical practice is primarily intended to persecute physicians. Concerns of this nature have contributed to the rise of *defensive medicine*, where physicians seek to confirm their diagnoses through numerous repetitive tests, ultimately delaying treatment, increasing costs, and reducing efficiency.[108] Medical professionals have long advocated for clearer guidelines on physicians' liability, and Spain's legal system has addressed these demands, as will be examined later.

---

105. *See* Urruela Mora and Libano Beristain, 'La ordenación de las profesiones sanitarias. Las agresiones a los profesionales sanitarios', *supra*, pp. 418 ff.; Segura Fuente/Martínez-Calcerrada, *Derecho Médico, I.*, *supra*, p. 58 on the need for regulation; Romeo Casabona, *El médico ante el Derecho*, *supra*, pp. 6 ff.

106. *See* Segura Fuente/Martínez Calcerrada, *Derecho Médico I*, *supra*, p. 56, in line with the views of Rico Pérez.

107. Romeo Casabona, *El médico ante el Derecho*, *supra*, pp. 5–10.

108. On this point *see* Romeo Casabona, *El médico ante el Derecho*, *supra*, 8–10; A. Perin, 'El fenómeno de la medicina defensiva como cuestión político-criminal. ¿Cómo conjugar autonomía y responsabilidad?', in C.M. Romeo Casabona/A. Perin (eds), *Derecho y medicina defensiva: legitimidad y límites de la intervención penal* (Comares, Granada 2020), pp. 1 ff.; J. Santos Briz, 'La responsabilidad civil de los médicos en el Derecho español', in *Revista de Derecho Privado* (julio-agosto) 1984, p. 644.

65. The various aspects of professional medical practice, including its activities and any resulting liability, can be analysed based on the legal nature of the provisions that govern them. A distinction is typically made between criminal and civil liability.[109]

II. Criminal Liability

66. The legislation governing this matter is the Spanish Criminal Code, which differentiates between liability arising from intentional conduct and that resulting from negligence.[110]

A. Liability in Respect of Intentional Conduct

67. Intentional conduct covered by the Penal Code presupposes a conscious and wilful attack on a legally protected asset. The perpetrator will be held liable if certain additional requirements are met. However, liability may be waived in specific cases, such as when a justifying cause applies – meaning the conduct, though harmful, is deemed lawful under the circumstances. This includes situations like acting in legitimate self-defence or out of necessity.

68. Clearly, this type of criminal liability applies to physicians in the same manner and under the same conditions as it does to any other citizen. While it is extremely difficult – though not impossible – to conceive of a physician, in the course of professional practice and while performing a curative action, intentionally committing homicide (Articles 138 and ff. of Spanish Criminal Code) or causing injury (Articles 147 and ff.), no specific criteria exist to differentiate the physician's scope of liability or to establish distinct rules of incrimination based solely on their professional status. Since there is nothing that sets apart a physician's intentional conduct from that of any ordinary person, and given that such offences are not commonplace in medical practice, the argument put forth by some – that physicians should be held criminally liable only for intentional offences they commit – should be rejected. A different scenario arises when a physician leverages their specialized knowledge to facilitate or ensure the commission of an offence or to prevent its punishment. However, this situation is by no means exclusive to physicians; rather, it applies equally to healthcare workers, pharmacists, chemists, biologists, gunsmiths, police officers, and others.

---

109. *See* E. Sola Reche/F. Sánchez Lázaro, 'Lección 19. Responsabilidad jurídica del profesional sanitario', in C.M. Romeo Casabona /P. Nicolás Jiménez/S. Romeo Malanda (Dirs) (2ª edición, Dykinson, Madrid 2025), pp. 511 ff. https://bioderecho.eu/manual-bioderecho/

110. *See* J. González Pernía/A. Hidalgo Carballal, 'Capítulo 44. Responsabilidad penal sanitaria', in A. Palomar Olmeda/J. Cantero Martínez (Dirs), *Tratado de Derecho Sanitario. Volumen II* (Thomson Reuters, Aranzadi, Cizur Menor 2013), pp. 99–102.

69. It is worth highlighting that the Spanish Criminal Code includes an article specifically dedicated to punishing the conduct of healthcare workers who deliberately fail to fulfil their duty to provide treatment: '*A medical practitioner who, while under obligation to do so, refuses to provide health assistance or abandons the provision of health services, when such refusal or abandonment causes a serious risk to personal health, shall be punished with the penalties established in the preceding article, in its upper half, along with a special disqualification from public employment and office, profession, or trade for a term of six months to three years*' (Article 196). Case law[111] and legal doctrine have determined the specific circumstances under which this article is applicable. These include:

a. When the perpetrator refused to provide necessary healthcare despite being aware of its necessity.
b. When healthcare assistance was required. However, this requirement would not apply if an alternative course of action were at least as effective as the one initially required. For example, if urgent home care by a medical professional (the most common course of action under Article 196 of the Spanish Criminal Code) was requested, but it was evident that transporting the patient to a healthcare facility would be equally effective, this requirement would not be applicable.
c. When the previously mentioned actions posed a serious risk to the patient's health.[112]

70. Nevertheless, consideration must also be given to the scenario in which a physician deliberately and consciously *fails to assist* not just any sick person or accident victim, as in the previously mentioned cases, but their own patient. If, as a result of this inaction, the patient dies or suffers irreparable harm to their health, jurists consider this to constitute an intentional or wilful offence – specifically, an offence committed by omission – which is legally equivalent to an offence committed through active (as opposed to passive) conduct. Depending on the specific circumstances of the case, this could qualify as either homicide or wilful injury. Beyond other requirements that need not be explored here, the legal basis for holding the physician criminally liable stems from the close relationship between doctor and patient, which arises either through a formal contract or a de facto connection – such as a hospital doctor on duty treating a patient in the emergency department. In such cases, given the privileged position the physician holds regarding the life and health of the patient, he has a special duty to guarantee 'his' patient's legally

111. *See* Supreme Court Rulings on 29 Nov. 2001 and 28 Jan. 2008.
112. *See* A. Urruela Mora/S. Romeo Malanda, 'Tendencias actuales de la jurisprudencia española en materia de responsabilidad penal médica', in *Revista de Derecho Penal*, 34, 2011, pp. 35–74; G. Portilla Contreras, 'La omisión del deber de socorro', in G. Quintero Olivares/F. Morales Prats (Coords), *El Nuevo Derecho Penal Español. Estudios Penales en Memoria del Profesor José Manuel Valle Muñiz* (Aranzadi, Pamplona 2001), pp. 1665–1696; C.M. Romeo Casabona, 'Artículo 196', in J. Luis Díez Ripollés/C. María Romeo Casabona (Coords), *Comentarios al Código Penal. Parte Especial. II* (Tirant lo Blanch, Valencia 2004); P. Esquinas Valverde, *El delito de denegación de asistencia o abandono de los servicios sanitarios. El artículo 196 del Código Penal* (Comares, Granada 2006), pp. 651–675.

protected assets. This duty obliges him to provide medical care in a manner that prevents harm to those interests, provided, of course, that he is able to do so under the given circumstances.

B. Liability in Respect of Negligent Conduct

1. Juridico-criminal Negligence: Features and Configuration in the Penal Code

71. In cases of negligent liability, the legally protected asset – namely, the life, integrity, and physical or mental health of the patient – is not intentionally harmed. Instead, liability arises from the perpetrator's – whoever they may be – failure to meet certain duties of care or diligence, resulting in harm to that legal interest. The perpetrator's intended purpose in such cases is of little relevance, or even entirely irrelevant, to Criminal Law; in fact, their purpose may be highly beneficial to society (e.g., treating a patient). What matters is the manner in which the perpetrator has acted – that is, the means they have used, how they have employed them, and their lack of due diligence, which may have led to an unintended, and perhaps even unforeseen, outcome. Given the nature of negligence-based offences, this type of liability is the most frequently encountered in professional practice, particularly in cases of unlawful acts committed by physicians.

72. The Spanish Criminal Code (1995) was reformed by Organic Law 1/2015, of 30 March, amending Organic Law 10/1995, of 23 November. This 2015 regulation defines criminal offences as 'intentional or negligent actions or omissions punishable by law'. As a result, negligence is considered a key element in several offences. There are five cases of particular relevance regarding healthcare workers' liability:

1. Homicide. Article 142.1 of the Penal Code states: '*Whoever causes the death of another by serious negligence shall be convicted of manslaughter and punished with a prison sentence of one to four years (…). When manslaughter is committed due to professional negligence, an additional penalty of special disqualification from practicing the profession, trade, or public office shall be imposed for a period of three to six years.*' Furthermore, Article 142.2 establishes that: '*Whoever causes the death of another by less serious negligence shall be punished with a fine of three to eighteen months.*'
2. Abortion. According to Article 146 of the Penal Code: '*Whoever causes an abortion due to serious negligence shall be punished with a prison sentence of three to five months or a fine ranging from six to ten months.*'
3. Injuries. The Criminal Code punishes:
   a. With a sentence of imprisonment from three to six months, in the case of the injuries described in Article 147.1 ('*injury that detracts from his bodily integrity or his physical or mental health, shall be convicted of the offence of grievous bodily harm, with a sentence of imprisonment of six months to three years, whenever the injury objectively requires medical or surgical treatment for health purposes, in addition to qualified first aid*').

b. With a sentence of imprisonment of one to three years, in the case of the injuries described in Article 149 (to forfeit or lose the use of a major organ or limb, or a sense, or sexual impotence, sterility, serious deformity or to suffer a serious physical or mental illness or to cause a genital mutilation in any form).
c. With a sentence of imprisonment of six months to two years in the case of the injuries in Article 150 (to forfeit or lose the use of a non-major organ or limb or a deformity).
d. '*Anyone who, through serious negligence, causes any of the injuries provided for in the previous Articles shall be punished, in accordance with the risk created and the result produced: 1. with a prison sentence of three to six months or a fine of six to eighteen months, in the case of the injuries referred to in section 147(1). 2° to imprisonment for a term of one to three years in the case of injuries under article 149. 3° Imprisonment for a term of six months to two years in the case of injuries under Article 150.*' (Article 152 Penal Code):

   Additionally, Article 152 states that: 'When the injuries are caused due to professional negligence, the punishment shall include special disqualification from practicing the profession, trade, or public office for a period of six months to four years.'

4. Injuries to the Foetus. Article 158 of the Spanish Criminal Code establishes that: '*Whoever, due to serious negligence, causes injury or disease to a foetus that seriously damages its normal development or results in severe physical or mental disability shall be punished with a prison sentence of three to five months or a fine ranging from six to ten months. When these acts are committed due to professional negligence, an additional penalty of disqualification from practicing the profession, trade, or public office for a period of six months to two years shall also be imposed.*' Notably, the pregnant woman shall not be penalized under this provision.
5. Gene Manipulation. Article 159 of the Criminal Code states: '*1. Those who manipulate human genes to alter the genome for purposes other than eliminating or reducing serious defects or diseases shall be punished with a prison sentence of two to six years, along with special disqualification from public employment, office, profession, or trade for a period of seven to ten years.*' '2. *If genome alteration is committed due to serious negligence, the punishment shall be a fine ranging from six to fifteen months and special disqualification from public employment, office, profession, or trade for a period of one to three years.*' Consequently, it is clear that gene modification due to negligence is prohibited under Spanish law.

The Spanish legislator has drawn an important distinction between serious negligence and less serious negligence. In principle, the difference[113] lies in the degree

113. *See* Cerezo Mir, *Curso de Derecho Penal Español. Parte General I, Introducción*, 6ª ed., Ed. Tecnos, Madrid, 2004, pp. 390 f.

of carelessness: serious negligence involves a more flagrant or reckless breach of the duty of care, whereas less serious negligence stems from a less severe but still improper breach of duty.[114] However, the Spanish Criminal Code does not explicitly define this distinction, leaving it to case law to determine how different degrees of negligence apply in each specific offence, as has been the case in the past.[115]

2. The Elements of Offences of Negligence: Aspects of Greatest Relevance to Medical Practice

73. Despite the clarifications provided above, a literal reading of the Penal Code alone is insufficient to fully comprehend the scope of liability for negligence and its implications for physicians. Therefore, it falls to those responsible for interpreting the law – ultimately, the judges tasked with applying it – to determine the specific elements through which liability must manifest in order to attain legal-criminal relevance.

In cases of negligence offences, as defined in the Penal Code, the following elements must always be present:[116]

a. Failure to uphold the duty of care required in professional practice.
b. The occurrence of death or injury to the patient.
c. A causal link between the physician's conduct and the resulting harm.
d. The existence of an unlawful connection between conduct and outcome or the objective imputation of the result.

Each of these elements will be examined in detail below, although we will focus only on the aspects which are of greatest relevance to the specific category of medical negligence.[117]

a. Failure to Observe the Duties of Care Entailed in Professional Practice

74. Let us first examine conduct in which due care is not exercised. This is undoubtedly the most complex element of the offence and the most challenging to assess. In practice, whether an offence of negligence exists ultimately depends on this element, although it is important to remember that the other components of the offence must also be present.

---

114. The representation of the result or the absence thereof (conscious or unconscious fault) may be present in both; *see* Cerezo Mir, *supra*, p. 392; S. Mir Puig, *Derecho Penal. Parte General* (10ª edic., PPU, Barcelona 2015), pp. 294 and ff.; M.ª Carmen Gómez Rivero, *La responsabilidad penal del médico* (2ª edición, Tirant lo Blanch, Valencia, 2008), pp. 329–432.
115. *See* Supreme Court Rulings of 1 Dec. 1989, 29 Feb. 1996, 3 Oct. 1997, 25 May 1999, 29 Nov. 2001.
116. *See* Urruela Mora and Romeo Malanda, 'Tendencias actuales de la jurisprudencia española en materia de responsabilidad penal médica', *supra*, pp. 35–74.
117. *See* C.M. Romeo Casabona, *El Médico y el Derecho Penal. I. La actividad curativa* (Bosch, Barcelona 1981), pp. 211 ff.

This requirement arises from the fundamental legal principle underlying negligence offences, which states that in social life (in all areas), individuals must adhere to specific duties or rules designed to prevent harm to legally protected assets, particularly in situations involving significant risk. These include not only activities such as traffic, public transport, hazardous industries, nuclear energy, certain sports, etc., but also seemingly innocuous actions, such as caring for plants placed on a balcony or windowsill. This principle is known as 'the duty of care'. Thus, individuals or professionals (in this context, physicians and healthcare professionals) who act in accordance with these duties of care are merely aligning their conduct with established legal guidelines. It is therefore essential to compare the required duty of care in a given professional or social context with the actual conduct of the individual.

75. As is well known, the precise legal content of the duty of care is not explicitly defined by law – a task that would be impractical given the vast number of behaviours subject to such duties. Instead, it is the judge's role, with the necessary expert guidance, to determine whether a breach of the duty of care has occurred in a particular case. All physicians treating a patient must adhere to fundamental professional standards to avoid committing a criminal offence, regardless of their level of training or specialization: the duty of care is an objective obligation. This was explicitly affirmed in a ruling by the Spanish Supreme Court (Second Chamber) on 14 February 1991, concerning a case related to healthcare. The Court stated that for negligence to be punishable, the following elements must be present: 'An act or omission in breach of cautionary or precautionary rules and regulations – based on the circumstances of the event, place, and time – intended to foresee and, where possible, prevent harm or damage.' This ruling establishes the minimum standard of care required, below which an individual has a duty to refrain from acting.

76. However, a number of authors raised the point that the duty of care should be established in accordance with individual ability, and assessment of this duty should be determined *not* from the standpoint of culpability, as the majority would hold, but should be based rather on the description of the offence included in the law. Put another way, the duty of care is only breached when the person, in accordance with his ability, could have foreseen the outcome, which means that the level of this duty will vary from person to person. This represents an individual or subjective duty of care.[118] This notion of the duty of care is extremely important in the medical profession, particularly with regard to professionals of much greater ability than others practising the same specialist branch, given that if they fail to make use of this extra-special ability, they will be in breach of the duty of care which is within their reach; from an objective point of view, this situation would also affect those of

118. *See* E. Orts Berenguer/J.L. González Cussac, *Compendio de Derecho Penal. Parte General* (5ª ed., Tirant lo Blanch, Valencia 2015), p. 328; G. Quintero Olivares, *Parte General del Derecho Penal* (5ª ed., Aranzadi, Cizur Menor 2015), pp. 437 f. (although with slight nuances). The issue is dealt with in greater depth in Cerezo Mir, *Curso de Derecho Penal Español. Parte General I*, *supra*, pp. 381 f.; A. Jorge Barreiro, *La imprudencia punible en la actividad médico-quirúrgica* (Tecnos, Madrid 1990), pp. 41 ff.; Mir Puig, *Derecho Penal. Parte General*, *supra*, pp. 299 ff.; Romeo Casabona, *El Médico y el Derecho Penal*, I, *supra*, pp. 215 ff.; A. Torío López, 'El deber de cuidado en los delitos culposos', in *Anuario de Derecho Penal y Ciencias Penales*, 1974, pp. 25 ff.

below-average ability: they would not be liable (not having breached the duty of care) if they used all the diligence they are capable of using, even though this is below the average ability of colleagues. The question arises only in relation to individual ability and not (exceptional) knowledge, since the latter is taken into account in the appraisal of objective foreseeability. Only insofar as failure to use this ability can be determined objectively can a case be made for the existence of a breach of the duty of care, which would give rise in turn to an offence of negligence;[119] if this is not the case, in certain situations an intentional offence may exist, whereas the rest would not be punishable.[120]

77. The objectively required duty of care is assessed using the intellectual criterion of objective foreseeability (adequate causation). However, this criterion is further refined and limited by a statutory criterion, which dictates that only dangerous actions – those leading to an objectively foreseeable outcome – are prohibited. In other words, a person of reasonable intelligence and sound judgment would recognize and refrain from such actions. This approach has been consistently upheld by the Spanish Supreme Court in recent years.[121]

i. Technical Fault, Breach of Lex Artis and of the Duty of Care

78. It is difficult to describe in more specific terms the content of the duty of care as conceived objectively, given the vast diversity and complexity of the behaviours that must be evaluated.

One could determine the content of the duty of care based on general laws applicable to cases that meet the legal definition of the offence or those of a similar nature. This body of technical rules and procedures is commonly referred to as *lex artis*, which naturally varies across different sectors and professions. Consequently, a physician or healthcare professional who adheres to the *lex artis* – acting in accordance with their expertise and judgment in each specific situation – will generally not be considered to have breached their duty of care. This is a topic we will revisit later.

The existence of a breach of the duty of care can also be determined – albeit less frequently in the case of physicians – based on technical or administrative regulations. As previously mentioned, if a breach of such provisions results in harm to the patient, the offender may be held liable for either serious negligence or less serious negligence due to regulatory non-compliance, depending on the specific circumstances.

79. A distinction must be made between three closely related, yet not entirely identical, concepts that, if confused, could lead to hasty and erroneous conclusions.

119. Mir Puig, *Derecho Penal. Parte General*, *supra*, p. 299.
120. For more details *see* Cerezo Mir, *Curso de Derecho Penal Español I. Parte General I*, *supra*, p. 382. Jorge Barreiro, *La imprudencia punible en la actividad médico-quirúrgica*, *supra*, p. 42, opts rather for the alternative of intentional or negligent homicide, depending on the case.
121. For instance, Supreme Court Ruling of 6 Jul. 2006.

These three concepts are breaches of the objective duty of care, technical error or fault, and infringements of the *lex artis*.[122] Conceptually, they are very similar, which is why it is crucial to clearly define the logical context of each as precisely as possible.

Technical error or fault, also known as professional error or fault, is a concept common to various professions, most of which are technical or experimental in nature (e.g., architects and engineers). In medicine, technical fault involves the *defective application of methods, techniques, or procedures at different stages of a physician's actions*[123] (examination, diagnosis, indication, or treatment administration). As used here, the concept of technical fault does not imply a legal assessment but rather a factual determination that a given medical situation is incorrect from a medical standpoint. This neutral legal interpretation means that once an error resulting in harm has been established, it must then be determined whether a breach of the duty of care has also occurred, as it is possible for a technical error to exist without such a breach. Technical fault or error, being a scientific concept, does not inherently imply negligence[124] (a legal concept). From a legal perspective, the decisive element is not the error itself but rather its cause. To sum up, then, the existence of technical fault alone is of no value other than as an indication (as long as it is accompanied by a result of harm to the patient), which leads us to ascertain subsequently that objectively due care has or has not been breached. Therefore, criminal liability cannot always be presumed in such cases unless the offence meets this requirement. Indeed, the Supreme Court has ruled that technical fault should only lead to liability if the mistakes committed are of extraordinary magnitude.[125]

Similarly, with regard to *lex artis*, we may conclude the following:

1. Technical error or fault does not necessarily constitute a breach of *lex artis*.
2. *Lex artis* is neither immutable nor singular in form; it must be reconciled with individual freedom in choosing different methods and should remain open to new techniques and procedures, including those that are less widely used.
3. *Lex artis* applies solely to 'typical' situations – such as those described in scientific literature – but does not extend to exceptional or 'atypical' cases.
4. It is not possible to establish a direct equivalence between technical regulations and legal rules, as each serves distinct purposes. Consequently, a breach of one does not necessarily imply a breach of the other.

---

122. *See*: D. Arias Madrigal, 'La responsabilidad penal en el ámbito médicosanitario: algunas consideraciones generales', in *Revista de Ciencias Penales*, Vol. 2, nº. 1, 1999, pp. 81–106; Gómez Rivero, *La responsabilidad penal del médico*, *supra*, pp. 329–336; E. Hava García, *La imprudencia médica* (Tirant lo blanch, Valencia 2001); A. Jorge Barreiro, *La imprudencia punible en la actividad médico quirúrgica* (Tecnos, Madrid 1990), pp. 145–150.
123. *See* Romeo Casabona, *El Médico y el Derecho Penal, I*, *supra*, pp. 233 ff.; M. Corcoy Bidasolo, *El delito imprudente*, (PPU, Barcelona 1989), pp. 101 ff.; Urruela Mora/Romeo Malanda, 'Tendencias actuales de la jurisprudencia española en materia de responsabilidad penal médica', *supra*, pp 35–74.
124. A. Quintano Ripollés, *Derecho penal de la culpa* (Bosch, Barcelona 1958), pp. 505 and 510.
125. *See* Supreme Court Rulings of 13 Nov. 2002 and 29 Feb. 2006.

In conclusion, although the principle that physicians should observe the *lex artis* (in the broad sense referred to earlier) is still very much in force, a breach does not as yet entail a breach of the duty of care, although it often does constitute an indication thereof.[126] Indeed, on occasions (in atypical situations), a physician's observance of the duty of care may even require him to distance himself from the *lex artis*.

80. The general considerations outlined above regarding these three concepts are also reflected in case law. For example, it has been stated that medical practice is 'subject to the *lex artis*, and that medical criminal liability does not arise merely from diagnostic errors or a lack of extraordinary expertise (since infallibility cannot be a requirement): rather, negligence is established when conduct fails to meet certain standards and requirements ...'[127]

ii. Determining the Existence of a Breach of the Objective Duty of Care: Special Features[128]

81. To begin with, several factors must be taken into account, such as how a practitioner's training or specialist knowledge is assessed (even though there is no outright prohibition against practising without the appropriate specialist qualification), the general obligation to stay updated on scientific advancements and techniques, the circumstances of time and place (e.g., whether the setting is a rural area or a hospital), and the duty of so-called therapeutic information, among others.

Within the various phases of the medical process – anamnesis, diagnosis, prognosis, treatment, and preventive or prophylactic measures – there are a number of specific circumstances that must be considered when determining whether duties of care have been breached. Given the inherent degree of uncertainty involved in diagnosis, a greater margin of discretion is permitted. However, as established by Supreme Court case law, this does not mean that criminal liability for negligence is entirely excluded.

b. Death of or Injury to Patient

82. For criminal liability due to negligence to exist, the mere occurrence of negligent conduct by a physician, as described above, is not sufficient. A harmful material result to the patient is also required, since, in medical practice, only a material result offence is possible. This principle was clarified in the Supreme Court ruling of 14 February 1991, which stated: 'Concrete damage and harm must be caused, and

126. *See See* Supreme Court Rulings of 23 Oct. 2001, 7 Oct. 1986, 4 Sep. 1991 and 1 Dec. 1989.
127. Supreme Court Ruling of 5 Feb. 1981, which uses these very terms and others. A Ruling of 7 Oct. 1986 develops the criterion further and summarizes doctrine on medical negligence: '1. No incrimination for scientific error; 2. A lack of extraordinary expertise is not deemed to be punishable either. 3. Culpability stems from cases where the doctor could have avoided the conduct which led to the harmful outcome; 4. Immutable general considerations should be avoided in the search for punishable medical liability'.
128. *See* Romeo Casabona, *El Médico y el Derecho Penal, I, supra*, pp. 242 ff. and 252 ff.

this must be a consequence of the negligent conduct in its twofold aspect – namely, the lack of foresight or the "duty to know" and the lack of care or the "duty to prevent".' In any case, it is not always easy to determine whether harm has been caused to the patient on the basis of how his condition has evolved.

This harm may manifest as damage to the patient's health or physical integrity and, in extreme cases, even loss of life. Consequently, inadequate action on the part of a physician who has failed to observe due care but which has not led to one of the aforementioned events or situations shall not give rise to criminal liability of any kind. Conversely, the mere presence of harm or injury does not automatically imply punishable negligence on the physician's part. It must be demonstrated that their conduct effectively breached the duty of care, as previously outlined. The existence of harm merely serves as the starting point for a subsequent analysis of the physician's or healthcare professional's actions.

c. The Causal Link Between the Physician's Conduct and the Outcome

83. Let us suppose that duties of care have indeed been breached, resulting in harm to the patient. Even in such a case, this alone is insufficient to establish liability; it must also be determined whether the negligent conduct directly caused the harm – that is, whether a causal link exists between the two. This principle was emphasized in the Supreme Court Ruling of 22 February 2024,[129] which stated that it is necessary 'to assess whether the victim's death has a direct causal relationship with the negligent medical care received'. As mentioned earlier, the negligent act itself does not extend to the subsequent outcome – this is a fundamental requirement of the offence – since the individual's intent was not to cause the harm in question. This is why the causal link between the action and the outcome – an essential element – forms part of the legal definition of the offence.[130]

This requirement has led to widespread difficulties as regards the furnishing of proof, and it is easy to understand that such difficulties arise most frequently in the field of health or medicine, given that medicine by definition is an inexact science involving a certain degree of guesswork and not everything is known about the physical and mental behaviour of human beings.[131] Hence, doubts as to the existence of this causal link shall lead to the person being acquitted, by virtue of the application of the principle of *in dubio pro reo* (presumption of innocence).

129. *See also* Supreme Court Ruling of 29 Oct. 1994 and Supreme Court ruling of 14 Feb. 1991.

130. Cerezo Mir, *Curso de Derecho Penal Español. Parte General I*, *supra*, p. 280; Guillermo Portero Lazcano, 'Responsabilidad penal culposa del médico: fundamentos para el establecimiento de la negligencia o impericia', *Rev. Latinoam.Der.Méd. Medic. Leg.*, 6(2), Diciembre 2001 – 7(1), Junio 2002, pp. 89–96. *See also* Supreme Court Ruling of 20 May 1981.

131. On the determination of the causal link in accordance with the criterion of 'the loss of life expectancy', *see* J.A. Gisbert Calabuig, *Nuevos aspectos de la responsabilidad médica: el ejercicio de la Medicina de grupo o en equipo* (Real Academia de Medicina de Valencia, 1979), passim; Romeo Casabona, *El Médico ante el Derecho*, *supra*, pp. 83 f.

d. Unlawful Link Between Action and Outcome: Objective Imputation of the Latter

84. In both specialist literature and case law, it is widely accepted that something else is required in addition to all the above.[132] (1) There must be a closer link between the action and the outcome than mere causation – the harm must be a direct consequence of the failure to observe objectively required care.[133] (2) The harm must be of the type that the regulations governing due care were specifically designed to prevent.[134]

Providing clear-cut examples in the field of medicine can be challenging, so let us consider an analogy from another field to illustrate the first criterion of imputation. Imagine a motorist who exceeds the speed limit while driving on a particular stretch of road. Ahead of him, a cyclist is riding erratically. The cyclist is struck and killed. Now, let us analyse the circumstances: The driver breached his duty of care by exceeding the speed limit; a death results from the incident and undoubtedly, a causal link exists between the driver's conduct and the fatal outcome. However, is the driver guilty of negligent homicide? According to the law, no – because the cyclist's death did not stem from the motorist's speeding. The fatal accident would have occurred even if the driver had been within the speed limit. Now, let us apply this reasoning to a medical scenario: Suppose an anaesthetist mistakenly administers cocaine instead of the correct substance during an operation. The patient dies, but a subsequent autopsy reveals that, due to the patient's severe condition, death was inevitable regardless of the anaesthetist's error. In this case, The duty of care was breached (administration of the wrong substance); the patient's death occurred and a causal link exists between the anaesthetist's action and the fatal outcome. However, the final requirement – the unlawful link between the action and the outcome (or objective imputation of the result) – is absent. Since the patient would have died regardless of the anaesthetist's mistake, the correct legal decision would

132. *See* M.A. Rueda Martín, *La teoría de la imputación objetiva del resultado en el delito doloso de acción* (Bogotá, Universidad Externado de Colombia, primera edición 2002), pp. 49–122. *See also* Supreme Court Ruling of 9 May 2011.

133. *See* Cerezo Mir, *Curso de Derecho Penal Español. Parte General I, supra*, pp. 396 f.; Mir Puig, *Derecho Penal. Parte General, supra*, pp. 306 ff. (in which further views and critical considerations are given); Romeo Casabona, *El Médico y el Derecho Penal, I, supra*, pp. 226 ff.; E. Sola Reche/J.U. Hernández Plasencia/C.M. Romeo Casabona, 'La responsabilidad profesional del médico en el Derecho español', en Carlos María Romeo Casabona (ed.), *Responsabilidad penal y responsabilidad civil de los profesionales* (Centro de Estudios Criminológicos-Universidad de La Laguna, Tenerife 1993), pp. 99–120.

134. *See* Cerezo Mir, *Curso de Derecho Penal Español. Parte General I, supra*, pp. 399 f.; Mir Puig, *Derecho Penal. Parte General, supra*, pp. 306 ff. (in which some further views and critical considerations are given); Romeo Casabona, *El Médico y el Derecho Penal, I, supra*, p. 228; Sola Reche/Hernández Plasencia/Romeo Casabona, 'La responsabilidad profesional del médico en el Derecho español', *supra*, p. 110. This second criterion of imputation by itself, without the first, is advocated by E. Gimbernat Ordeig, 'Infracción del deber de diligencia y fin de la norma en los delitos culposos', in *Revista de Derecho de Circulación*, 1965, p. 675.

be to acquit the accused. Determining whether the harm would have occurred even if the duty of care had been observed often depends on the defence lawyer's ability to present compelling evidence. However, as long as it is *possible* or *likely*[135] that the result was inevitable, any existing doubt should be resolved in favour of the accused, in accordance with the principle of *in dubio pro reo* (benefit of the doubt).

3. Aggravated Liability in Respect of Professional Negligence or Lack of Expertise

85. Regarding aggravated offences, there is little to add beyond what has already been stated.[136] While both 'lack of expertise' and 'negligence' pertain to professionals, they have distinct meanings. Professional negligence involves a breach of technical duties that apply specifically to professionals in the course of their work.[137] However, not every act of negligence by a professional automatically warrants an aggravated sentence – such liability arises only if the professional also breaches their duty of care.[138]

Although this aggravation of the offence is questionable, bearing in mind that there are other activities in society which may be performed by professionals and laypersons alike (e.g., the driving of motor vehicles), it is not as wide of the mark as might at first seem (provided it is kept within the appropriate limits). It is important to recognize that some professions, including medicine, architecture, engineering, and pharmacy, can only be practised by qualified professionals. Authorization to practice is contingent upon obtaining the necessary qualifications (which carries with it a presumption of aptitude). For this reason, breaches of the duty of care, particularly those outlined in technical regulations or the illegal practice of a profession by an unqualified individual, are understandably regarded as more serious offences. However, based on this rationale, there would be no justification for an objective aggravation of liability – meaning that any aggravation must be tied to the specific circumstances of the case rather than applied automatically.[139]

---

135. There has been a great deal of debate as to the degree of likelihood, or even certainty, which can be required. *See* C. Roxin, 'Infracción del deber y resultado en los delitos imprudentes', in *Problemas básicos del Derecho penal* (Spanish translation and notes by D.M. Luzón Peña) (Reus, Madrid 1976), pp. 147 ff.
136. *See* Romeo Casabona, *El Médico y el Derecho Penal, I, supra*, pp. 229 ff.
137. *See* J. Córdoba Roda, 'Zum Verkehrsstrafrecht in Spanien', in *Zeitschrift f.d.g. Strafrechtswissenschaft*, 1961, pp. 122 f.
138. *See* Supreme Court doctrine, which is similar, on such types of lack of expertise or professional negligence: rulings of 24 Nov. 1984, 21 Feb. 1986, 5 May 1988, 27 May 1988; 6 May 1990 (Barcelona Provincial Court).
139. *See* Cerezo Mir, *Curso de Derecho Penal Español. Parte General I, supra*, pp. 393 ff. A critical view is taken also by J. Bustos Ramírez, *Manual de Derecho Penal. Parte General* (3ª ed., Ariel, Barcelona 1989), p. 236.

C. Teamwork in Medical and HealthCare

86. Teamwork,[140] which is becoming increasingly common in hospital medicine, presents particular challenges in determining liability. However, it can also be a crucial factor in assigning responsibility, given that criminal liability is strictly personal – each individual is accountable for their own conduct. In such cases, the principle established by Spain's Supreme Court in a road traffic ruling can be applied. This principle, known as the 'principle of trust', states that each participant in a shared activity may reasonably rely on others to fulfil their respective duties competently. This principle also extends to the sharing out of functions in joint professional activities. For example: A surgeon may trust that the anaesthetist is applying the correct parameters and performing the necessary verifications during surgery and that the nurse will hand him/her the appropriate instruments. For her part, the nurse may trust that the instrument or drug requested is the correct one (and the dosage indicated is correct); the internist may trust that the nurse will administer the prescribed doses at the indicated times. Both physicians and nurses may assume that pharmaceutical laboratories have correctly manufactured medications, labelled them accurately, and indicated the proper expiration dates.

The sharing out of functions also means that superiors will not ask their subordinates to perform any tasks which exceed their level of training or their allotted work or which they themselves should do. If such tasks are assigned, it becomes the superior's duty to supervise and ensure that their instructions are carried out correctly.

III. Civil Liability

87. Civil liability (whether linked to an offence or not)[141] aims to provide reparation for harm caused to an individual and, where appropriate, to compensate for any damages resulting from a punishable event. This typically takes the form of financial compensation, although other remedies may occasionally be employed. Such liability may arise from the contractual relationship between the patient and the healthcare professional, in accordance with the provisions of Article 1101 of the Civil Code (CC) (*'Persons who, in the performance of their obligations, incur in*

140. For an extremely thorough study of this issue, *see* Jorge Barreiro, *La imprudencia punible en la actividad médico-quirúrgica*, *supra*, pp. 113 ff. *See also* Romeo Casabona, *El Médico y el Derecho Penal, I*, *supra*, pp. 247–252; G. Stratenwerth, 'Arbeitsteilung und ärztliche Sorgfaltspflicht', in *Eb. Schmidt-Fest.*, (Vandenhoeck und Ruprecht, Göttingen 1961), pp. 383 ff.; D. Wilhelm, 'Probleme der medizinischen Arbeitsteilung aus strafrechtlicher Sicht', in *Medizinrecht*, 1983, pp. 45 ff.

141. On the legal nature of liability stemming from a physician's acts, *see* E. Llamas Pombo, *La responsabilidad civil del médico* (Trivium, Madrid 1988), pp. 92–109; on jurisdictional limits *see* L. González Morán, *La responsabilidad civil del médico* (Bosch, Barcelona 1990), pp. 19–32; M. Barahona Migueláñez/M.C. González García, 'Capítulo 42. Error sanitario y responsabilidad jurídica por asistencia sanitaria', *Tratado de Derecho Sanitario. Volumen II*, *supra*, pp. 56–61.

willful misconduct, negligence, or default, and those who in any way contravene the content of the obligation, shall be subject to compensation for any damages caused'), along with related articles. Alternatively, liability may be based on extra-contractual fault, giving rise to extracontractual liability, as governed by Article 1902 of the CC ('*A person who, through an action or omission, causes damage to another through fault or negligence shall be obliged to repair the harm caused*').[142]

The distinction between these two forms of liability in the field of medicine has generated considerable doctrinal debate, as well as controversy.[143] Both legal doctrine and case law have widely recognized the existence of a contractual relationship between physician and patient when such a relationship stems from a prior legal relationship *inter partes*.[144] Although contractual medical cover is becoming increasingly common, the importance of situations where this exists – emergency operations, occasional gaps in contractual cover, etc. – makes it inappropriate to examine here the contractual basis of civil liability derived from medical practice.[145] Despite the distinct legal frameworks governing contractual and extracontractual liability[146] – differences in legal capacity requirements for entering into a contract, statutes of limitations, burden of proof regarding fault, etc. – case law has, on occasion, blurred the distinction between them in rulings on reparations.[147] The theoretical grounds for this lie in the circumstance that here both types of liability come into play; that is, it can be ascertained that the general duty of *alterum non laedere* has been breached, as has a duty stemming from contractual obligations,[148] even though both become merged in one single claim for compensation. Moreover, as laid down in the Supreme Court Ruling of 11 November 1990,[149] these obligations are derived from another which is common to all health professionals, whether or not they are under contract, namely, the obligation which is not necessarily to ensure the recovery of the patient. Put another way, it is not an obligation which involves a specific result, but rather one involving means: the professional's

142. The starting point for contractual and extracontractual liability is the same, namely, the notion of reparation and compensation; on this point, *see* Supreme Court Ruling of 19 Jun. 1984. The same ruling outlines the differences between both types of liability, which are governed by different legal systems despite the fact that the basic goal involved is one and the same. On situations where both contractual and extracontractual liability may be involved, *see* González Morán, *La responsabilidad civil del médico*, *supra*, pp. 36–48.
143. *See* E. Ruiz Vadillo, 'La responsabilidad civil y penal de los médicos (especial referencia a los anestesistas)', *Derecho y Salud,* Vol. 3, núm. 1, enero-junio, 1995, p. 74.
144. On this point, *see* Supreme Court Ruling of 19 Jun. 1984.
145. As argued by Llamas Pombo, *La responsabilidad civil del médico*, *supra*, p. 100.
146. *See* in this regard the Supreme Court Ruling of 30 Dec. 1980.
147. Note, for example, how the Supreme Court Ruling of 16 Dec. 1986 admits the possibility of extra-contractual liability even where a contract exists.
148. *See* G. García Valdecasas, 'El problema de la acumulación de la responsabilidad contractual y delictual en el Derecho español', in *Revista de Derecho Privado*, 1962, pp. 834 ff.; González Morán, *La responsabilidad civil del médico*, *supra*, pp. 36 ff.; Llamas Pombo, *La responsabilidad civil del médico*, *supra*, pp. 100 ff.
149. In line with the Rulings of 6 Nov. 1990, 7 Feb. 1990, 12 Jul. 1988 and 13 Jul. 1987.

obligation is not to cure the patient but rather to provide him with all the care required in accordance with the state of the art in science.[150]

88. This provides all the more reason not to draw a strict distinction between contractual and extracontractual liability when addressing cases of civil liability.[151] For our purposes, it will suffice to focus on the common elements shared by both, using Articles 1101 and 1902 of the CC as our starting point, as they pertain to the failure to uphold certain duties of care incumbent upon the liable party.[152] The conditions or circumstances surrounding this form of liability include the following:[153]

1. *Harmful conduct*: this consists of an action or omission,[154] which leads to a result of harm to the patient. In order for this conduct to be relevant in terms of civil liability, it must be unlawful; that is, it must transgress a legal rule based on the principle that one shall not harm others.[155] Moreover, 'the harm on which the alleged liability is grounded must be a consequence of an action or omission circumscribable to the scope of activities related to the health-medical profession'.[156]

   In cases where the physician-patient relationship is governed by a contract, there is debate as to whether 'liability waiver' clauses should be deemed valid. However, the limitations imposed by Articles 1102–1104 – which invalidate waivers with respect to liability derived from fault or an intentional act – and

150. *See*, for instance, Supreme Court Rulings of 24 May 1999.
151. In this regard, *see* Supreme Court Rulings of 24 Mar. 1952, 7 Feb. 1990 and 22 Feb. 1991.
152. Article 1101: '*Any person who, in the performance of his obligations, commits wilful misconduct or negligence or defers his obligations excessively, or who in any way transgresses the spirit of said obligations, shall be liable to compensate for any damage or harm caused by his actions.*'
    Article 1902: 'Any person who through his actions or omissions causes harm to another either wilfully or negligently is obliged to make good the harm caused.' In addition to this statutory requirement, one has to consider also Art. 1903, which allows a claim to be brought against the centre or institution in which the physician provides his services. In this regard, the Supreme Court Ruling of 5 May 1988 is significant: 'there existed culpable action on the part of the institution (...) in consenting to the use of health equipment in a deteriorated condition without providing sufficient guarantees that it was working properly and could be used in such a delicate health situation. This was responsible for the death of the patient being treated; the harm sustained was clear and substantial and was the result of an undeniable relationship of cause and effect, which was directly attributable to INSALUD because of the poor state of the material used in the hospital'.
153. *See* Supreme Court Rulings of 6 Nov. 1990 and 11 Mar. 1991.
154. This active or omissive conduct must be voluntary. A degree of confusion surrounds the possibility of inferring civil liability from involuntary acts when the basis used is the antinomy which exists between 'voluntary behaviour' and 'negligent behaviour'. Attributing a harmful outcome to negligent behaviour supposes that the outcome was not intended by the author, although this does not mean that the behaviour itself was not voluntary; the author voluntarily breaches the duty of care, even though it is not his wish to produce the harm in question. Cf. Llamas Pombo, *La responsabilidad civil del médico*, *supra*, p. 210; J.L. Lacruz Berdejo, *Elementos de Derecho Civil II. Vol. Primero*, (Bosch, Barcelona 1985), pp. 498 f. A similar line to that taken here can be found in J. Santos Briz, *La responsabilidad civil. Derecho sustantivo y Derecho procesal*, (5th edition revised and updated, Montecorvo, Madrid 1989), pp. 26–27. The distinction between voluntary and involuntary behaviour is not valid either to explain civil liability; cf. *infra*.
155. On this point *see* Santos Briz, *La responsabilidad civil*, *supra*, pp. 28 ff.
156. Llamas Pombo, *La responsabilidad civil del médico*, *supra*, p. 211.

Articles 1255[157] and 1258[158] of the CC – which annul the validity of clauses which are contrary to the law, to morals or public order or which entail consequences that do not conform to good faith or proper usage – substantially curb the efficiency of agreements which exonerate the professional from civil liability in cases where strict liability is involved.

2. *The causing of harm*: although this element is extremely difficult to determine, in the field of health or medical care, it entails so-called bodily harm (although in the broad sense, which also includes harm of a mental nature) as well as material and moral harm, mental and physical pain and loss of profit or earnings.[159] The harm caused must be real in all cases. Even more complex than the determination of harm is the question of how it can be assessed for the purpose of compensation: the importance of the harm caused depends on personal circumstances, which are difficult to compare in absolute terms for all patients alike. Hence, to a large extent it is the law, having weighed up the specific circumstances of the case, which has to establish the nature and *quantum* of any reparation to be awarded in respect of civil liability.[160]
3. *Causal connection between the conduct and the harm caused*: this is a perfectly logical requirement and is explained above;[161] it might be appropriate here to recall once more the difficulties involved, although not so much those regarding the furnishing of proof (which we will examine in a moment) as those which arise in seeking a general criterion which will enable us to construct – or rule out – the causal connection satisfactorily. In the area of negligence, for example, Spanish case law has adopted the notion that causation should be deemed to exist if the harmful result would have been avoided with diligent conduct; although this criterion appears clear and defendable, it is somewhat imprecise as regards the weighing up the likelihood that the result would have been avoided.[162] Furthermore, a lack of diligence – which would enable the conduct to be viewed as being negligent – is often associated with causation, when it is more correct initially, at least to analyse the two separately. Only after a causal link has been seen to exist between conduct and result is it appropriate to assess the matter of whether the action was negligent

157. 'The contracting parties may establish any covenants, clauses and conditions deemed convenient, provided that they are not contrary to the laws, to morals or to public policy.'
158. Contracts are perfected by mere consent, and since then bind the parties, not just to the performance of the matters expressly agreed therein but also to all consequences which, according to their nature, are in accordance with good faith, custom and the law.
159. *See also* J. Ataz López, *Los médicos y la responsabilidad civil* (Montecorvo, Madrid 1985), pp. 323 ff.
160. In this regard *see* Ataz López, *Los médicos y la responsabilidad civil*, *supra*, pp. 327–329.
161. On this issue *see infra* and particularly Ataz López, *Los médicos y la responsabilidad civil*, *supra*, pp. 335–346; J. Fernández Costales, *Responsabilidad civil médica y hospitalaria* (La Ley, Madrid 1987), pp. 154–159; Llamas Pombo, *La responsabilidad civil del médico*, *supra*, pp. 239–244.
162. *See* Romeo Casabona, *El médico y el Derecho Penal, I*, *supra*, p. 227; Cerezo Mir, *Curso de Derecho Penal español. Parte General I*, *supra*, p. 396. Moreover, this criterion should be complemented (restricted) by that of foreseeability, even where the causal link between conduct and harmful outcome can be established; *see* Cerezo Mir, *supra*, p. 396 and also the Supreme Court Rulings of 13 Jul. 1987 and 7 Jun. 1988 mentioned above.

or not.[163] Perhaps it is for these reasons that case law is not guided by one single criterion alone in establishing the causal connection: although the *conditio sine qua non* formula is widely accepted, there is another current in case law (backed by a sector of doctrine) which stresses the failings of this principle. For example, it is not capable of settling correctly cases involving several causal processes which lead to harm being caused, and it would rule out finding possible grounds for objective liability, etc. This second body of opinion prefers other criteria and is supported by the Supreme Court ruling of 11 July 1987, which sided with the theory of adequation. Having said that, the *conditio sine qua non* formula continues to afford the surest means of establishing the causal link between conduct and harm. This does not mean, however, that it is not possible to perfect the legal relevance of causation either by extending civil liability of cases of objective liability – given that the problem is one of culpability, that is, strict liability – or by limiting it in accordance with the modern-day category of objective imputation.

Objective liability will be dealt with in the next section, although it is important to recall here that objective imputation is a category which covers a range of criteria, which can be used to rule out liability in respect of a conduct which has been considered previously to have been the cause of a harmful result. This is why objective imputation may be considered acting in the opposite sense to objective liability,[164] which broadens the scope of liability, whereas the former serves to limit the attribution of harmful results to conducts for which a causal connection can be established and thereby reduces the scope of civil liability. In this way, the ruling of the Supreme Court (2nd Chamber) of 11 February 1987 acknowledges that 'the causal link between the action and the result is not in itself sufficient, (...) it is necessary also to add to the notion of cause, as understood by the natural sciences and as translated into the doctrine of *conditio sine qua non* or equivalence of conditions, the legal-criminal relevance of any such causal connection'. Furthermore, objective imputation leads to the author being made responsible for conducts which, strictly speaking, are not the actual causes of the harmful result – as is the case, for example, with acts of omission.[165]

Objective imputation is being introduced into Spanish civil law doctrine particularly in view of its potential as a criterion which limits criminal liability and any derived civil liability consequences. However, at present moment, it does not play a decisive role in the determination of the legal relevance of causal conducts in medical practice yet.

4. *Culpability of the causer of the harm*: although civil law specialists acknowledge that there are two accepted meanings of the term fault – in the broad sense as comprising intention also, and in the stricter sense as the breach of certain duties of diligence and foresight[166] – it is used more frequently in the

---

163. Cf. Supreme Court (2nd Chamber) Ruling of 11 Feb. 1987.
164. *See infra.*
165. *See* Cerezo Mir, *Curso de Derecho Penal español. Parte General I*, *supra*, pp. 280–281.
166. In this regard *see* M. Traviesas, 'La culpa', in *Revista de Derecho Privado*, 1926, pp. 273 ff. (reference taken from Ataz López, *Los médicos y la responsabilidad civil*, *supra*, p. 274 and p. 370).

stricter of the two senses, and in particular in relation to the health professions to denote negligent conduct from which civil liability may be derived.[167] The sense of Article 1104 of the CC is adopted therefore.[168] Moreover, here, one can discern the influence of French doctrine; the category of 'medical fault' has gradually been introduced into Spanish law to denote breaches of duties of diligence by medical professionals in the course of professional practice.[169]

Here again, we encounter difficulties in attempting to arrive at a precise definition of what constitutes a breach of said duties. These difficulties stem from the relative nature of the two factors, which are generally advanced by our case law as requirements for an act to be deemed to be blameworthy, namely, the degree to which the harmful result is foreseeable and avoidable.[170]

Objective liability is a crucial issue in civil liability and has considerable implications for medical practice. In order for it to be deemed to exist and thus give rise to an obligation to make reparation, the causal link between the conduct and the harm suffices and no fault needs to be present. This could be taken to mean that the requirement of culpability is replaced by the assumption of risk in the performance of the dangerous conduct.[171] To date, this type of liability has been used only exceptionally in Spanish law, as we shall see shortly. However, the use of the reversal of the burden of proof may be understood as meaning that some Supreme Court rulings have opened the way to objective liability.[172]

89. This factor further increases the significance of the problem of proof, a subject that remains widely debated today. As previously mentioned, harm is a necessary condition for establishing civil liability, yet assessing it within the physician-patient relationship is particularly complex. Generally speaking, this relationship arises when an ailing patient consults a doctor, seeking assistance either to improve their condition or to mitigate the negative effects of an illness or injury. Unfortunately, these objectives are not always achieved, giving rise to the challenge of evaluating a lack of improvement or a deterioration in the patient's condition. Clearly, a decline in the patient's health may be attributable to the physician's actions, necessitating an assessment of whether those actions were inadequate. However, it should not be ruled out that the worsening state may be due to the very process of the illness or the accident sustained by the patient and could not have

---

167. *See* Llamas Pombo, *La responsabilidad civil del médico*, *supra*, pp. 213–230. In our opinion, this is the sense in which one has to understand the 'element of intent' which, according to the Supreme Court (1st Chamber) Ruling, is required along with the causal connection in order for liability to be found to exist.
168. Article 1104; '*Fault or negligence consists in the omission of the diligence which is required by the person's obligations and which corresponds to the circumstances of people, time and place* (...)'.
169. *See* Ataz López, *Los médicos y la responsibilidad civil*, *supra*, p. 290.
170. Significant in this regard is the Fourth Principle of Law of the Supreme Court Ruling of 11 Mar. 1991.
171. On all these points *see* Ataz López, *Los médicos y la responsabilidad civil*, *supra*, pp. 257–262.
172. *See*: Supreme Court Rulings of 23 of Jun. 2005.

been halted by the physician's diligent action.[173] Thus, other essential elements of civil liability come into play, and several key aspects must be demonstrated: the existence of harm,[174] the nature of that harm, the causal connection, and fault or lack of fault – depending on who has to furnish the proof – on the part of the physician.

A fundamental principle of civil liability is that the burden of proving harm falls upon the party alleging its existence, with the judge responsible for assessing the validity of such claims.[175] Abundant examples exist in civil law and case law of attacks on people's honour, privacy and personal image,[176] which show how interesting the perspective described here is; that is, splitting the concept of culpable harm into its two elements and conferring a separate identity on the problem of the determination of harm (of a moral nature in the above-mentioned case law examples). In the field of medical liability, this perspective is justified in view of the conflict which exists between the two categories of bodily and moral harm: partial recovery of sight,[177] causing of blindness, worsening of one's physical appearance following plastic surgery designed to do just the opposite, etc.[178] and even death (from the point of view of the moral harm caused to next-of-kin).[179] The number of circumstances in which it would be necessary to ascertain and prove the existence of harm in order to make the physician answerable for unlawful conduct could well be endless. For instance, in organ transplantation, how should the rejection of an organ – leading to a worsened post-operative condition – be evaluated? How can the success or failure of plastic surgery be objectively assessed? To what extent and in which circumstances does a breach of professional secrecy result in moral damages? These questions, among many others, highlight the complexities involved.

Meanwhile, the other key issues – proving the causal link and establishing fault on the physician's part – are addressed in the Supreme Court Ruling (First Chamber) of 11 March 1991,[180] which states:

---

173. *See* Ataz López, *Los médicos y la responsabilidad civil*, *supra*, pp. 340 ff.
174. It is quite a different matter if the harm is caused by an unlawful intervention. As was stated, the existence of harm is indicated by the impairment sustained by the patient's health, but this does not necessarily mean that it can be made good through civil liability. This acceptance can be inferred from Arts 1101 and 1902 of the CC: the obligation to make good the harm arises when said harm is caused by someone who commits, for instance, negligence, that is, it arises when the harm is culpable; however, there exists also harm caused by non-culpable behaviour; cf. Santos Briz, *La responsabilidad civil*, *supra*, pp. 140–141.
175. *See* González Morán, *La responsabilidad civil del médico*, *supra*, pp. 118–119 and Supreme Court Ruling of 14 Apr. 1999.
176. The need to lay down the precise content of such rights and guidelines for determining whether infringement constitutes moral harm led the Constitutional Court to give rulings (in sentences handed down on 23 Mar. and 5 Oct. 1987 and 2 Dec. 1988).
177. In Supreme Court Ruling of 6 Nov. 1990; the appeal was dismissed for lack of proof that the doctor concerned had acted negligently.
178. An abundance of examples of case law on bodily harm can be found in González Morán, *La responsabilidad civil del médico*, *supra*, pp. 121–124.
179. Although it is not a case involving medical liability, it is cited as an example by González Morán, *La responsabilidad civil del médico*, *supra*, pp. 115 and 117.
180. Rapporteur Luis Martínez Calcerrada y Gómez. Prior to this, Supreme Court Ruling of 6 Nov. 1990, following others of 13 Jul. 1987, 12 Jul. 1988 and 7 Feb. 1990. One possible argument in this sense is that based on the liability which could be established in cases involving omission, where the causal link could not be determined.

> The contractual or extracontractual obligation of physicians and healthcare professionals is not necessarily to ensure the recovery of the patient. In other words, their duty is not to achieve a specific result but rather to employ all necessary means: the professional is not obliged to cure the patient but to provide all required care in accordance with the state of medical science. Moreover, more or less objective liability of all types is generally ruled out in the case of health professionals and their conduct, while the reversal of the burden of proof (which has been accepted by this Chamber with respect to harm arising out of circumstances of a different nature) is also excluded, and hence it is up to the patient to prove the existence of a causal connection or link and of fault.[181]

This and other rulings have firmly established the current case law, which places on the shoulders of the plaintiff the burden of proving each and every one of the requirements.

As mentioned earlier, reversing the burden of proof may lead to the objectification of liability, meaning the plaintiff would not need to prove negligence in the medical act that caused the harm.[182] However, such cases are rare in Spanish case law.[183] One notable exception is the Supreme Court ruling of 1 December 1987,[184] which recognized the evidentiary challenges faced by patients in proving a physician's fault in radiotherapy treatments. In that case, the court reversed the burden of proof, establishing liability based solely on the causal link between the patient's injuries and the excessive radiotherapy dosage administered, without requiring the defendant to prove that they exercised due diligence in handling what is inherently a hazardous medical procedure.[185]

Despite this, legal doctrine[186] generally acknowledges that placing the entire burden of proof on the patient in medical liability cases is inappropriate. Several key arguments support this position. First, the patient or their heirs may be in a state of helplessness due to the harm caused by medical intervention. Second, and more

181. On the reference to the reversal of the burden of proof in harm of a different origin, *see* Supreme Court Rulings of 29 Dec. 1975, 2 Apr. 1986, 20 Mar. 1987 and 24 Jun. 2024, which based civil liability on the existence of a harm that can be indemnified and, where appropriate, the presumption of culpability in the causal behaviour.
182. The reversal of the burden of proof does not lead to objectivation of liability in the strict sense of the term: in fact liability shall not be deemed to exist where the defendant can prove that he acted diligently. However, where this, and culpability, cannot be proven, he will have to answer for the harm caused by his action and thus it is in this sense that one can speak of objective liability; cf. Ataz López, *Los médicos y la responsabilidad civil*, *supra*, p. 259.
183. Cf. Supreme Court Ruling of 13 Jul. 1987 (rapporteur Santos Briz), cited by González Morán, *La responsabilidad civil del médico*, *supra*, p. 93.
184. *See also* Supreme Court Ruling of 19 Jul. 2001.
185. For more details on objective medical liability in case law *see* González Morán, *La responsabilidad civil del médico*, *supra*, pp. 215–230.
186. *See,* for instance, González Morán, *La responsabilidad civil del médico*, Bosch, Barcelona, 1990, pp. 92–94 and 207 ff.; Llamas Pombo, *La responsabilidad civil del médico*, *supra*, pp. 423 ff. Also Santos Briz, *La responsabilidad civil de los médicos*, *supra*, p. 673, in which he shoulders the patient or his heirs with the burden of proving both the negligence of the physician and also the causal link between the negligence and the harm. However, it is generally acknowledged that the injured party is not in a position to furnish full and convincing proof of the negligence, the harm caused and the causal connection between the two; *see* González Morán, *supra*, p. 133.

commonly, they may lack access to comprehensive information regarding the medical-surgical process undergone, the necessary evidence, or even the ability to identify the individuals truly responsible when multiple professionals were involved in the treatment. Neither will they be in a position to assess all these elements properly. Above all, patients often face an insurmountable obstacle in the form of the 'cruel corporatism of professionals'.[187] For these reasons, and based on the principle that both parties in a legal dispute should have equal means to defend their positions – a principle recognized by the German Constitutional Court in its ruling of 1 April 1979 – Spanish legal doctrine has increasingly turned to objective liability as a means of mitigating the inherent inequalities in medical liability cases, which stem from the general principle that the burden of proof lies with the plaintiff. However, it is important to stress here that this form of the reversal of the burden of proof should not be taken to mean that strict liability or liability without fault is accepted fully – given that lack of fault would not necessarily prevent the physician from being held responsible. It is a case rather of the burden of proof being displaced in the direction of the person who is better placed to furnish evidence that he acted with the necessary diligence.

IV. The Liability of the Public Health System

90. Where strict criminal liability does not apply, Spanish law recognizes several cases in which an individual or entity that did not directly cause the harm is nonetheless obliged to provide reparation. For example, as established in the Constitution (Article 106), the State is held liable for harm resulting from the operation of public services. This means that it must assume responsibility for the actions of professionals working within the various national health authorities.[188]

A. Direct State Liability

91. Although the CC establishes provisions for civil liability on the part of the State (Article 1903, paragraph 5), this liability is further reinforced by additional administrative legislation, such as 'Law 40/2015, of October 1, on the Legal Regime of the Public Sector.' Article 32 (Principles of Liability) of this law states that: '1.

187. González Morán, *La responsabilidad civil del médico*, *supra*, p. 207.
188. *See supra*. Supreme Court (1st Chamber) Ruling of 22 Feb. 1991 (rapporteur Francisco Morales Morales), which is based on Art. 1903 of the CC, establishes direct not vicarious liability, which can be demanded directly of the employer because of his own *culpa in vigilando* or *in eligendo*, regardless of the type of liability attributable to the material author of the deed. The ruling follows Supreme Court Rulings of 22 Jun. 1988 – which held INSALUD alone responsible for the lack of diligence of an unidentified nurse – and of 17 Jun. 1989 and 30 Jan. 1990. For its part, the Contentious-Administrative Chamber of the Spanish Supreme Court has repeatedly upheld this doctrine, as reflected in rulings concerning the financial liability of the public healthcare administration, such as those issued on 7 Sep. 2005; 26 Jun. 2008; 23 Sep. 2010; 13 Jan. 2015; 24 Apr. 2018; and more recently, 14 May 2020.

Individuals shall have the right to be compensated by the relevant Public Administrations for any damage or injury suffered to their property or rights, provided that such damage results from the normal or abnormal operation of public services, except in cases of force majeure or damages that the individual has the legal duty to bear in accordance with the law. The annulment of administrative acts or regulations, whether through administrative proceedings or by the contentious-administrative jurisdiction, does not in itself imply a right to compensation. 2. In all cases, the alleged damage must be real, financially assessable, and specifically attributable to an individual or a group of individuals'. This type of liability is enforced using administrative channels and expires one year after the date of the event giving rise to the claim for compensation.[189]

Notably, this liability is not considered an indirect or vicarious responsibility for the actions of others but rather a direct liability.[190] It is not based on the unlawfulness of the harmful act or the negligence of the public servant involved. Instead, it falls under the principle of objective liability.[191]

92. These provisions form the fundamental legal framework governing harm or injury caused in State-run hospitals. Such liability is not rooted in contractual obligations (even in cases where a contractual relationship exists between patient and physician) but rather in statutory law, making it extracontractual in nature.

93. It is evident that liability is contingent upon the existence of injury, which, as previously discussed, is a requirement under Article 32 of the Act. Here again, it may be understood that the concept of injury is a purely de facto one and is accepted in a manner similar to the way the notion of harm is accepted by civilists, as was explained above ('injury' in the criminal law denotes an attack made on a legally-protected interest and implies that the interest in question is undermined, even though this cannot always be assessed in monetary terms).

94. In exceptional cases, the State has assumed liability beyond what is expressly provided for in existing legislation. One such instance was its assumption of responsibility for the consequences of the so-called toxic syndrome, in which thousands of people were poisoned by adulterated cooking oil, as recognized by Royal Decrees of 19 October 1981 and 18 June 1982. A similar case occurred in 1993 when the State took responsibility for haemophilic patients who had contracted HIV due to contaminated blood transfusions.

---

189. L.A. Panes Corbelle, 'Capítulo 43. Responsabilidad patrimonial de los servicios de salud', in A. Palomar Olmeda/J. Cantero Martínez (Dirs), *Tratado de Derecho Sanitario. Volumen II, supra,* pp. 71–77.
190. *See also* González Morán, *La responsabilidad civil del médico*, *supra*, p. 149, and Supreme Court Ruling of 11 Mar. 1991.
191. In this regard, Supreme Court Ruling of 16 Dec. 1987, which, 'without there being a clearly negligent action on the part of the professional, independently of whether said professional or other health professionals in the hospital incurred in organisational liability (...)', establishes the direct and objective liability of the hospital and INSALUD in respect of the serious harm caused to the patient; ruling cited by González Morán, *La responsabilidad civil del médico*, *supra*, p. 218. *See also*, Supreme Court Rulings of 11 Nov. 2002 and 17 May 2002.

B. Liability on the Part of the Social Security System

95. Let us now examine the case of a person covered by Social Security who files a liability claim regarding medical assistance received in a Social Security hospital.

First and foremost, it should be noted that Social Security is a public yet autonomous entity, although it is explicitly excluded from the regulatory framework governing autonomous state-run institutions. As we shall see in a moment, this consideration is important for the question of the most appropriate avenue of jurisdiction to be used.

It is also important to point out that two very different types of legal relationships are involved in healthcare, which is provided under the Social Security system. The first is the employer-employee relationship between the healthcare professional and the Social Security system. The second is the statutory national insurance link between Social Security and the insured individual. From this, it is evident that no contractual legal relationship exists between the healthcare professional and the patient. Consequently, liability arising from the professional's actions is extracontractual and is based on the aforementioned statutory provisions of the CC. This implies that a claim may be filed *jointly* against both the Social Security system and the healthcare professional under Article 1903 of the CC (*see also* Supreme Court rulings – Civil Chamber – of 20 February 1981 and 28 March 1983).

96. It is also possible to file a claim *directly* against Social Security through the labour courts, based on the national insurance relationship between the system and its beneficiaries. Support for this approach can be found in Articles 1 and 2(o) of Law 36/2011, of 10 October, which regulates labour jurisdiction. Such claims would hold the Spanish NHS directly liable for the alleged improper provision of services it is obligated to deliver (*see* Supreme Court rulings – Labour Disputes Chamber – of 20 November 1982 and 21 November 1983). As previously mentioned, given that no legal relationship of any kind exists between Social Security-employed physicians and system beneficiaries, this avenue of direct liability (or the legal basis thereof) cannot be extended to include the employees of the system (although, as we have also seen, extracontractual liability remains a viable option).

Similar to cases where the State is held directly liable (as was mentioned above in the previous section), the advantages afforded by this avenue of jurisdiction – Social Security liability – are clear for all to see. The physician who may have provided imperfect services is relegated to a secondary role and his professional competence and prestige are not compromised to the same extent. Furthermore, bearing in mind the rather closed nature of the medical profession, this approach promotes greater objectivity in establishing the facts and presenting evidence. As a result, the patient-beneficiary is provided with stronger assurances of receiving fair compensation for the harm suffered. It should be said, however, that much will hinge on the flexibility and breadth of the criteria adopted by case law until such times as doctrine governing the matter becomes fully consolidated.[192]

---

192. *See* for instance the Supreme Court Ruling of 1 Nov. 1991, with regard to 'a private hospitalisation contract. It adopted a criterion of fault, as opposed to the objectivation of liability and different to

C. Vicarious Liability on the Part of the Administration

97. We shall now briefly examine the issue of vicarious liability on the part of health authorities.[193] Vicarious liability arises when the law holds one party responsible for the misconduct of another, even when the former is free from personal blame or fault.[194] As defined in legal doctrine, 'Vicarious liability is liability for the tort of another person. (…) The most common form of vicarious liability is based on the principle of respondeat superior. Under this principle, both private and public employers are generally held jointly and severally liable, along with the employee responsible for the tort, provided the wrongful act was committed within the scope of employment. (…) However, respondeat superior may also apply to impose liability on an employer for contracts made by an agent within their authority, as well as for various types of torts, including fraud and other wrongful acts that do not necessarily involve physical harm.'[195]

In principle, all criminal offences give rise to civil liability. The determination of both criminal and civil liability is generally made within the criminal law procedure unless the private accuser expressly indicates otherwise. The Penal Code makes provision for – or perhaps it would be more accurate to say that it can be deduced from the Code – vicarious civil liability of the State and other public health authorities for offences or negligent acts committed by employees who are found criminally liable but are unable to pay the compensation ordered by a court. Specifically, Article 121 of the Spanish Criminal Code states: 'The State, the Autonomous Community, the province, the island, the municipality, and other public entities, as applicable, shall be subsidiarily liable for damages caused by those criminally responsible for intentional or negligent offenses when such individuals are authorities, agents, contractors, or public officials acting in the exercise of their duties or functions. This liability shall apply provided that the harm is a direct consequence of the functioning of the public services entrusted to them, without prejudice to the patrimonial liability arising from the normal or abnormal functioning of such services, which may be claimed in accordance with the rules of administrative procedure, and ensuring that no double compensation may occur in any case. If civil liability is sought in criminal proceedings against an authority, its agents, contractors, or public officials, the claim must be simultaneously directed against the Administration or public entity presumed to be the subsidiary civilly liable party.'

As a result, the institutions mentioned above are obligated to assume civil liability for an insolvent healthcare professional, as determined by a court ruling. Additionally, Spanish courts interpret vicarious civil liability in an objective sense, meaning that the institution or entity deemed liable is held accountable even in the

---

the criterion established for public hospital liability'; in P. Andrade, 'Ejercicio de los derechos y reclamaciones de los usuarios. Diversas vías de actuación', in *Jornadas sobre los derechos de los pacientes* (Instituto Nacional de la Salud, Madrid 10–14 Dec. 1990), pp. 581–589. *See also* Supreme Court Ruling of 24 Apr. 1990 and the legal grounds provided by Art. 1089 of the CC.

193. *See* P. Salvador Cordech et al., 'Respondeat Superior I', *InDret,* Barcelona, marzo 2002.
194. J.G. Fleming, *The Law of Torts* (9th ed., Law Book Company, Sydney 1985), Ch. 19, p. 409.
195. D.B. Dobbs, *Law of Torts* (West Group, St. Paul 2000), Ch. 22, §333, p. 905.

absence of direct fault. That is, fault *in eligendo* (failure to select qualified personnel) or *in vigilando* (failure to supervise) is presumed, and no evidence demonstrating due diligence or care can be admitted as a defence.

§3. Quality Assurance: Review Boards

I. Quality Assurance

98. Like its neighbouring countries, Spain has based its health model on the notion of the coexistence of public and private action. However, it falls upon the authorities to guarantee the right to health protection (Article 43.1 CE), regardless of private sector involvement, because health is viewed as a public service;[196] these are the principles which have shaped medical care in Spain.

When speaking of quality assurance, it is necessary to return once more to the constitutional principle contained in Article 43.2 of the Spanish Constitution, which defines the role of the public administrations in this regard as follows:

> the public authorities are charged with the organisation and assurance of public health through preventive measures and the necessary services and facilities. The Law shall lay down the rights and duties of all concerned.

The principle is taken up once again in Article 1.1. of the LGS, the goal of which is '*the general regulation of all actions to give effect to the right to the protection of health, as recognised in Article 43 and others of the Constitution*'; Article 6.1.4 of the Law stipulates that the actions of public health authorities shall aim, among other things, to assure health assistance in all cases where a loss of health occurs; Article 9 sets out the duty of the authorities to inform users of public health services, or associated private services, of their entitlements and duties; Article 10 (which nowadays has to be complemented with the dispositions of the Law 41/2002, of 14 November, basic law regulating Patient Autonomy and the Rights and Obligations regarding clinical information and documentation) lists the rights of patients in relation with the various public health administrations; Article 30 deals with the intervention of the authorities in the inspection, control and appraisal of the activities and functions of all health centres and institutions; Articles 32–37 deal with health-related infringements and sanctions. More specifically, Articles 32 and 33 regulate the disciplinary powers of the Administration where civil and criminal actions are also involved; Articles 34 and 35 set out guidelines and principles governing the classification of infringements of regulations as minor, serious and very serious, while Article 36 lists the sanctions applicable in each case.[197]

Mention should be made at this point that Title V of the Law, governing pharmaceutical products, confers quality assurance powers on the Administration. These

196. *See* Beato Espejo, 'El sistema sanitario español', *supra*, p. 403 note 41. Fuller treatment is given in Rodríguez Pastrana, *El servicio público de la Sanidad: el marco constitucional*, *supra*, pp. 26–39.
197. *See infra.*

powers include the evaluation of the suitability of drugs, medicines and other health products (Article 95.1). Authorization of medicines and drugs is subject to their being safe and efficient and of sufficient quality and purity; moreover, they must have been manufactured by suitably able natural or legal persons endowed. All these aspects must be guaranteed by the procedure for authorization, which extends also to other aspects such as tolerance, purity, stability and information, in accordance with statutory requirements (Article 95.3 and 95.4). The Administration is also charged with drawing up standards governing the quality, production, storage, advertising and dispensing of drugs and medicines (Articles 98–103).[198]

These provisions are developed fully in the Legislative Royal Decree 1/2015 of 24 July, which approves the refunded text of the Law on guarantees and rational use of medicines and health products of 2006. The explanatory memorandum to the Legislative Royal Decree 1/2015 states that 'pharmaceutical services includes medicines and medical devices, as well as a set of actions to ensure that patients receive and use them adecuately to their clinical needs and in precise doses according to their individual requirements, for an adequate period of time with the necessary information for their proper use and at the lowest possible cost'. After setting forth a series of principles, the Legislative Royal Decree 1/2015 proceeds to lay down regulations relating to quality (Article 11), safety guarantees and others governing non-toxicity or tolerance (Article 12), efficacy (Article 13), identification (Article 14), information (Article 15), authorization procedure (Articles 16 and 17), exclusivity of data (Article 18) and conditions of prescription and dispensing of drugs (Article 19). Of note also is Chapter 6 Title II, which deals with pharmacoepidemiology and risk management (Article 55) and objectivity in the evaluation of security (Article 56). The latter article also stipulates which bodies are competent to draw up security control programmes.[199]

These provisions provide the basis for the control of healthcare activities.

99. In addition to the above, a further and complementary avenue through which quality control is assured in medicine, this time from the perspective of citizens as users of the healthcare system, is opened up by the Constitution itself. The opening paragraphs of Article 51 state that:

1. The public authorities shall guarantee the defence of consumers and users by protecting, through efficient procedures, their safety, health and legitimate economic interests.
2. The public authorities shall promote consumer and user information; they shall encourage the setting up of such organizations and shall hear them in matters affecting consumers and users, in accordance with the terms laid down by the Law.

---

198. *See* Beato Espejo, 'El sistema sanitario español', *supra,* p. 413.

199. The RD 1090/2015, of 4 December, which regulates clinical trials with medicines, the Research Ethics Committees with medicines and the Spanish register of clinical trials (Real Decreto por el que se regulan los ensayos clínicos con medicamentos, los Comités de Ética de investigación con medicamentos y el Registro español de estudios clínicos). Thus, it regulates the functions and responsibilities of participants in clinical trials and the requirements for authorization in the drugs and medicines sector accordingly to European provisions.

These stipulations were developed further by the Consumer and User Protection Law 26/84 of 19 July 1984, which set out as its objective the defence of consumers and users in accordance with Article 53.3 of the Constitution. The in-force regulation in this field is the Royal Legislative Decree 1/2007, of 16 November, which approves the refunding text of the General Law for the defence of the consumers and users and other complementary laws. This defence is one of the general principles which shapes Spain's legal order. Notwithstanding, as we have seen above, nowadays, specific legislation on health quality has been implemented much more deeply.

Chapter III Title I of the Law is devoted specifically to the protection of health and safety. Of particular note is Article 57 (Chapter II, Title V of Royal Legislative Decree 1/2007 *Judicial and extrajudicial proceedings of protection of consumers and users*), which puts in place a system of arbitration which is empowered to give binding decisions for the settlement of complaints or claims filed by consumers or users.

100. A concern and a central objective of the Spanish HealthCare System is to ensure and improve the quality in which such services are implemented, and there is no doubt that ensuring patient safety throughout the care process is a key factor in achieving these objectives. The Quality Plan for the NHS of 2010 presents a set of six major areas that seek to address the issues affecting the major principles and challenges of the Spanish health system:

i. Protection, health promotion and prevention.
ii. Promoting equity.
iii. Development and Support for human resource planning in healthcare.
iv. Promoting clinical excellence.
v. Using information technology to improve care of citizens.
vi. Increased transparency.

The Law on Cohesion and Quality of the National Health System implemented the framework of the LGS in 2003,[200] which maintained the basic lines of the former but modified and broadened the articulation of that law to reflect an existent social and political reality. By 2003, all of the Autonomous Communities had gradually assumed purview in matters of health and had established stable models to finance the assumed purview. Therefore, the Law on Cohesion and Quality establishes coordination and cooperation of public health authorities as a means to ensure citizens the right to health protection, with the common goal of ensuring equity, quality and social participation in the NHS. The law defines a core set of functions common to all of the autonomous health services. Without interfering with the diversity of forms of organization, management and services inherent in a decentralized system, it attempts to establish certain basic, common safeguards throughout the country. This law attempts to establish collaboration of public health

200. Law 16/2003 of 28 May, on Cohesion and Quality of the National Health System (Ley 16/2003 de 28 de mayo, de cohesión y calidad del Sistema Nacional de Salud).

authorities with respect to benefits provided, pharmacy, health professionals, research, health information systems, and the overall quality of the health system.

Toward these ends, the law created or empowered several specialized organs and agencies, all of which are open to the participation of the autonomous communities:

- Agency of Evaluation of Technologies (*Agencia de Evaluación de Tecnologías*). In the current structure, the Spanish Network of Agencies for the Evaluation of Health Technologies and Services of the National Health System (*Red Española de Agencias de Evaluación de Tecnologías Sanitarias y Prestaciones del Sistema Nacional de Salud*).
- Spanish Agency of Medicines and Medical Products (*Agencia Española de Medicamentos y Productos Sanitarios*).
- Human Resources Committee (*Comisión de Recursos Humanos*).
- Committee to Assess Health Research (*Comisión Asesora de Investigación en Salud*).
- Instituto de Salud Carlos III.
- Institute of Health Information (*Instituto de Información Sanitaria*).
- Quality Agency of the National Health System (*Agencia de Calidad del Sistema Nacional de Salud*). In the current structure, Subdirectorate General for Quality and Cohesion (*Subdirección General de Calidad y Cohesión*).
- Observatory of the National Health System (*Observatorio del Sistema Nacional de Salud*).

The basic organ of cohesion is the Interterritorial Council of the Spanish National Health Service, which has great flexibility in decision-making, as well as mechanisms to build consensus and to bring together the parties taking such decisions. A system of inspection, the *Alta Inspección*, assures that accords are followed.

101. This system of control of medical services was historically complemented in Spain by further provisions concerning treatment provided in a public hospital or care centre. RD 571/1990 of 27 April, which dictates norms on the peripheral structure of management of health services managed by the INSALUD, provided for the creation of Citizens Participations Commissions (Article 10.1), 'a body of community participation in the planning, monitoring and evaluation of the management and quality of care provided by the National Institutes of Health in the field of healthcare'. The functions of the Committee included: (a) knowing and developing proposals for action assistance programmes of the INSALUD in the health sector; (b) knowing and developing proposals on the economic programmes of the INSALUD in the Health Sector for each exercise; (c) identifying and reporting the annual management report of the INSALUD in the health sector; (d) receiving information and making proposals on personnel policy, the policy on services concerted with other entities, public or private ones, as well as on purchases and supplies of the INSALUD in the health sector; (e) proposing to the bodies of the health sector to adopt whatever measures are appropriate to the adequacy of the activities of the National Institutes of Health to the needs of the health sector and, in general, those relating to improving the quality care (Article 10.3). Article 23 RD 521/1987, of 15 April, governing the structure, organization and functioning of hospitals under the management of the INSALUD provided for the setting up of a Social Welfare Committee, a collegiate advisory body charged among other things with 'examining specific aspects which might improve care' (Article 23.2c); finally, Article 32 provided for the creation of a Patient Care Service to channel and give written form to any claims which might arise. These claims were forwarded to the heads of the Division concerned, and replies should be given in writing and signed by the director or person appointed by him. Two representatives of Consumer and User Organizations sit on both Committees.[201] It should be pointed out, however, that in practice, the application of the Decree provisions was far from satisfactory: in 1989, only 28% of the Social Welfare Committees had been set up and were working; Patient Care Services received 13,005 complaints – less than 1% of the total number of activities carried out in hospitals.[202] It is considered that the 'chief cause of the low number of complaints would appear to be people's misgivings that lodging a complaint serves any useful purpose'.[203]

Nowadays, once the institutional Health System in place in Spain was fully decentralized by means of Law 16/2003, of 28 May, on Cohesion and Quality of the National Health System, Autonomous Communities had completely assumed purview in matters of health and had established stable models to finance the assumed purview, and consequently the basic regulations in this fields are the ones issued by each of the Spanish Autonomous Communities.[204]

II. Adverse Events Reporting and Learning Systems

102. In the last twenty years, the Spanish Ministry of Health has done intense work aimed at the implementation of a system for the reporting of adverse events in the health field. Some of the key milestones in this process are, in the first place, the different studies of the prevalence of adverse events in the Spanish health system (ENEAS[205] and APEAS[206]) and, second, the creation of a committee of experts at the legal level with the purpose of preparing a series of reports that showed the

201. Cf. Elola Somoza, *Crisis y Reforma de la Asistencia Sanitaria Pública en España* (1983–1990), *supra.*, p. 195.
202. Figures taken from the 'Memoria Fundacional de S.G. de Gestión de la Atención Hospitalaria de 1989' (Hospital Care Management Report for 1989), cited by Elola Somoza, *Crisis y Reforma de la Asistencia Sanitaria Pública en España* (1983–1990), *supra*, p. 195.
203. Elola Somoza, *Crisis y Reforma de la Asistencia Sanitaria Pública en España* (1983–1990), *supra*, p. 195.
204. Ministerio de Sanidad y Consumo, *Análisis y benchmarking del tratamiento de las reclamaciones y sugerencias en el Sistema Nacional de Salud* (Ministerio Sanidad y Consumo, Madrid 2008), https://seguridaddelpaciente.sanidad.gob.es/informacion/publicaciones/2008/docs/InformeIReclamaciones.pdf.
205. J.M. Aranaz (Dir.), C. Aibar/J. Vitaller/P. Ruiz, *Estudio Nacional sobre los Efectos Adversos ligados a la Hospitalización. ENEAS 2005* (Ministry of Health and Consumer Affairs, 2006), https://seguridaddelpaciente.sanidad.gob.es/proyectos/financiacionEstudios/estudiosEpidemiologicos/docs/ENEAS.pdf.
206. J.M. Aranaz (Dir.), C. Aibar et al., *Estudio APEAS. Estudio sobre la seguridad de los pacientes en atención primaria de salud* (Ministry of Health and Consumer Affairs 2008), https://

juridical issues linked to the implementation of such a notification system and the technical characteristics that this system should have in order to be fully integrated in the Spanish legal order.[207]

The Spanish Patient Safety Reporting and Learning System (SiNASP: *Sistema de Notificación y Aprendizaje para la Seguridad del Paciente*) was implemented in 2010 by the Quality Agency of the Ministry of Health in collaboration with the Avedis Donabedian University-Institute (dependent on the Autonomous University of Barcelona). SiNASP is currently applied in various Autonomous Communities (10). Others (Andalusia, Castile and Leon, Catalonia, the Valencian Community, the Basque Country, the Balearic Islands and Madrid)[208] have implemented their own reporting systems. The regulatory framework for the development of a notification structure is constituted by Law 16/2003, of 28 May, on the Cohesion and Quality of the National Health System, whose provisions (Articles 59 and 60) are absolutely generic and lack the minimum level of specificity (as well as being limited to the national system and not extendable to those of the Autonomous Communities).

Law 16/2003, of 28 May, on the Cohesion and Quality of the National Health System:

> Article 59. Quality infrastructure:
>
> 1. The improvement of quality in the healthcare system must preside over the actions of both public and private healthcare institutions.
> 2. The infrastructure for the improvement of the quality of the National Health System shall be made up of the following elements:
>   a) Quality and safety standards, which shall contain the requirements that must guide healthcare centres and services in order to be able to carry out a healthcare activity safely.
>   b) Indicators, which are statistical elements that will make it possible to compare the quality of different health centres and services in a standardized, risk-adjusted and reliable manner.

---

seguridaddelpaciente.sanidad.gob.es/proyectos/financiacionEstudios/estudiosEpidemiologicos/docs/APEAS.
pdf.

207. The different works and reports prepared in the framework of a Collaboration Agreement signed between then Ministry of Health and Consumer Affairs of Spain and the Interuniversity Chair, BBVA Foundation-Foral Provincial Council of Bizkaia, of Law and Human Genome, University of Deusto-University of the Basque Country, led to the publication of a monograph: C.M. Romeo Casabona and A. Urruela, *El establecimiento de un sistema nacional de notificación y registro de eventos adversos en el sector sanitario: aspectos legales* (Comares, Granada 2011). The criteria maintained by the authors of the monograph, in particular in Ch. III (Legal configuration of the system for the notification and recording of adverse events and incidents), constitute the normative criteria taken as a reference by the Spanish Ministry of Health for the implementation of the Patient Safety Reporting and Learning System (SiNASP).

208. Specifically, at the regional level, the existing systems other than SiNASP are the following ones: NotificASP (*Sistema de Notificación de Incidentes y Aprendizaje para la Seguridad del paciente)* in Andalusia, SNiSP Cat (Catalonia), SISNOT (*Sistema de notificación de incidentes sin daño en los centros del Servicio Regional de Salud de Castilla y León*, Castile and Leon), SINEA (*Sistema de Información de Registro de Incidentes y Efectos Adversos*) in the Valencian Community, SNASP (*Sistema de Notificación y aprendizaje en seguridad del paciente)* in the Basque Country, Not-i-Fic (Balearic Islands) and CISEMadrid.

c) Clinical practice guidelines and care practice guidelines, which are descriptions of the processes by which a health problem is diagnosed, treated or cared for.
d) The register of good practices, which will collect information on those practices that offer an innovation or a way of providing a better service than the current one.
e) The register of adverse events, which will collect information on those practices that have resulted in a potential patient safety problem.
This infrastructure shall be at the disposal of both the Ministry of Health and Consumer Affairs and the Autonomous Communities.

Article 60. National Health System Quality Agency:

1. The National Health System Quality Agency shall be created, a body under the Ministry of Health and Consumer Affairs, which shall be responsible for the development and maintenance of the elements of the quality infrastructure.
Its creation shall be carried out in accordance with the procedure provided for in Article 67.1 of Law 6/1997, of 14 April, on the Organisation and Functioning of the General State Administration.
2. The Agency will elaborate or adopt the elements of the infrastructure with the advice of scientific societies and experts in the sector, based on national and international experience. It may also promote agreements with scientific institutions to develop or manage the elements of the infrastructure. It shall also disseminate the elements of the infrastructure for their knowledge and use by the Autonomous Communities and the centres and services of the National Health System.

The SiNASP is based on the following pillars:[209]

- The unique goal is constituted by the improvement of patient safety from the analysis of situations, problems and incidents that caused, or could have caused, harm to patients.
- In principle, the nature of the notification is merely voluntary, although there is an evident institutional interest in the notification to be produced, as the system collaborates with the professionals' learning and, in this way, with the patient's own safety.
- The information introduced in SiNASP is completely confidential and the most advanced security systems protect it.
- Initially, its scope of action was hospital level, although progressively, the implementation of the system has also taken place in primary care centres.

209. Sistema de noficación y aprendizaje para la Seguridad del paciente (SiNASP), Ministerio de Sanidad. https://www.sinasp.es.

Regarding its configuration at a chronological level, the current extension of SiNASP responds to a process that began (in terms of system design and configuration) in 2007, when the following steps were taken for its implementation:

- Review of the literature and visits to national systems for the notification and recording of adverse events and incidents in other countries.
- Survey of representatives of Autonomous Communities and also of experts in patient's safety.
- Constitution of two focus groups with patients.
- Definition of the basic principles of SiNASP.

In 2008, through the Scientific Societies, a survey of professionals was carried out, and for this purpose, the data collection questionnaire as well as the computer application itself were developed. Two fundamental actions were put into practice in 2009. Both involved the first steps of the implementation of SiNASP in the healthcare sector (even with a merely exploratory character). In this way, throughout that year, the pilot test of the system was done in two hospitals of different Autonomous Communities (Catalonia and Castille-La Mancha), as well as later, an extended pilot test was carried out in twenty-three hospitals of these two Spanish regions. 2010 was the year of the progressive implementation of the system and of the consolidation of the two Autonomous Communities already participating as pioneers; the subsequent incorporation of the Communities of Galicia and Murcia was also achieved. Since then, there has been a gradual incorporation of new Autonomous Communities into SiNASP. According to the information provided by the Spanish Ministry of Health and corresponding to 2020,[210] ten Autonomous Communities (Aragon, Canary Islands, Cantabria, Castille-La Mancha, Estremadura, Galicia, The Rioja, Murcia, Navarre and Principality of Asturias) and the cities of Ceuta and Melilla (INGESA) are part of SiNASP.

SiNASP has a pyramidal structure in which different levels of information aggregation are established:

- In essence, the system is locally configured in the health centre itself. At this level a Security Nucleus, in charge of receiving incidents as well as managing and analysing them, is established. This allows that the learning obtained from the events notified in each centre is primarily carried out at the same centre.
- Aggregation of the information derived from the notifications at the Autonomous Community level and, subsequently, from the NHS itself. Aggregation at a supralocal level makes it possible to highlight trends that would go unnoticed in the exclusively local field, giving rise to the development of strategies and projects to improve patient safety at the level of the Autonomous Community itself or at the NHS. In any case, at the higher levels (Autonomous Community and NHS), the information received is not personal (data of the notifier, health professionals involved, name of the centre, etc.) but only aggregated.

---

210. *See* https://seguridaddelpaciente.sanidad.gob.es/proyectos/financiacionEstudios/sistemasInformacionNotificacion/incidentesEASNS/sinasp2019.htm.

SiNASP has an application consisting of a website (so no special installation requirements are needed in the health centres) that gives access to a public and a private area. Regarding the notification management process, a series of basic characteristics of the system should be highlighted:

- All types of incidents connected to patient safety are included in the reportable events, that is, events or circumstances that have caused or could have caused harm to a patient (adverse events, incidents without personal injury and incidents related to safety that did not directly affect the patient).
- Incidents are classified within SiNASP using an adaptation of the Severity Assessment Code (SAC) matrix.[211]
- For analysis and management purposes, incidents with extreme risk (SAC1) are analysed by Root Cause Analysis (RCA); high-risk incidents (SAC2) are analysed using the simplified version of the RCA or similar technology, and medium and low-risk incidents (SAC3 and SAC4) are analysed using aggregated data analysis.
- Improvements, which pretend to solve the underlying causes of the reported incidents, are introduced through the development of risk reduction plans. Feedback on the information collected and the results of the analysis are provided to the professionals during the different phases of the process by means of alerts, periodic reports of the notifications received, cases' analysis, etc.

III. Review Boards

103. One of the most important recommendations of the Helsinki (1964) and Tokyo (Helsinki II, 1975) Declarations was the setting up of independent committees to oversee medical research protocols, particularly where experiments involving human beings are concerned. In the United States, these recommendations led to the creation of Institutional Review Boards, which have had a major influence on the regulations governing Clinical Trials Committees throughout the world and also on recent Spanish provisions.[212] These committees were set up primarily to review medical research protocols and those governing the consent of subjects once they have been duly informed of the importance, consequences and risks entailed in the treatment or operation to be undergone.[213]

The review carried out by the Committees prior to the clinical test is designed to protect the patient by ascertaining whether he has given his/her free consent and also the scope of any such consent, the appropriateness of the information given, particularly with regard to potential risks and benefits. The overall aim is to ensure

211. The SAC (acronym for the Severity Assessment Code) matrix helps staff to prioritize and classify incidents in accordance with the Incident Management Policy. The SAC is a matrix that provides a method to quantify the level of risk associated with an incident and gives the incident a numerical value. Thus, it is intended to guarantee an appropriate management of the incident. The grading system assures the fulfilment of the notification requirements. Appropriate management of the incident will depend on the level of risk incurred for the patient(s) and for the organization.
212. F. Abel, 'El Comité de ética', in *Labor Hospitalaria*, No. 209, 1988 (3), p. 210.
213. *supraIbid.*, p. 207.

that he is not subjected to any experimentation to which he has not given his/her express consent and authorization and that his/her rights are protected. The rights of the researchers involved are protected also in that a clear framework of responsibility is created. The same is true also of the host institution, whose reputation is thus kept intact.[214] Appraisal and control by Committees of this type are strictly scientific and legal-administrative in nature. They do not enter into the ethical considerations of the test performed. On this last point, notice has been drawn[215] to the confusion which traditionally exists in Spanish legislation between Clinical Trials Committees, which limit themselves to the purely scientific and medico-legal aspects, and Bioethics Committees, whose job it is to settle conflicts of values which arise in the course of medical practice. Article 60 of the Legislative Royal Decree 1/2015 of 24 July, which approves the refunded text of the Law on guarantees and rational use of medicines and health products, under the heading 'Guarantee of respect for the ethical principles', stipulates that no clinical test may be performed without a preliminary report drawn up by a Clinical Research Ethics Committee (Comité de Ética de Investigación Clínica, CEIC), which shall be independent of the instigators of or the researchers involved in the test and of the health authorities and shall be duly authorized by the competent body of the corresponding Autonomous Community, which shall notify such authorization to the Spanish Agency of Medicines and Medical Products. The Committee shall weigh up the methodological, ethical and legal aspects of the proposed protocol, as well as the anticipated risks and benefits of the test. CEICs shall be made up of, at the very least, an interdisciplinary team comprising doctors, hospital and primary care pharmacists, clinical pharmacologists, nursing staff and non-health professionals, of whom at least one shall be a jurist.

104. The attribution of scientific-legal and ethical supervisory functions had already been included in the MO of 3 August 1982, which developed Royal Decree 944/1978 governing clinical trials on human beings of pharmaceutical and medicinal products. The Order itself was updated several times during its term of validity, and nowadays, the in-force regulation in this field is the Royal Decree 1090/2015, of 14 December, which regulates clinical trials with medicines, the Research Ethics Committees with medicines and the Spanish register of clinical trials which sets out in Article 12 the general functions of the Ethics Committees on clinical trials with medicines, namely, to weigh up the methodological, ethical and legal aspects of the proposed protocol and to issue an opinion; to assess the substantial changes in approved clinical studies and issue the corresponding report; and to track the study, from its approval until the reception of the final report. Research with human beings excluding the one related to clinical trials with medical products and medical devices which are submitted to their specific set of legislation is regulated in Spain by Law 14/2007, of 3 July, on Biomedical Research Law (LIB). In order to practice such research, Title II Law 14/2007 (*Researches that imply invasive procedures in*

---

214. *See Ensayos Clínicos en España* (Monografías Técnicas 17, Ministerio de Sanidad y Consumo, Dirección General de Farmacia y Productos Sanitarios, Madrid 1990), p. 17; Abel, 'El Comité de ética', *supra,* p. 210.
215. Abel, 'El Comité de ética', *supra,* p. 210.

Human Beings – Articles 13–27) requires, among other conditions, the previous evaluation of the Research Project by a CEI (Article 16). The mentioned CEIs are regulated under Article 12 LIB.

105. In 2024, 122 CEIs exist in Spain, 90 of which are also CEIs with medicines.[216]

§4. Biomedical Ethics Committees

I. Introduction

106. Biomedical Ethics Committees were first regulated in Spain by a Royal Decree in 1978, which referred to these committees as 'CECs'. This was the first legal text to establish that all drug clinical trials had to be evaluated by these committees and that any centre conducting such studies was required to have a CEC. Since then, the Spanish Parliament has enacted a significant number of laws related in some way to Biomedical Ethics Committees.[217] One of the most recent legal instruments addressing this issue is Royal Decree 1090/2015, of 4 December, which regulates clinical trials with medicines, Research ethics committees with medicines and the Spanish Clinical Trials Register.

107. This situation has led to a complex and somewhat confusing legal framework, as there are – at least – three main types of committees regulated under different laws, along with specialized bodies such as the Spanish Committee of Bioethics. The terminology used in the statutory provisions governing these committees is, at the very least, ambiguous. The three primary types of committees are: (a) CEIs, (b) HealthCare Ethics Committees (Comités de Ética Asistencial, CEAs), and (c) Animal Research Ethics Committees (Comités de Ética de Experimentación Animal, CEEAs). However, additional names, such as CEICs, remained in use during a transitional period.

For a long time, the so-called CEICs were the most prominent type of Research Ethics Committees in Spain. However, Royal Decree 1090/2015 introduced two new categories of committees: the aforementioned CEIs and the CEIms. For the purpose of this book, we will focus and explain the functions only of the most prominent bodies in the Spanish context: CEIs (Comités de Ética de la Investigación), Spanish Committee on Bioethics and the Commission on Guarantees for the Donation and Use of Human Cells and Tissues.

---

216. Agencia española de medicamentos y productos sanitarios, 'Listado de Comités de Ética de la Investigación que pueden evaluar proyectos de investigación biomédica que no sean estudios clínicos con medicamentos o investigaciones clínicas con productos sanitarios', 19 Jul. 2024, at: https://www.aemps.gob.es/investigacionClinica/CEIm/doc/Listado_Comites_Etica_de_la_Investigacion.pdf.

217. *See* C.M. Romeo Casabona/P. Nicolás Jiménez, 'Research Ethics Committees in Spain', in D. Beyleveld/D. Towned/J. Wright (eds), *Research Ethics Committes, Data Protection and Medical Research in European Countries* (Sheffield Institute of Biotechnological Law and Ethics, Ashgate 2005), pp. 233–244.

II. Research Ethics Committees

108. In response to the terrible experiences related to human experimentation carried out during World War II, the need to establish multidisciplinary and independent committees responsible for assessing the ethics of medical research was outlined in various international instruments – some binding and others not.[218] Currently, this obligation is included in Spanish national legislation, specifically in the LIB. Its Article 2.e establishes that any research involving human beings or their biological material must, as a requirement, have the authorization and a favourable report issued by a CEI before its initiation.

109. As stated, the CEI are responsible for evaluating the ethical, social, and legal aspects of research projects involving human beings, their data, or biological samples. Article 2 of Royal Decree 1090/2015 establishes that a CEI is an 'independent and multidisciplinary body whose primary purpose is to safeguard the protection of the rights, safety, and well-being of subjects participating in a biomedical research project and to provide public assurance in this regard through an opinion on the relevant documentation of the research project, taking into account the perspectives of laypersons, particularly patients, or patient organizations'. It should be noted that Spanish legislation establishes a very specific type of CEIs, known as the CEIms. These committees have a specific accreditation that allows them to evaluate clinical trials related to medicines and medical devices, ensuring compliance with the ethical and regulatory requirements in this particular field.[219] In this regard, Article 2 of Royal Decree 1090/2015 also establishes that a CEIm is a CEI that is additionally accredited in accordance with the terms of this Royal Decree to issue an opinion on a clinical study with medicinal products and on clinical research with medical devices.

110. The CEIs are the competent bodies to evaluate any research 'on' human beings or their biological samples.[220] The LIB, in its Article 12, establishes some general issues regarding their activity: (1) The CEIs corresponding to the centres conducting biomedical research must be properly accredited by the competent authority of the relevant Autonomous Community or in the case of centres dependent on the General Administration of the State, by the competent authority of the

218. For example, *see* s. 23 of the Declaration of Helsinki of the World Medical Association, on the Ethical Principles for Medical Research Involving Human Subjects, from 1964; Art. 15 of the European Convention on Human Rights and Biomedicine, from 1997; as well as Art. 19 of the Universal Declaration on Bioethics and Human Rights, from UNESCO, in 2005.

219. After successive reforms, many aimed at incorporating community regulations into our legal system, clinical trials are currently regulated by Royal Legislative Decree 1/2015, of 24 July, which approves the consolidated text of the Law on Guarantees and Rational Use of Medicines and Health Products, and by Royal Decree 1090/2015, of 4 December, which regulates clinical trials with medicines, Research Ethics Committees for medicines and the Spanish Clinical Trials Registry, in implementation of Regulation (EU) No. 536/2014, of 16 Apr. 2014, on clinical trials of medicinal products for human use.

220. Article 2(e) of the LIB establishes that: 'The authorization and development of any research project involving human beings or their biological material will require the prior and mandatory favourable opinion of the Research Ethics Committee.'

State itself, to ensure their independence and impartiality. For the accreditation of a CEI, at least the following criteria will be considered: the independence and impartiality of its members in relation to the promoters and researchers of the biomedical research projects, as well as its interdisciplinary composition. The competent authorities may order the creation of CEIs that carry out their functions in two or more centres conducting biomedical research. (2) The CEI corresponding to the centre will perform the following functions: (a) Evaluate the qualifications of the principal investigator and the research team, as well as the feasibility of the project. (b) Assess the methodological, ethical, and legal aspects of the research project. (c) Assess the balance of risks and anticipated benefits arising from the study. (d) Ensure the implementation of procedures that guarantee the traceability of human-derived samples, without prejudice to the provisions of personal data protection legislation. (e) Inform, after evaluating the research project, all biomedical research involving interventions on human beings or the use of human biological samples, without prejudice to other reports that need to be issued. The research project may not be authorized or developed without the prior and mandatory favourable opinion of the CEI. (f) Develop codes of good practices in accordance with the principles established by the Bioethics Committee of Spain and manage the conflicts and cases arising from non-compliance. (g) Coordinate their activities with similar committees from other institutions. (h) Ensure confidentiality and perform any other functions that may be assigned by the regulations implementing this law. (3) To carry out their functions, the CEIs may request the information they need, particularly concerning the sources and amounts of funding for the studies and the distribution of expenses. (4) Members of the CEIs must declare their activities and interests and abstain from participating in deliberations and votes where they have a direct or indirect interest in the matter being examined.

Without prejudice to the above, Spanish regulations also assign other functions to the CEIs: (a) Evaluate population genetic screening, even though it is not a research procedure (Articles 48.3 and 54 of the LIB). (b) Evaluate research projects involving personal data (specifically, the Seventeenth Additional Provision of ‘Organic Law 3/2018, of December 5, on the Protection of Personal Data and the Guarantee of Digital Rights’ establishes two scenarios that require evaluation by CEIs: (1) cases involving the reuse of personal data for research purposes in the field of health and biomedicine, when data initially collected with consent for a specific purpose is later used for other purposes or research areas related to the scientific field of the original study – as set out in point ‘c’; and (2) cases involving the use of pseudonymized personal data for research purposes in public health and, in particular, biomedicine – as set out in point ‘g’).

111. For their part, the operation and activities of the CEIm, due to the specificity and complexity of the studies they oversee, are specifically regulated in Royal Decree 1090/2015, which includes the regulation of key aspects such as: (1) Coordination with the ‘Spanish Agency for Medicines and Health Products’ AEMPS (Article 11 emphasizes the need for collaboration between the CEIm and AEMPS in the evaluation of clinical trials). (2) Functions (Article 12 establishes that, in addition to the functions they may have as CEIs, the CEIm is responsible for evaluating the methodological, ethical, and legal aspects of the study and issuing the corresponding opinion; evaluating substantial modifications of authorized clinical studies and issuing the corresponding opinion; and, finally, monitoring the study from its initiation to the receipt of the final report. Furthermore, Royal Decree 957/2020, of 3 November, which regulates observational studies with human medicines, establishes that CEIms are also responsible for evaluating observational studies with medicines). (3) Accreditation and Renewal (Article 13 establishes that the accreditation, which corresponds to the health authority, must be periodically renewed and notified to AEMPS). (4) Resources and Personnel (Article 14 regulates the nature, functions, means, and infrastructure of the CEIm's Technical Secretariat). (5) Composition of the Committee (Article 15 establishes the number and profiles of the CEI members. The number and profiles of its members are specified). (6) Operating Rules (Article 16 sets out general rules on the operation of the CEIm, establishing criteria to ensure the independence, transparency, and quality of the evaluation process, as well as the obligation to apply standardized working procedures).

III. The Spanish Committee on Bioethics

112. The Spanish Committee on Bioethics[221] was established by Law 14/2007, of 3 July, on LIB as a 'collegiate, independent, and advisory body that shall perform its functions with full transparency on matters related to the ethical and social implications of Biomedicine and Health Sciences'. The Committee – composed of thirteen members – was constituted on 22 October 2008 and is attached to the Ministry of Health. According to Article 78 LIB, its main functions are: 'a) To issue reports, proposals and recommendations for the State and autonomous public powers in matters with relevant ethical implications. b) To issue reports, proposals and recommendations on matters that the Committee considers relevant, relating to the ethical and social implications of biomedicine and the health sciences. c) To establish general principles for the drafting of good practices codes for scientific research that shall be developed by the Research Ethics Committees. d) To represent Spain in the supranational and international forums and organisations that deal with bioethics. e) To draft an annual memorandum of activities. f) Any other functions that are attributed to it, through regulations develop under this Law'.

The LIB also stipulates that the Spanish Committee on Bioethics shall collaborate with other state and autonomous committees that serve advisory functions on the ethical and social implications of biomedicine and the health sciences. Additionally, it shall promote communication among these bodies, without prejudice to their respective functions. The reports, proposals, recommendations, and other documents produced by the Spanish Committee on Bioethics are typically published to ensure broad awareness and dissemination in full compliance with constitutionally recognized fundamental rights.

221. At present, its official website is: https://comitedebioetica.isciii.es/.

IV. The Commission on Guarantees for the Donation and Use of Human Cells and Tissues

113. There is a very special Ethics Committee that plays an essential role in the Spanish Legal Framework. We are referring to the Guarantees Commission for the Donation and Use of Human Cells and Tissues, which was also created by Law 14/2007, of 3 July, on LIB. It is composed of twelve members and aimed at providing counsel and guidance on research and experimentation with human embryonic biological samples and contributing to the updating and dissemination of scientific and technical knowledge in this matter. The regulation of the composition, organization, operation, and functions of the Commission is established through Royal Decree 1527/2010, of 15 November, which regulates the Commission on Guarantees for the Donation and Use of Human Cells and Tissues, as well as the Registry of Research Projects. In accordance with Articles 38 of the LIB and 3.1 of Royal Decree 1527/2010, the Commission is assigned the following functions: (a) Ensuring compliance with the necessary scientific, ethical, and legal safeguards concerning the research referred to in Article 35 of the LIB, annually evaluating its results, issuing a prior favourable opinion on the research projects and activities specified in Article 6 of Royal Decree 1527/2010, monitoring authorized research projects, and issuing a final evaluation report on such projects. (b) Issuing reports, at the request of the State and regional health authorities, on biomedical research involving human embryonic cells and tissues, as well as on their clinical applications in the field of regenerative medicine. (c) Issuing a mandatory report on research projects requiring the entry and/or exit of embryonic material from Spain. In the case of research projects involving embryonic stem cell lines from non-EU countries, the Commission shall issue its report only if the project includes documentation certifying the origin, procedures, and safeguards in the acquisition and handling of the stem cell lines, as well as the regulatory framework of the country of origin governing this matter.

Part II. The Physician-Patient Relationship

Chapter 1. General Description

§1. Rights and Duties of Physicians and Patients

I. General Context

114. Traditionally, the relationship between physicians and their patients in Spain has been built on trust, although physicians have been widely recognized for their overtly paternalistic approach. Over the years, Spain has become increasingly aware of the need for effective protection of patient rights, with particular emphasis on respecting the principle of patient autonomy and promoting more humane treatment – an aspect that has been conspicuously lacking in hospitals. Furthermore, the growing involvement of medical practice in ethically contentious issues, along with the increasing complexity of medical procedures, has highlighted the need to clearly define physicians' specific rights and duties, as well as those arising from their relationship with patients.

In this regard, it is important to highlight the significant role played by the Spanish Constitution, which remains scrupulously committed to respecting individual rights while embracing social and ideological pluralism. This commitment has gradually permeated various sectors of society, although the process of integrating these rights into the legal framework took considerable time to mature. Ultimately, it led to the enactment of three landmark laws: the LGS of 25 April 1986; the Convention for the Protection of Human Rights and Dignity of the Human Being with regard to the Application of Biology and Medicine – commonly known as the Oviedo Convention – which came into effect in Spain on 1 January 2000, following its ratification by Parliament; and Law 41/2002, of 14 November, basic law regulating Patient Autonomy and the Rights and Obligations regarding clinical information and documentation. However, the recognition, protection, and respect of the rights of both patients and physicians do not depend solely on their acknowledgement as ethical values upheld by society. Rather, as will be demonstrated below, these rights are, first and foremost, civil or constitutional rights granted to patients[222] and physicians as citizens. This implies that it is the responsibility of the

222. *See* J. Escrihuela Morales, 'Los derechos del enfermo', in *Jano*, nº. 664, 1985, p. 1279; C.M. Romeo Casabona, 'Configuración sistemática de los derechos de los pacientes en el ámbito del derecho español', in *Jornadas sobre los derechos de los pacientes 1990* (INSALUD, Madrid 1992), pp. 173 ff.

legal system to provide the necessary legal foundation for safeguarding these rights. Therefore, it is essential to first examine how and where these rights have been formally established in positive law.

115. The Spanish Constitution of 1978, which serves as the foundation of the country's political and legal system, contains a series of provisions that allow for the identification of both the core principles of the legal-health framework, as envisioned by the Constitution, and a set of individual rights. Some of these rights are particularly relevant to hospital patients. Several of the aforementioned rights are classified as public rights and freedoms, benefiting from special privileges and enhanced constitutional protections, particularly when they are recognized as 'fundamental rights' (Article 53.1 and 53.2, as well as Article 54 of the Constitution). In such cases, direct protection may be granted by ordinary courts and, in certain instances, even by the Constitutional Court (Article 53.2). Other rights, meanwhile, stem from obligations assumed by the authorities under the Constitution, based on the principles that guide the State's economic and social policies. The protection of these rights is ensured through the legislation enacted to implement them (Article 53.3).

Among these laws, several have direct implications for healthcare and, more specifically, for hospital care. The list provided here is by no means exhaustive and should not be viewed as reflecting priorities of any kind:[223]

1. The right to equality before the law, with no discrimination on the grounds of birth, race, sex, religion, opinion or any other personal or social condition or circumstance (Article 14 of the Constitution).
2. The right to life and to physical and moral integrity; in no circumstances can a person be subjected to torture or to inhuman or degrading punishment or treatment (Article 15).
3. The right to freedom and security (Article 17.1).
4. The right to ideological and religious freedom and freedom of worship (Article 16.1).
5. The right to one's honour, personal and family privacy, one's image, and legal restrictions on the use of computerized information (Articles 18.1 and 4).
6. The right to secrecy in communications (Article 18.3).
7. The right to strike (Article 37.2).
8. The right to health protection (Article 43.1).
9. The right to have public health organized and protected by the authorities (Article 43.2), with special consideration to be given to persons suffering physical, sensory and mental handicaps (Article 49), the elderly (Article 50) and consumers and users (Article 51.1).
10. The right to health and physical education (Article 43.3).

After listing the rights that affect patients, it is appropriate to highlight two crucial legal provisions. The first establishes freedom, justice, equality, and political

223. *See* L.C. Martínez Aguado, *Los derechos del paciente en el hospital publico* (unpublished dissertation) (Zaragoza 1986), p. 26.

pluralism as supreme values of the legal system (Article 1.1), while the second declares that human dignity, inherent rights, the free development of personality, respect for the law, and respect for the rights of others form the foundation of political order and social peace (Article 10.1). Despite the significant complexity involved in interpreting these provisions – particularly regarding their direct applicability (at least in the case of Article 1) and their status as statutory regulations alongside the fundamental rights enshrined in the Constitution (as well as the hierarchical relationship between them) – experts unanimously recognize their importance. At the very least, they serve as guiding principles for interpreting fundamental rights and exert a significant influence on their scope. It is essential to emphasize that these values take on even greater significance in the context of hospital patients.

II. Rights and Duties of Physicians

A. *Objection on the Grounds of Conscience*

116. Objection on the grounds of conscience by physicians and other healthcare professionals primarily arises in relation to abortion, particularly in cases where professionals, either due to their specialization or their assigned duties, are required to perform a legal abortion that conflicts with their ideological views, religious beliefs, or personal ethics. The issue of conscientious objection arises mainly in public hospitals (such as those within the Social Security system), although it can also affect private healthcare centres, albeit to a much lesser extent. Additionally, since 2021, conscientious objection can also be invoked in cases of euthanasia following the entry into force of 'Organic Law 3/2021 of 24 March on the Regulation of Euthanasia.' In the past, it has occasionally been invoked in cases of non-therapeutic sterilization or, more rarely, in relation to certain forms of assisted reproduction.

In Spain, the right to conscientious objection is linked to the fundamental right to 'ideological and religious freedom', as established in Article 16.1 of the Spanish Constitution: '*The ideological and religious freedom of individuals and communities is guaranteed, with its expression limited only insofar as necessary to maintain public order as protected by law.*' However, there is no unanimous consensus on whether conscientious objection should be recognized as an autonomous right directly associated with ideological and religious freedom. Nevertheless, Parliament has the authority to regulate it, resolving specific conflicts by exempting individuals from certain legal obligations when they can demonstrate a genuine conflict between those obligations and their moral convictions. This does not imply that all forms of objection must be protected but rather that such protection should be reserved for matters of significant ethical importance. It would be equally unacceptable to disregard the conscience of objectors as it would be to ignore the interests and rights protected by the legal framework giving rise to the objection.[224]

---

224. Comité de Bioética de España, 'Opinión del Comité de Bioética de España sobre la objeción de conciencia en sanidad', 2011, p. 6, at: https://comitedebioetica.isciii.es/wp-content/uploads/2023/10/La-objecion-de-conciencia-en-sanidad.pdf.

For a long time, Spanish legislation largely overlooked the issue of conscientious objection. For example, it was not addressed in the law that legalized abortion in 1985 (Organic Law 9/1985, of 5 July, amending Article 417 of the Criminal Code). Similarly, the LGS, which emphasized patient rights, did not extend the same consideration to the rights of healthcare professionals. The first legally binding document to address the issue, apart from case law, was the 1990 Code of Medical Ethics, which stated:

> '1. It is ethical for a physician, on the basis of their ethical or scientific beliefs, to refrain from participating in abortions, matters related to human reproduction, or organ transplants. The physician must promptly notify the relevant authorities of their decision and, when necessary, offer alternative treatment options for the medical issue in question. At all times, the physician must respect the right of patients to seek a second opinion from other medical professionals.
> 2. The physician must not be conditioned by actions or omissions which are immaterial to his own right to object on the grounds of conscience. In all cases, the College of Physicians shall provide all necessary advice and help to the physician'. (article 27).

Thus, for many years, conscientious objection by physicians and other healthcare professionals was primarily recognized based on Constitutional Court Ruling 53/1985 (11 April), legal principle No. 14. This ruling, in the context of the decriminalization of abortion, explicitly acknowledged conscientious objection as a fundamental right, stating that the right to object 'exists and may be exercised' regardless of whether it has been expressly recognized by Parliament. Subsequent rulings reaffirmed this position. For instance, a 1988 ruling by the Territorial Court of Oviedo[225] recognized the right to conscientious objection concerning abortion. The court held that 'on-call doctors who are conscientious objectors cannot be compelled to perform any medical acts that directly or indirectly lead to abortion, whether before or during the termination of pregnancy'. However, the ruling also imposed a limitation, stating that 'physicians must provide all necessary medical assistance to patients admitted for such a purpose in any other medical situations or pathological conditions that may arise, even if they result directly from the abortion procedure'. Similar criteria were applied to conscientious objection in other medical practices, provided that the refusal to act did not pose a serious risk to the life or health of the patient.

On the other hand, Spanish Organic Law 2/2010, of 3 March, on sexual and reproductive health and voluntary termination of pregnancy provided a concrete legal response to this issue. It codified case law, granting conscientious objection to abortion the status of a legal right. Thus, conscientious objection is now explicitly recognized under section 19.2 of Organic Law 2/2010, which states that while abortion services must be provided within the public healthcare system, 'the health care providers directly involved in the voluntary interruption of pregnancy shall be entitled to exercise conscientious objection, with no detriment to the access to and

---

225. Ruling of the Territorial Court of Oviedo (Court for Administrative Disputes), 29 Jun. 1988.

quality of the assistance due to the exercise of conscientious objection. Refusal to carry out an interruption of pregnancy for reasons of conscience shall at all times be a personal decision of the medical staff directly involved in performing that voluntary interruption of pregnancy, which must be expressed in advance and in writing. Health care providers shall, in any case, provide adequate medical attention and treatment to women requiring them before and after an abortion'.

Shortly after, the Spanish Bioethics Committee issued several recommendations regarding the regulation of conscientious objection in lawful medical procedures, particularly concerning specific cases within the field. These recommendations included the following key points: '4.1. Conscientious objection must be exercised by individuals. It must be exercised by individual persons, this right cannot be exercised in a collective or institutional manner. 4.2. Hospitals cannot invoke conscientious objection at an institutional level. Private hospitals that are approved and their services contracted by the Social Security can exclude the objected service from their contract. 4.3. The person exercising objection must be involved in the service. The regulation must specify the possible extent and scope of the objection, which medical practitioners or other employees in medical or pharmaceutical centres are entitled to allege conscientious objection, respecting the principle of equality. The opinion of those medical practitioners and other health care providers must be taken into account when establishing these provisions. 4.4. The objection must be specific and refer to specific actions. The objection cannot be extended to all care cases deriving from possible incidents produced by the medical service giving rise to the objection and forming part of the usual obligations of health care providers. 4.5. Hospitals must have the necessary information on the objectors to enable them to guarantee hospital management and ensure the necessary health care provisions. 4.6. "Subsequent objection" and reversible conscientious objection are accepted, because life is a dynamic process in which the opinions of the individuals might change. 4.7. It must be possible to check the coherence of the objector's actions with his/her ideology and beliefs within his/her overall activity in the medical profession. It would not be coherent to object in the public health system and not in private practice. 4.8. The recognition of conscientious objection is consistent with the establishment by Parliament of an alternative service by the objector. This service would be established to avoid any imbalance in the provision of medical services. 4.9. The Spanish Bioethics Committee understands that both the compliance with the law and the objection must be performed in a responsible way and that the provision of the services established by law must be guaranteed at all times'.[226]

Regarding the context of euthanasia, as mentioned above, the 'Organic Law 3/2021 of 24 March on the Regulation of Euthanasia' states that *Conscientious objection in healthcare* is the individual right of healthcare professionals to refuse to comply with healthcare demands regulated by this law when such demands are incompatible with their personal convictions. Article 16 of Organic Law 3/2021 establishes two important criteria for the exercise of this right: (1) Healthcare professionals directly involved in providing aid to dying may exercise their right to

226. Comité de Bioética de España, 'Opinión del Comité de Bioética de España sobre la objeción de conciencia en sanidad', 2011, p. 6, at: https://comitedebioetica.isciii.es/wp-content/uploads/2023/10/La-objecion-de-conciencia-en-sanidad.pdf.

conscientious objection. Refusal to perform this service for reasons of conscience is an individual decision of the healthcare professional directly involved in its execution, which must be expressed in advance and in writing. (2) Health authorities shall establish a register of healthcare professionals who declare themselves conscientious objectors to the provision of aid in dying. This register will serve to provide the necessary information to health administrations to ensure the proper management of aid-in-dying services. The register will be subject to strict confidentiality and compliance with personal data protection regulations. To conclude, Organic Law 3/2021, in its Seventh Additional Provision, states that competent health authorities have the duty to facilitate the exercise of the right to conscientious objection for healthcare professionals.[227]

117. To summarize, the Spanish legal framework recognizes conscientious objection by physicians and other healthcare professionals[228] as a fundamental right. Healthcare professionals, including doctors and other medical staff, may invoke conscientious objection in cases of abortion, euthanasia or other medical procedures that conflict with their ethical beliefs. However, certain legal limitations apply. These include restrictions imposed by the Penal Code regarding failure to provide assistance and omissions leading to harm, as well as constitutional restrictions outlined in Article 16. Additionally, Article 3.1 of the Organic Law on Religious Freedom (5 July 1980) establishes that 'the safeguarding of public safety, *health*, and morals' imposes certain limits on religious and ideological freedom. There is ongoing debate about whether 'health' in this context refers solely to public health or also includes individual health. The interpretation of this provision – whether narrowly or broadly – could significantly impact the scope of conscientious objection. In the field of abortion, ultimately, conscientious objection should be limited to acts that directly contribute to the termination of pregnancy.[229] Physicians must still provide all necessary medical care to patients admitted for abortion in any other medical circumstances, including complications arising from the performed abortion. The same principles apply to conscientious objection in other medical contexts, provided that refusal to act does not pose a serious risk to the patient's life or health.

B. The Right to Strike

118. The right of health professionals to strike is also recognized by the Spanish legal framework. However, it is governed by an extremely outdated law – Royal

227. F. Flores Mendoza, 'Lección 17. Objeción de conciencia', in C.M. Romeo Casabona/P. Nicolás Jiménez/S. Romeo Malanda (Dirs), *Manual de Bioderecho* (2ª edición, Dykinson, Madrid 2025), pp. 463 ff. https://bioderecho.eu/manual-bioderecho/.
228. I. de Miguel Beriain, 'La objeción de conciencia del farmacéutico: una mirada crítica', *Revista de Derecho UNED*, nº. 6, 2009, pp. 173–198.
229. A. Cuerda Riezu, 'El delito de aborto ante la Propuesta de Anteproyecto del Nuevo Código Penal', in *Documentación Jurídica. Monográfico dedicado a la propuesta de Anteproyecto del Nuevo Código Penal (vol. I)*, 37/40, 1983, pp. 376 and f.; M. García Arán, 'La objeción de conciencia del médico en relación a la interrupción del embarazo', in *El aborto: un tema para el debate*, Ayuso, Madrid, 1982, p. 128.

Decree-Law 17/1977 of 4 March[230] – which was enacted before the 1978 Spanish Constitution. Although there have been attempts to amend it, none have been successful. Some specific issues, such as ensuring minimum services in public hospitals during strikes, have been addressed in subsequent regulations, generally providing adequate protection for patients' fundamental right to healthcare. Unfortunately, isolated cases have been reported in which patients have died due to lack of treatment during a strike. If proven, such cases should, at the very least, give rise to criminal liability for negligence.

C. *The Right of Exclusive Practice*

119. The high level of scientific and technical qualification required for medical practice justifies limiting it exclusively to qualified physicians. Those who lack proper qualifications, have not registered with the relevant professional college, or lack official authorization are prohibited from practising medicine. This restriction forms the exclusive right of practice granted to physicians, which is legally protected against unauthorized or insufficiently qualified individuals engaging in medical practice. As previously explained (Part I, Chapter 2), the illegal practice of medicine is a punishable offence under the Spanish Criminal Code, referred to as 'encroachment' or 'impersonation'.

120. Another aspect of exclusive practice is the prohibition of *prescription issuance* by unauthorized individuals. Social Security or Municipal Welfare prescriptions are considered 'official documents', and unauthorized issuance is classified as forgery under Article 392 of the Penal Code.[231] However, prescriptions from private practice physicians working in private hospitals or healthcare companies are not regarded as official documents, although forgery is still punishable if it results in harm or is intended to cause harm. Courts have recognized such harm in certain cases. For example, in a Supreme Court ruling (Second Chamber) of 22 January 1981, it was stated: 'Where the name, prescription book, and signature of a physician who has not actually issued the prescription have been used, it must be considered that the physician's prestige, professional reputation, and practice have been damaged, as the unscrupulous use of his name and title is sufficient to cause moral harm, affecting the reputation and professional honor to which he is entitled.'[232] Nowadays, most prescription forgeries are still committed by drug addicts seeking to obtain psychotropic substances from pharmacies.[233]

230. The right to strike is regulated generally in Royal Decree-Law 17/1977 of 4 March.
231. *See* Rulings of Supreme Court (2nd Chamber) of 18 Apr. 1989 and 22 Apr. 1991.
232. Rulings of Supreme Court (2nd Chamber) of 19 Dec. 1996, 21 May 1993, 23 Mar. 1990, 28 Dec. 1984 and 27 Feb. 1982.
233. *See* Ruling of Provincial Court of Valencia, 18 Jan. 1990, Rulings of Supreme Court (2nd Chamber) of 24 May 1990 and 21 May 1993.

D. Duties of Physicians

121. A physician's most important duties stem from the recognition and respect of patients' rights, as will be detailed below. However, there are also specific statutory duties that must be observed.

122. Duty to report criminal offences. The Spanish Criminal Procedure Act imposes specific reporting obligations on physicians when they become aware of criminal offences in the course of their work (Articles 259 and 262, regarding the general obligation to report an offence, and Article 355, related to reporting harm).

This obligation has been widely criticized on the grounds that disclosing a patient's involvement in a crime may constitute a breach of medical confidentiality, thus violating the confidential relationship between physician and patient. This creates a conflict of duties – the duty to report the offence versus the duty to maintain confidentiality. The resolution of this conflict is complex; however, the duty of confidentiality is generally prioritized, as it is linked to personal privacy, a fundamental right recognized in Article 18.1 of the Spanish Constitution.

123. Duty to assist. Physicians have a general duty of human solidarity, which obliges them to provide assistance in emergencies – whether as medical professionals, public servants, or ordinary citizens. Physicians who fail to provide assistance in situations of serious health risk may face criminal liability. According to Article 196 of the Criminal Code: '*A medical practitioner who, while under obligation to do so, refuses to provide healthcare assistance or abandons the provision of health services, when such refusal or abandonment causes a serious risk to personal health, shall be punished with the penalties outlined in the preceding article, in the upper half of the range, and with special disqualification from public employment and office, profession, or trade for a term of six months to three years.*' However, convictions of physicians under this provision are extremely rare.[234] In some cases, physicians have been convicted for failing to visit a patient's home when they were under a legal obligation to do so.[235]

III. Rights and Duties of Patients

124. The primary legal sources governing patient rights at the national level in Spain are the LGS of 1986 and Law 41/2002 (LAP). Patient rights were first introduced into the Spanish legal framework through the LGS of 1986. This Act, which remains in force, establishes a series of rights and duties for patients[236] and users of public health services (and, in some cases, private ones) in Articles 10 and 11. These rights are genuinely subjective and enforceable. The most significant ones include:

234. Rulings of Supreme Court (2nd Chamber) of 22 Oct. 2015.
235. Rulings of Supreme Court (2nd Chamber) of 21 Jun. 1989 and 2 Oct. 1989.
236. *See* Romeo Casabona, 'Configuración sistemática de los derechos de los pacientes en al ámbito del derecho español', *supra*, pp. 178 ff.

- The right to one's personality, to human dignity and intimacy, and the right not to be discriminated against on the grounds of race, gender, sexual tendencies, etc.
- The right to information concerning health services to which they are entitled and concerning any requirements governing the use thereof.
- The right to confidentiality in respect of all information concerning their medical condition and their stay in public health institutions and in private institutions which co-operate with the public system.
- The right to be notified if the prognosis, diagnosis and therapeutic procedures applied to them are likely to be used as part of a teaching or research project. In no way shall the project entail any additional danger to their health and in all cases the patients' prior written consent must be sought and authorization given by the physician and the management of the health institution concerned.
- The right to have a physician assigned to his case. The physician's name shall be notified to the patient and he shall serve as his main healthcare interlocutor. In the absence of the physician appointed, responsibility shall be assumed by another member of the team.
- The right to participate, through community institutions, in health activities, in accordance with the terms laid down in Law 14/1986 and any statutory provisions which develop the Law further.
- The right to make use of channels created to enable patients to lodge complaints or propose suggestions within the appropriate time limits. In either case, the patient shall receive a written reply within the stipulated time limit.
- The right to choose his physician and other qualified healthcare professionals in accordance with the conditions laid down in Law 14/1986, as well as in any provisions drawn up to develop the Law further and those regulating the functioning of healthcare centres.
- The right of a patient to obtain drugs and medicines and health products considered necessary to promote, conserve or restore his health, in accordance with the terms laid down by the State Administration.

The LGS (Law 14/1986) also established the main obligations of citizens towards health institutions and bodies (Article 11):

1. To comply with general health regulations governing the population and also with any specific health service regulations.
2. To treat facilities with care and to co-operate in the upkeep of healthcare institutions.
3. To ensure that appropriate use is made of the services provided by the healthcare system, in particular the use of services, procedures for certifying sick leave and permanent disability, and therapeutic and social services.

125. Afterwards, several Acts complemented the LGS, either by introducing new rights or modifying those already established. By the late 1990s, it had become evident that the list of rights included in the LGS was insufficient, mainly due to a shift in attitudes toward healthcare relationships and a corresponding need to define these rights and their scope more precisely. This need was addressed through two key instruments. The first was the Convention for the Protection of Human Rights and Dignity of the Human Being with regard to the Application of Biology and Medicine: Convention on Human Rights and Biomedicine (commonly known as the Oviedo Convention), which entered into force in Spain on 1 January 2000, following its ratification by Parliament. Although the Convention was directly applicable, its ratification prompted a reform of the existing healthcare legislation. This reform was necessary not only because certain aspects of the existing legal framework contradicted the Convention but also because some of the new rights established by the Convention had not yet been recognized in Spanish healthcare legislation.[237]

This legislative reform was carried out through Law 41/2002 (LAP), which partially repealed the LGS of 1986, particularly in relation to patient rights. The new law regulated aspects that the 1986 Act had failed to adequately address, such as the right to health information, informed consent, health documentation, clinical records, and other clinical information. It also established the conditions under which a patient's capacity may be limited and granted physicians the authority to assess such limitations. As a nationwide primary law, this legislation represented a major advancement in physician-patient relationships.[238] Its overarching purpose is to regulate patient autonomy and the rights and obligations related to information and clinical documentation, not only for patients and users but also for healthcare professionals, as well as public and private healthcare centres and services (Article 1). The Exposition of Reasons (Explanatory Memorandum) of the law states the following: 'this Law completes the provisions enunciated by the General Health Act as general principles. In this regard, it reinforces and provides special treatment for the right to autonomy of the patient. In particular deserving of special mention is the regulation on prior instructions which, in accordance with the criterion set down in the Oviedo Convention, considers the wishes of the patient stated in advance within the scope of informed consent'. According to the Act, patient rights include:

a. Right to informed consent. The right of a patient to informed consent is one of the basic patient rights in Spain. The Patient Rights Law defines an informed consent as the free, voluntary and conscious decision of a patient, stated in the full use of his faculties after receiving proper information, so that an action concerning his health can be undertaken.[239] Of course, it includes the patient's right to take part in the decision-making process and the right to refusal of treatment.
b. Right to information about health as a right independent of the right to informed consent. Article 4 of the Act recognizes a double right of the patients (the positive and the negative aspect): the right to know all the information about their health with the purpose of any action that may be carried out on it and the right not to know, that is, to be respected in the decision to not receive any information as long as the individual requests so.

---

237. S. Defloor et al., 'Patient Rights in the EU: Spain', *European Ethical-Legal Papers* No. 15, Leuven, 2008, p. 7.
238. *See* C. García Ortega et al., 'Patient autonomy and information and clinical documentation-related rights within the context of Spanish Law 41/2002', *Revista española de salud pública*, 78:4, 2004, pp. 469–479.
239. *See* Centre for Biomedical Ethics and Law, Katholieke Universiteit Leuven, *Patient Rights in the EU – Spain*, 2008, at: https://kuleuven.limo.libis.be/discovery/search?query=any,contains,LIRIAS1948866&tab=LIRIAS&search_scope=lirias_profile&vid=32KUL_KUL:Lirias&offset=0.

c. Right regarding access to medical files. All patients or users of healthcare services have the right for a record to be kept of the information gathered during all their provided healthcare services. They also have a whole right to gain access to this record.
d. Right to intimacy. Article 7 of the Law states the right of all people to have the confidential nature of information about their health respected and that no one may access this information without previous authorization as established by law.

126. Apart from all these fundamental acts, there are a number of Laws and Royal Decrees ruling some specific issues. For instance, rules for patients related to genetic testing are included in Basic Law 14/2007 of 3 July 2007 on Biomedical Research, which contains a comprehensive regulation regarding genetic analyses.

A. *Respect for Human Dignity and Equality*

127. The LGS is explicitly linked to the Spanish Constitution, as made clear in the first section of the rights it establishes (Article 10.1), which specifically refers to respect for dignity and personality (Article 10.1 of the Constitution). It also includes references to privacy and equality (non-discrimination), both of which are enshrined as constitutional rights (Articles 18.1 and 14, respectively): '[All persons have the right] to respect for their personality, human dignity, and privacy, and not to be discriminated against on the grounds of race, social background, sex, morals, or economic, ideological, political, or trade union grounds'. This provision can be seen as the cornerstone of the patient rights listed in Article 10 of the LGS. References to human dignity are also present in both the Oviedo Convention – which states its primary purpose as the protection of 'the dignity and identity of all human beings and to guarantee everyone, without discrimination, respect for their integrity and other rights and fundamental freedoms with regard to the application of biology and medicine' – and Basic Law 41/2002 (LAP) (Article 2, which outlines fundamental principles).

Lastly, human dignity takes on even greater relevance with regard to research and experimentation involving human beings, as we shall see in a moment; however, personal dignity cannot be considered independently but rather only from the point of view of its bearing on other fundamental rights, and thus it is with regard to these rights that one has to ascertain whether dignity has been harmed.[240]

B. *Rights of Access to HealthCare*

128. The Spanish Constitution of 1978 guarantees the right to healthcare and health protection. According to Article 43.1: 'It is incumbent upon the public

240. Constitutional Court Ruling of 27 Jun. 1990, nº. 4.

authorities to organize and oversee public health through preventive measures and the necessary benefits and services. The law shall establish the rights and duties of all in this respect.'

The Spanish healthcare system is entirely decentralized. Following the decentralization of the Spanish state, various healthcare powers were transferred to regional authorities. In practice, however, this reform was not fully completed until 2002, when the governance of the system was decentralized across all seventeen Autonomous Communities.[241] Each of these regions now holds significant legislative and executive authority in the fields of public health, community care, and most social services. There is no hierarchical relationship between the central government and regional governments in the areas that have been devolved.[242] This means that, although all Spanish citizens share the same constitutional right to healthcare, the quality of service may vary depending on the Autonomous Community and the resources available to its regional healthcare administration – even though Article 3 of the LGS explicitly states otherwise (*see* below).

129. The most significant Spanish law governing healthcare access is the LGS, which establishes that all Spanish citizens and foreign residents in Spain are entitled to health protection and medical assistance (Article 1.2). It also includes provisions for non-resident Spaniards and foreign nationals (Article 1.3). As a result, any Spanish citizen who falls ill has the right to medical care, a principle of crucial importance to patients, even though it is not explicitly stated in Article 10 of the LGS.

The law also mandates that public healthcare services must be accessible to the entire population, that access to facilities and services must be based on effective equality, and that health policy should aim to eliminate territorial and social disparities (Article 3). When significant delays occur in the public healthcare system or when a specific treatment is unavailable, a patient who seeks care through a private physician or facility is entitled to full reimbursement of incurred expenses. However, the courts require that the patient must have first formally requested assistance from the public system and that such assistance must have been denied. Merely alleging that the waiting time would have been excessive is not sufficient – except in emergency situations where there is a life-threatening risk, making it necessary for the patient to seek care from private healthcare providers.[243]

Several of the rights outlined in Article 10 of the LGS are directly derived from the right to healthcare, including: The right to information about available health services and their conditions of use (Article 10.2), The right to have a physician assigned to their case (Article 10.7), The right to participate in health-related activities (Article 10.10), The right to use complaint and suggestion channels (Article 10.12), The right to choose a physician (Article 10.13), and The right to obtain medications and pharmaceutical products under conditions of equality (Article 10.14). Beyond these rights, the LGS also establishes the duty of public authorities

241. A. Durán/J.L. Lara/M. Van Waveren, 'Spain: Health System Review', in V. Bankauskaite (ed.), *European Observatory on Health Systems and Policies,* Vol. 8, nº. 4, 2006, p. 19.
242. S. Defloor et al., 'Patient Rights in the EU: Spain', *European Ethical-Legal Papers* No. 15, Leuven, 2008, p. 7.
243. Supreme Court Rulings of 12 Dec. 1991 and 15 Jan. 1992.

to provide users with information about public or associated healthcare services, their rights and obligations (Article 9), and to ensure that the assistance provided meets appropriate standards.

C. Patients' Rights to Self-determination

130. General principle. Today, there is no dispute regarding a patient's right to decide on their own medical treatment. This entails the requirement for informed consent, meaning that a patient (or, if they are incapable, their legal representative) must provide authorization after receiving the necessary medical information. It also includes the right to refuse treatment if the patient deems it contrary to their personal interests. The Spanish legal framework governing this right is based on the Oviedo Convention and Law 41/2002 (LAP).

131. The right to refuse life-saving treatment. One of the most controversial rights under Law 41/2002 (LAP) is the right of a patient to refuse life-sustaining treatment (Article 2.4). This issue typically arises in cases involving terminally ill patients and will be examined in greater depth in Chapter 2, §3.

132. Refusal of a blood transfusion on religious grounds. Serious medical and legal conflicts can arise when adults refuse certain medical treatments for religious reasons. A well-known example is the case of Jehovah's Witnesses, who object to blood transfusions.[244]

This type of religious belief can create serious dilemmas for healthcare providers, particularly in life-threatening situations, such as severe haemorrhages following an accident or surgical procedures where a transfusion is likely to be required. Some hospitals abroad address this issue by pre-collecting the patient's own blood (autotransfusion) before surgery for use if needed – an approach that Jehovah's Witnesses generally accept.

From a legal standpoint, physicians must respect a patient's religious freedom, especially when medical interventions conflict with their beliefs or moral convictions. Failure to do so could lead to legal liability, such as accusations of coercion. Respect for the wishes of a patient poses no major problems and should prevail if the physician has foreseen the situation and can offer alternative, albeit more difficult and risky, forms of treatment.

The situation is vastly different where no therapeutic options are available to replace or mitigate a life-saving blood transfusion. The fundamental issue here is whether the refusal can be deemed to constitute a suicidal attitude. Jehovah's Witnesses stress that they are not suicidal, nor are they exercising the 'right to die' when

244. *See* M. Bajo Fernández, 'La intervención médica contra la voluntad del paciente', in *Anuario de Derecho Penal y Ciencias Penales*, 1979, pp. 492 ff.; by the same author, 'Agresión médica y consentimiento del paciente', in *Cuadernos de Política Criminal*, 1985, pp. 127 ff.; L. Martín-Retortillo Baquer, 'Derechos fundamentales en tensión (¿Puede el juez ordenar une tranfusión de sangre en peligro de muerte, aún en contra de la voluntad del paciente?)', in *Poder Judicial*, 1984, pp. 31 ff.; C.M. Romeo Casabona, *El Médico y el Derecho Penal, I*, *supra*, pp. 372 ff.

they refuse a transfusion.[245] Such arguments are acceptable and easy to explain: their view is that they wish to live but without transgressing their religious beliefs, a stance which is deserving of respect. However, when no other therapeutic alternative exists and the blood transfusion is considered to be the only means of eliminating the immediate danger to the life of a patient of that religious persuasion and if, in order to remain faithful to his religion, he continually refuses to undergo a transfusion, it must be acknowledged that in adopting such a stance, the patient is contemplating the possibility of death, and thus, if he is aware that there are no other means of saving his life, the patient is expressing a desire (albeit an indirect one) to die. This acceptance of death, from a legal standpoint, is equivalent to a suicidal attitude,[246] which is equally to be respected from the ethical standpoint in that it seems from a personal valuation based on individual conscience. From a legal perspective, the correct solution is awkward, given that at stake is an interest of particular value to which the legal order affords reinforced protection. However, insofar as the decision is a conscious one taken by an adult after great thought and without undue pressure, it should be respected and even supported by the Constitution (Articles 15, 16 and 18).

133. The *right to free movement* and the *right to security* (Article 17.1 of the Constitution) can become particularly complex when a patient suffers from certain illnesses. This complexity finds parallels in the European Convention for the Protection of Human Rights and Fundamental Freedoms of 1950, which in Article 5(e) considers detention lawful in cases involving the lawful internment of a person liable to spread a contagious disease, a mentally deranged person, an alcoholic, a drug addict, or a vagrant. Similarly, the International Covenant on Civil and Political Rights of 1966 (Article 12.3) addresses restrictions on freedom of movement. Both international instruments have been signed and ratified by Spain.

The Spanish Constitution states that no person may be deprived of their freedom except in situations outlined in the Constitution itself and in cases provided for by law (Article 17.1). Consequently, in situations of emergency or necessity, competent health authorities are empowered to protect public health by implementing measures such as examination, treatment, hospitalization, or control, as stipulated in the Organic Law on Special Public Health Measures of 14 April 1986. These measures are not deemed to infringe constitutional rights.[247] In this respect, Law 41/2002 includes exceptions to the requirement of consent (Article 9.2).

D. The Right to Information

134. Although it is closely bound up with consent to the medical act, it should not be forgotten that the right to information is justified in its own right and is

245. *See also* Bajo Fernández, 'La intervención médica contra la voluntad del paciente', *supra*, p. 498.
246. J.L. Díez Ripollés, 'La huelga de hambre en el ámbito penitenciario', in *Cuadernos de Política Criminal*, nº. 30, 1986, p. 609; Romeo Casabona, *El médico y el Derecho Penal, I*, *supra*, p. 375.
247. On this and the following situation, *see* E. Cobreros Mendazona, *Los tratamientos sanitarios obligatorios y el derecho a la salud*, (HAEE/IVAP, Oñati 1988), pp. 334 ff. and 369 ff.

wholly independent of all others. Information provided to a patient entails multiple considerations. The first is directly tied to consent, as mentioned earlier: only after receiving all relevant material information can a patient give conscious and valid consent. However, the right to information extends beyond consent and does not necessarily require a voluntary act by the patient. Article 9 of Law 41/2002 explicitly recognizes that information is not always a prerequisite for a patient's free choice and consent. This right also includes the patient's entitlement to knowledge about their condition and treatment process, as well as the right to receive therapeutic information. Additionally, patients have the right to a discharge report upon leaving the hospital (Article 20) and access to their health or clinical records (Article 18). Given the close connection between information and consent in medical procedures, this topic merits further discussion.

§2. Informed Consent

135. As we have already mentioned, informed consent is another patient right which has been naturalised in Spanish legislation, particularly in the Oviedo Convention and in Law 41/2002.[248] According to Article 5 of the Oviedo Convention, 'An intervention in the health field may only be carried out after the person concerned has given free and informed consent to it. This person shall beforehand be given appropriate information as to the purpose and nature of the intervention as well as on its consequences and risks. The person concerned may freely withdraw consent at any time.' This approach was reinforced by Law 41/2002, which includes informed consent as one of its basic principles.[249] According to the second paragraph of its Article 2, all actions within the scope of health require in general the prior consent of patients or users of health services. The consent, which must be obtained once the patient has received prior information, shall be given in writing when a law provides this. The same article (paragraphs 3 and 4) determines that the patient has the right to decide freely between the clinical options available, once he has received proper information. This includes a right to freely refuse a treatment. The Law also declares that all professionals involved in care activities are obligated not only to perform their techniques correctly but also to comply with the duties of information and clinical documentation. They are also obligated to respect the decisions taken freely and voluntarily by the patient (Article 2(6)). The third article of the Patient Rights Law defines an informed consent as the free, voluntary and conscious decision of a patient, stated in the full use of his faculties after receiving proper information, so that an action concerning his health can be undertaken.

Law 41/2002 dedicates its fourth chapter to regulate the autonomy of the patient. According to the first paragraph of Article 8, any action regarding the health of a patient requires the free and voluntary consent of the concerned party, once the

248. J. Núñez Fernández, 'Capítulo 4. El consentimiento informado', in A. Serrano Maíllo/J.A. Sánchez Sánchez (eds), *Una introducción criminológica a la Medicina Legal y Forense* (Dykinson, Madrid 2020), p. 158.

249. *See* S. Defloor et al., 'Patient Rights in the EU: Spain', *European Ethical-Legal Papers* No. 15, Leuven, 2008, p. 10.

patient has assessed the options inherent to the case and after he received the information provided for in Article 4, which regulates the right to healthcare information.The Law establishes as a general rule that informed consent must be given orally, unless otherwise stipulated by law, a solution that has been welcomed by practitioners and scholars as the LGS of 1986 required a written consent in all cases. However, this was not workable in practice and was even unnecessary in many healthcare processes.[250]

The same Law describes the cases in which written informed consent is compulsory: in case of surgical operation, invasive diagnostic and therapeutic procedure, and in general when the application of procedures implies risks or drawbacks having a notable and foreseeable negative repercussion (Article 8.2). The written consent has to contain sufficient information on the application procedure and its risks. The physician has to assess the need for a written consent on the basis of the degree of incertitude as regards the result of the intervention (Article 10(2)).

It is worth mentioning that the Law establishes two exceptions to the requirement of informed consent, which clarify Article 8 of the Oviedo Convention ('When because of an emergency situation the appropriate consent cannot be obtained, any medically necessary intervention may be carried out immediately for the benefit of the health of the individual concerned'). The physician shall in the first place be able to conduct clinical interventions which are essential for the health of the patient without the informed consent of the patient in case there exists a risk for public health. In the second place, informed consent does not have to be obtained when there is an immediate serious risk to the physical or mental integrity of the patient and it is not possible to obtain his consent, consent of the family or the consent of persons tied to the patient for de facto reasons.[251]

136. Some observations are necessary with regard to consent-related information.[252] In general, information is a requirement which conditions the validity of subsequent consent to the medical act; however, the act need not necessarily lead to treatment or intervention, which is why information in its own right is construed as an autonomous right enjoyed by the patient, regardless of whether he is to give his consent. However, consent and information are frequently linked, and hence, the two rights are not entirely unrelated, given that when the patient has to give his consent, he must know what he is consenting to and needs information to do so. Moreover, whoever provides him with the information should be person(s) who will treat him or perform the intervention (Article 4.3 Law 41/2002).

---

250. *See* Defloor et al., 'Patient Rights in the EU: Spain', *supra*, p. 7.
251. *See* Centre for Biomedical Ethics and Law, *Patient rights in the EU – Spain*, (Katholieke Universiteit Leuven 2008), at: https://kuleuven.limo.libis.be/discovery/search?query=any,contains,LIRIAS1948866&tab=LIRIAS&search_scope=lirias_profile&vid=32KUL_KUL:Lirias&offset=0.
252. S. Gallego Riestra, 'Capítulo 23. Información y consentimiento informado: De la Ley General de Sanidad a la Ley 41/2002', A. Palomar Olmeda/J. Cantero Martínez (Dirs), *Tratado de Derecho Sanitario. Volumen I* (Thomson Reuters, Aranzadi, Cizur Menor 2013), pp. 811–821; Núñez Fernández, 'Capítulo 4. El consentimiento informado', *supra*, pp. 159–161.

Very little needs added to what has been said above, especially with regard to the need for information, the amount of information, disclosure, understanding ('comprehensible information'), form ('verbal and written'), and persons to whom it shall be given (the patient and his next-of-kin, although, in the case of the latter, without violating the respect for the privacy of the patient), etc., given that everything can be inferred from the aforementioned paragraphs of Law 41/2002.

From the legal standpoint, and in the light of the explicit wording of the Law 41/2002, the duty to inform admits an only exception, the so-called therapeutic privilege (Article 5.4). According to this clause, information is not provided to the patient due to therapeutic reasons. Keeping this in mind, it could be said that in the Spanish legal framework, restrictions on the right to information on the grounds of therapeutic privilege can be justified to a certain extent. This clause is based on a simple reason: although the physician is obliged to give clear and adequate information to his patient, it is possible for him to give partial or gradual information only, provided that in doing so, his intended purpose is not to fraudulently evade his duty and that in his sound judgment, and in view of the specific circumstances of the case, he considers that full information might seriously impair the patient's recovery and hinder beyond repair the success of the treatment. Where information is restricted, the patients should be given an approximate idea of the seriousness of their condition, and under no circumstances should they be totally misinformed. Brief or limited information given to a patient should in all cases by accompanied and compensated for by fuller information given to the next-of-kin, since, at the end of the day, they will have to serve as substitutes for or complement the self-determination of the former.

137. As was stated above, there can be no doubt that an adult patient who has received adequate information, that is, a patient who is conscious of the repercussions of his decision, is entitled to refuse treatment. To sum up, physicians must respect a patient's refusal of treatment where the latter is aware of the repercussions of his decision. If, in spite of this – and notwithstanding opposition on the part of the patient or, in the case of an incompetent patient, his guardian, next-of-kin or those close to him – a physician chooses to intervene and performs surgery or any other form of treatment requiring hospitalization, he shall be held to be criminally liable as the author of arbitrary curative treatment, provided that all the measures taken were of a clearly curative nature (otherwise liability would probably be more serious, if the patient's personal integrity were undermined), or even for having unlawfully deprived the patient of his freedom, if the appropriate authorization was not sought and obtained from a judge. An attack of this nature on the patient's personal freedom shall be liable to punishment under the offence of coercion (or that of unlawful detention, depending on the case). Physical or moral compulsion must be present or actual deprivation of freedom – displacement – of the patient for the purpose of carrying out the intervention shall be required; if this is not the case, civil liability may be claimed. Spanish criminal courts, however, have not tried any of the above cases, except for a number involving involuntary confinement in psychiatric hospitals of mentally ill patients or violent or threatening persons, where it was deemed that the offences of coercion and unlawful detention, respectively, were applicable.[253]

§3. Privacy

138. The right to personal privacy has traditionally been one of the most frequently disregarded rights in hospitals, likely reflecting the limited importance historically attached to it by society. However, awareness of this right has been increasing, primarily due to its inclusion in the Constitution (Article 18.1, which states that the law shall restrict the use of data processing to protect the honour, personal and family privacy of citizens, as well as the full exercise of their rights), the LGS, the LAP, Regulation (EU) 2016/679 of the European Parliament and of the Council of 27 April 2016 on the protection of natural persons with regard to the processing of personal data and on the free movement of such data, and repealing Directive 95/46/EC (General Data Protection Regulation – GDPR) and Organic Law 3/2018, of 5 December, on the Protection of Personal Data and the guarantee of digital rights.[254] Various aspects of this right can be inferred both directly and indirectly.

139. First and foremost, this right implies that medical examinations should be limited to what is strictly necessary (e.g., inquiries into the patient's private, family, or social life) to ensure an accurate diagnosis. More importantly, however, it directly entails the *corresponding duty of confidentiality* and professional secrecy – an obligation that was historically afforded little protection in legislation and remains inadequately safeguarded in certain fields, including healthcare. This duty covers all aspects of a patient's illness, including hospitalization, and, if the patient so requests, obliges the physician to withhold information even from next-of-kin (despite the fact that Law 41/2002, Article 5.3, lists next-of-kin among those entitled to receive information). Contrary to common belief, this duty is binding on *all* healthcare professionals, regardless of rank or function, not just physicians and nurses. The LGS (Article 10.1 and 10.3) and Organic Law 3/2018 (Articles 5, 9 and Seventeenth additional provision) also clearly affirm the right to confidentiality.

This constitutional right to privacy, along with the right to one's image – both of which hold equivalent constitutional standing (Article 18.1 of the Constitution) – prohibits the publication of photographs or any other identifying information in scientific works (and, of course, in the media) without the patient's prior consent. The

---

253. Supreme Court Rulings of 16 Apr. 1959 and 24 Oct. 1978, respectively.

254. *See* B. Andreu Martínez, 'Lección 8. Intimidad, confidencialidad y documentación clínica', in C.M. Romeo Casabona/P. Nicolás Jiménez/S. Romeo Malanda (Dirs), *Manual de Bioderecho* (2ª edición, Dykinson, Madrid 2025), pp. 197–201 ff. https://bioderecho.eu/manual-bioderecho/; C.M. Romeo Casabona/P. Nicolás Jiménez, 'The Implementation of Directive 95/46/EC in Spain', in D. Beyleveld et al. (eds), *Implementation of the Data Protection Directive in Relation to Medical Research in Europe* (Ashgate, Aldershot 2004), p. 357.

duty of confidentiality is waived only in cases expressly provided for by law[255] or when a judge grants authorization on legal grounds.

140. A true test of the right to privacy arises in the context of the *computerized processing of personal data* related to hospital patients and outpatients. While this technology brings numerous advantages, it also increases the risk of patients becoming more vulnerable to privacy breaches.[256] In Spain, this matter is regulated by GDPR and Organic Law 3/2018, of 5 December, on the Protection of Personal Data and the guarantee of digital rights. Article 4.1 of the GDPR defines 'personal data' as 'any information relating to an identified or identifiable natural person ('data subject'); an identifiable natural person is one who can be identified, directly or indirectly, in particular by reference to an identifier such as a name, an identification number, location data, an online identifier or to one or more factors specific to the physical, physiological, genetic, mental, economic, cultural or social identity of that natural person' while Article 4.2 defines 'processing' as 'any operation or set of operations which is performed on personal data or on sets of personal data, whether or not by automated means, such as collection, recording, organisation, structuring, storage, adaptation or alteration, retrieval, consultation, use, disclosure by transmission, dissemination or otherwise making available, alignment or combination, restriction, erasure or destruction'.

Personal data concerning health is classified as a special category of personal data under GDPR (Article 9) and Organic Law 3/2018 (Article 9). It may only be collected, processed, and disclosed under specific conditions: either when the data subject has given explicit consent for reasons of general interest or when provided for by law. Additionally, the processing of personal health data is permissible when necessary for preventive medicine, medical diagnosis, the provision of care or treatment, or the management of healthcare services. In such cases, data processing must be carried out by a healthcare professional bound by professional secrecy or by another person subject to an equivalent obligation of confidentiality.

141. Patients' freedom and confidentiality of correspondence and communications are recognized as fundamental rights in the Spanish Constitution (Articles 20.1 and 18.3, respectively) and are protected under criminal law.

---

255. *See* Cobreros Mendazona, *Los tratamientos sanitarios obligatorios y el derecho a la salud*, *supra*, p. 267.

256. *See* F. Madrid Conesa, *Derecho a la intimidad, informática y Estado de Derecho* (Publ. Universidad de Valencia, Valencia 1984), passim; F. Morales Prats, *La tutela penal de la intimidad: privacy e informática* (Ed. Destino, Barcelona 1984), passim; F. Morales Prats, 'Confidencialidad, intimidad e informática: la protección de los datos del paciente. Perspectiva jurídico-penal', *Jornadas sobre los derechos de los pacientes 1990* (INSALUD, Madrid 1992), pp. 131 ff.; C.M. Romeo Casabona, *Poder lnformático y Seguridad Jurídica* (Fundesco, Madrid 1988), pp. 25 ff.; C.M. Romeo Casabona, 'La reforma penal ante las nuevas tecnologías de la información', in *Informática e Diritto*, 1987, pp. 115 ff.; C.M. Romeo Casabona/E. Domínguez García, *El Derecho ante las nuevas tecnologías en el ámbito sanitario* (Report commissioned by the Ministry of Health and Consumer Affairs, La Laguna 1991); E. Sola Reche, 'La protección penal de la intimidad informática', in *Anales de la Facultad de Derecho de la Universidad de La Laguna*, No. 11, 1991, pp. 179 ff.

142. Ideological and religious freedom, as well as freedom of worship, are also entitlements of hospitalized patients. However, while the LGS explicitly prohibits discrimination based on ideology (Article 10.1), it does not explicitly recognize freedom of worship. This right ensures that patients are allowed to engage in religious practices in accordance with their beliefs and that they are not compelled to undergo medical treatment that conflicts with their convictions. Where adherence to religious beliefs makes treatment impossible, competent adult patients have the right to refuse treatment. However, this right does not extend to minors when their parents refuse life-saving treatment on their behalf, as previously discussed in the case of Jehovah's Witnesses. This raises broader ethical and legal questions regarding an individual's right to control their own life, particularly when the treatment in question is life-sustaining.

Although the LGS does not explicitly recognize freedom of worship, this right is enshrined in the Constitution (Article 16.1) and further reinforced by various statutory provisions, beginning with Organic Law 7/1980 of 5 July on Religious Freedom. This law guarantees the right to practice religious acts, receive religious assistance in accordance with one's beliefs, and be free from the imposition of other religious practices (Article 2.1d). Moreover, the rights recognized by this law are granted constitutional protection (Article 4). Religious assistance in hospitals[257] is ensured through agreements between the Spanish State and the Holy See. The Agreement on Legal Affairs[258] establishes provisions for religious assistance in hospitals, stating:

> '1. The State recognizes and guarantees the right to religious assistance for citizens confined in prisons, hospitals, psychiatric institutions, orphanages, and similar public and private centers. 2. Catholic religious assistance and pastoral activities within these public institutions shall be regulated through mutual agreements between Church and State authorities. In all cases, individuals' rights to religious freedom and respect for their religious and ethical principles shall be upheld' (Article 4).

§4. Secrecy

143. The obligation to uphold medical secrecy is established in Article 199(2) of the Spanish Criminal Code, the Oviedo Convention, the LAP, the LGS, the GDPR, and Organic Law 3/2018.

Article 199 of the Spanish Criminal Code states: '*1. Whoever discloses the secrets of others obtained through their trade or professional relationships shall be punished with imprisonment from one to three years and a fine of six to twelve months. 2. Professionals who, in breach of their obligation of secrecy or confidentiality,*

257. Recognition has existed for some time of patients' right to spiritual assistance in hospitals belonging to the Social Security system: General Regulation governing the regime, government and services of Social Security healthcare centres (MO of 7 Jul. 1972, Art. 148.5).
258. Signed on 3 Jan. 1979, and ratified on 4 Dec. of the same year (*Official State Journal*, 15 Dec. 1979).

reveal the secrets of another person shall be punished with imprisonment from one to four years, a fine of twelve to twenty-four months, and special disqualification from their profession for a period of two to six years'. In recent years, several physicians who violated professional secrecy have been sentenced to prison under this provision. However, if the offender is not a healthcare professional authorized to access the data, Article 197 of the Criminal Code applies. This article states: '*1. Whoever, in order to discover the secrets or breach the privacy of another person, without their consent, seizes their papers, letters, electronic mail messages, or any other personal documents or belongings, or intercepts their telecommunications, or uses technical devices for listening, transmitting, recording, or reproducing sound or image, or any other communication signal, shall be punished with imprisonment from one to four years and a fine of twelve to twenty-four months*'.

Regarding healthcare legislation, Article 16 of Law 41/2002 regulates access to medical records by healthcare professionals and other individuals who, while not healthcare professionals, perform tasks within the healthcare context. According to the first paragraph of this provision, healthcare professionals responsible for diagnosing or treating a patient have access to the clinical record as a fundamental tool for ensuring proper patient care. Each healthcare centre must establish procedures that allow the attending professional to access the clinical record at all times (Article 16(2)). Administrative and management personnel of healthcare centres may only access medical record data relevant to their specific functions (Article 16(4)). However, it remains unclear whether these functions might provide them with exhaustive information about a patient's health. Additionally, healthcare personnel involved in inspection, evaluation, accreditation, and planning may also access medical records within the scope of their duties (Article 16(5)). According to Article 16(6), all personnel who access medical records during the course of their work are bound by confidentiality obligations. Furthermore, Article 16(3) establishes that access to clinical records for judicial, epidemiological, public health, research, or teaching purposes is governed by the provisions of current legislation on the protection of personal data, as well as by Act 14/1986 of 25 April (LGS) and other applicable regulations in each case. Access to clinical records for these purposes requires that the patient's personal identification data be kept separate from clinical and healthcare-related data, ensuring anonymity as a general rule unless the patient has explicitly consented to keeping them together. Exceptions apply to research cases outlined in section 2 of the seventeenth additional provision of the Organic Law 3/2018. Additionally, exceptions are made for judicial investigations where the unification of identification data with clinical and healthcare data is deemed essential. In such cases, the provisions established by judges and courts within the corresponding legal proceedings shall apply. Access to data and documents within clinical records is strictly limited to the specific purposes of each case. When necessary to prevent a serious risk or danger to public health, the health administrations referenced in Law 33/2011, of 4 October, General Public Health Law, may access patients' identification data for epidemiological reasons or to safeguard public health. In all cases, access must be granted by a health professional bound by professional secrecy or by another individual subject to an equivalent confidentiality obligation. Additionally, access must be preceded by prior justification from the requesting administration. Finally, Organic Law 3/2018, in Articles 71 to 78, establishes the sanctioning regime for administrative offences related to non-compliance with data protection mechanisms, including those concerning health data, as provided for in the law. It is also important to highlight the civil protection of professional secrecy in medical practice, as provided by the Organic Law on Civil Protection of the Right to Honor, Personal and Family Privacy, and One's Own Image (5 May 1982). Article 7(4) of this law establishes that the disclosure of private data concerning an individual or their family, obtained during professional or official activities, constitutes an unlawful invasion of privacy. In the previous section on patient privacy, we addressed the implications of this right concerning a physician's duty of confidentiality.

144. Nevertheless, it is necessary to highlight that the Spanish Legal Framework imposes an obligation on healthcare staff to facilitate information to the health authorities or their agents (Articles 35, B.5 and C.5 LGS), an obligation which must be rendered compatible with the duty of the confidentiality imposed by the very same Law. Similarly, the duty to report any offences which come to their knowledge is incumbent upon physicians also, as we saw earlier, despite the fact that this represents a clear restriction on the duty of secrecy.[259] Indeed, it is worth mentioning the Spanish Penal Code (Article 450 states that '*1. Whoever is able, by his immediate intervention and without risk to himself or another, and does not prevent a felony being committed that affects the life, integrity or health, freedom or sexual freedom of persons, shall be punished with a sentence of imprisonment of six months to two years if the offence is against life, and that of a fine from six to twenty-four months in the other cases, except if the offence not prevented is subject to an equal or lower punishment, in which case a lower degree punishment than that for the actual felony shall be imposed. 2. The same penalties shall be incurred by whoever, being able to do so, does not resort to the authority or its agents in order for them to prevent a felony of those foreseen in the preceding Section when informed that it is about to be, or is being committed.*'). Therefore, it seems that a healthcare worker who knows that a patient is planning to commit a felony that affects life, integrity, health, freedom or sexual freedom of persons is obliged to avoid it personally or by resorting to the authority or its agents. However, it is important to highlight that this obligation only exists when a felony is foreseen. It does not directly involve the same duty in the case of a general danger. Indeed, this is a much more conflictive case.

§5. COMPLAINTS

145. Introduction. A patient whose rights have been violated may seek legal protection through the courts and request compensation for any harm sustained, particularly in serious cases. Patients or their relatives, as users of healthcare services,

259. *See* Part II, Ch. 1, §1, §2 and §6.

have several avenues available to submit complaints regarding the care received or the treatment experienced during their hospital stay.

The Spanish legal framework on this matter is primarily based on the Oviedo Convention and the LGS, which constitute the most significant legally binding documents on the subject, given that the LAP does not address it at all. According to Article 23 (Infringement of the rights or principles) of the Oviedo Convention, 'The Parties shall provide appropriate judicial protection to prevent or to put a stop to an unlawful infringement of the rights and principles set forth in this Convention at short notice.' Similarly, Article 24 (Compensation for undue damage) states that 'The person who has suffered undue damage resulting from an intervention is entitled to fair compensation according to the conditions and procedures prescribed by law.' These principles are reflected, to some extent, in Article 10.12 of the LGS, which establishes that all patients have the right to access channels for submitting complaints and suggestions. In practice, all healthcare centres within the Autonomous Communities must provide guidelines outlining the rights and obligations of healthcare users, the services available at the facility, their characteristics, and the procedure for submitting suggestions or complaints.[260]

146. Complaints concerning the violation of patient rights.[261] The LGS outlines a list of healthcare user rights in Article 10, which has been further developed and amended by Law 41/2002, as previously mentioned. However, for these rights to be effectively upheld, a disciplinary system is necessary to ensure compliance and to sanction healthcare professionals who violate them. One of the initial steps patients can take is to file a complaint against the hospital through the Patient Care Service.

If the violation constitutes an offence or results in civil liability[262] – whether on the part of the professional, the healthcare facility, or vicariously through the Administration – the patient may pursue the appropriate legal action.[263] In other cases, the lack of clarity surrounding the issue makes it difficult to determine which system of infringements and sanctions should apply. However, it is essential to consider the corrective measures available to health authorities to address violations or neglect of certain rights. These include the disciplinary powers of the Colleges of Physicians and the relevant disciplinary regulations that may be inferred from the Legal Statutes of Social Security Medical Personnel and the General Law on Consumer and User Protection.

260. A. Durán/J.L. Lara/M. Van Waveren, 'Spain: Health System Review', in V. Bankauskaite (ed.), (European Observatory on Health Systems and Policies, 2006), pp. 38–39.
261. *See* A. Pedreira Andrade, 'Ejercicio de los derechos y reclamaciones de los usuarios: diversas vías de actuación', *Jornadas sobre los derechos de los pacientes* (INSALUD, Madrid 1992), pp. 199 ff.
262. For example, for breaches of privacy 'resulting from the disclosure of private data concerning a person or family which come to be known in the course of the professional or official activity of the person who discloses them', the specific regime contained in Art. 7.4 of the Organic Law on the protection of honour, personal an family privacy and one's image of 5 May 1982 is applicable.
263. *See* Part I, Ch. 3, §2.

§6. Access to Medical Records

I. Patient Access to Hospital Records

147. Access to Clinical Records in Spanish Law has addressed the issue of patients' access to their hospital records by granting unrestricted access under the LGS, which states that hospital or health records 'shall be made available to patients' and that 'the authorities shall adopt measures to guarantee these rights and duties' (Article 61).[264] This regulation was later amended by Law 41/2002, which regulates patient rights regarding medical records in its fifth chapter. According to Article 15 of this law, all patients or healthcare users have the right to have a clinical record kept – either in writing or in the most suitable technical format – containing information gathered throughout their medical care. Article 14(1) defines the clinical record as the set of documents related to a patient's care process, including the identification of the doctors and other healthcare professionals involved. The purpose of a clinical record is to ensure the maximum integration of a patient's health data, at least within each healthcare centre. The medical file must be compiled by the professionals directly involved in the patient's treatment (Article 15(3)), and each healthcare centre is required to store patient records in a manner that guarantees security, proper maintenance, and easy retrieval (Article 14(2)). Furthermore, Article 15(4) mandates that clinical records be kept in accordance with the principles of unity and integration to ensure that physicians have appropriate access to a patient's medical history. Regarding data retention, Article 17(1) establishes that medical files must be preserved for at least five years from the date of discharge following each medical care process.[265]

Law 41/2002 also regulates the right to access the medical file. Its Article 16, the right of the patient or his duly accredited representative to access his medical file is guaranteed by Article 18. According to the first paragraph of this provision, the healthcare centres have to regulate the procedures which enable the patient to exercise this right. The right to access the medical file cannot be exercised to the prejudice of a third party's right to confidentiality of his data noted in the medical file for the therapeutic interest of the patient, nor to the prejudice of the right to confidentiality of the subjective annotations made by the professionals who elaborate the clinical record (Article 18(3)).

The clinical record must contain all information deemed significant for an accurate and up-to-date understanding of the patient's health condition. Article 15(2) outlines the minimum content of the medical file, which includes: (a) Clinical-statistical documentation, (b) Admission authorization (if required), (c) Emergency report (if required), (d) Anamnesis and physical examination, (e) Evolution of the condition, (f) Medical orders, (g) Inter-consultation report, (h) Reports of complementary examinations, (i) Informed consent (if required), (j) Anaesthesia report (if required), (k) Surgical report or delivery record (if required), (l) Pathological report

264. R.A. Millán Calenti, 'Capítulo 22. Historia Clínica Electrónica: accesos compatibles', *Tratado de Derecho Sanitario. Volumen I, supra*, pp. 779–781.

265. *See* Defloor et al., 'Patient Rights in the EU: Spain', *supra*, p. 23.

(if required), (m) Evolution and planning of nursing care, (n) Therapeutic nursing applications, (o) Vital signs chart (if required), and (p) Clinical discharge report (if required).

148. Two key aspects need to be highlighted regarding this statutory provision: First, in referring to hospital records in a general sense, regardless of whether they are stored in a computer or in written form, the provision covers all forms in which records may be kept; hence, the right of access to the record as recognized in Law 41/2002 extends also to any information stored in a computer.

Second, a question mark surrounds exactly which parts of the record a patient is entitled to from the point of view of the precautions provided for in comparative law to avoid negative consequences for a patient who is granted direct access, which is not 'filtered' by the physician. Similarly, the requirements of the physician who wishes to safeguard his own privacy if the record includes his subjective opinions concerning the patient have been borne in mind, as far as our legislation describes a file entitled 'subjective notes', which is devoted to store this type of information. Indeed, Law 41/2002 clarifies that the right to access the medical file cannot be exercised to the prejudice of a third party's right to confidentiality of his data noted in the medical file for the therapeutic interest of the patient, nor to the prejudice of the right to confidentiality of the subjective annotations made by the professionals who elaborate the clinical record (Article 18(3)). Thus, it is perfectly possible to reconcile the recognition of access to the hospital record ('shall be made available') with the presence of highly subjective components (the physicians' subjective appreciations concerning the patients' attitudes or behaviours and their reactions), which might affect the physician's own privacy.

II. Third-Party Access to Data

149. Patient relatives cannot access medical records without the patient's prior authorization. Nevertheless, Article 18(4) of Law 41/2002 establishes that the clinical record of a deceased patient may be accessed by family members or individuals related to the patient for de facto reasons, unless the patient has explicitly prohibited such access and this prohibition has been duly recorded – Organic Law 3/2018 adopts the same criterion in its Article 3. Additionally, a third party may access relevant medical data when their own health is at risk.[266] However, it is unclear whether this provision applies only to deceased patients or whether it extends to the medical records of living patients as well.[267] The right to access the medical file cannot be exercised by family members or third parties when it concerns subjective annotations made by the professional who elaborated the clinical file or when the obtained information would affect the privacy of the patient or would be harmful to third parties.

266. *supraIbid.*
267. M.T. Requejo, 'Legal Analysis of the Spanish Basic Law 41/2002 on the Autonomy of the Patient and the Rights and Obligations with Regard to Clinical Information and Documentation', *European Journal of Health Law*, 10(3), 2003, p. 266.

III. Access for Research or Statistical Purposes

150. Access to clinical records for research or statistical purposes is subject to strict legal regulations, primarily aimed at protecting patient confidentiality and ensuring compliance with data protection laws. Several key Spanish legal frameworks govern this field.

Organic Law 3/2018 establishes that access to clinical records for research purposes must adhere to the principles of data minimization and proportionality. Patients' personal identification data must be anonymized or pseudonymized unless explicit consent has been obtained. Additionally, an exception to data protection requirements may be made for research purposes if the study meets ethical and legal standards and has been approved by an Ethics Committee.

Law 41/2002 mandates that clinical records must be maintained for healthcare purposes. However, access may be granted for research under strict conditions. Researchers must justify the necessity of accessing patient data and ensure compliance with confidentiality safeguards.

LGS and General Public Health Law allow public health authorities to access patient records for epidemiological studies and health protection, provided that confidentiality is maintained at all times. This legal framework ensures that research and statistical analyses are conducted while upholding patient privacy and adhering to ethical and legal requirements.

IV. Access to Records for Judicial Enquiries

151. Hospital records can be of crucial documentary importance as elements of proof in legal processes. In the case of a criminal process, the accused may be either the physician or the patient. In the latter case, physicians and hospital authorities in general can allege professional secrecy which, as is known, is afforded scant guarantees in our legal order, a situation which has posed problems for certain professions, notably journalism and medicine. It has already been mentioned above that the Constitution of 1978 stipulates that it is up to the law to regulate the cases in which, on the grounds of professional secrecy, a person shall not be obliged to give testimony with regard to alleged offences (Article 24.2). To date, however, no law has done so, although in view of the fact that this legal principle is placed alongside other fundamental rights in the Constitution, it has been suggested by some that professional secrecy may be used as a direct argument not to hand over hospital records to a judge.[268] It is doubtful whether this can in fact be done, since – as the Constitution itself indicates – the law shall determine the situations in which it is possible. In practice, physicians do collaborate with judges in criminal processes, provided that the ruling asking for their cooperation describes the information requested in detail and justifies its necessity adequately.

The situation seems rather more complex when records have to be handed over in proceedings in which the physician himself is the defendant, probably on charges

268. In this respect, *see* R. de Ángel Yagüez, 'Problemas legales de la historia clínica en el marco hospitalario', *La Ley*, 1987, p. 5.

of alleged negligence in treating one of his patients (the person to whom the records refer). It has been argued on occasions that the physician is not obliged to deliver up the records on the basis of his right not to testify against himself (Article 24.2 of the Constitution); neither is the hospital, since it is merely the depository of the records.[269] However, it does not seem to us that a physician incriminates himself by handing over the records, given that such records and any interpretations which are made of them are merely one of the elements which, taken together with the other elements of proof, will lead the judge to decide whether or not he was at fault. Furthermore, as part of their fundamental rights, patients are entitled to receive effective protection by courts and judges in exercising their legitimate rights and interests, and under no circumstances can they be placed in a situation of defencelessness (Article 24.1 of the Constitution). This means that access to the full records is legitimate. Where the request for access is made by the patient's next-of-kin (e.g., where a patient dies during treatment and his death leads the family to take legal action), it should be noted that no right of access is actually recognized in their case, although it should be granted for the same reasons outlined just now, so that they may take the appropriate legal action.

In the case of other civil, labour or administrative proceedings, account must be taken at all times of patients' right to confidentiality and the protection of their privacy – which, as we have seen, is reinforced in matters pertaining to health – so that no hospital records are made available to a judge without the patient's consent. Similarly, patients' right of access to their records must be taken into account. Note also that on occasions, they may stand to lose from such access, while on others, access will be to their benefit.

---

269. As understood by De Ángel Yagüez, 'Problemas legales de la historia clínica en el marco hospitalario', *supra*, p. 6.

Chapter 2. The Physician-Patient Relationship in Specific Terms

§1. The Minor Patient

I. The Relevance of the Wishes of the Minor Patient

152. The relationship between the physician and a minor patient poses specific problems, primarily concerning the obtaining of consent for treatment and other necessary measures, as well as ensuring that the minor is not subjected to abusive conduct. Two main statutes must be considered, namely the Spanish CC and Law 41/2002, of 14 November, basic law regulating Patient Autonomy and the Rights and Obligations regarding clinical information and documentation, whose purpose is to regulate patient autonomy and the rights and obligations regarding information and clinical documentation for patients, users, professionals, as well as public and private health centres and services.

The age of political and civil majority in Spain is 18 (Articles 12 of the Constitution and 240 of the CC). However, before reaching this age, a minor has the capacity to carry out certain acts, which means that he or she must give valid consent to such acts. This is true notwithstanding the CC's statement that 'parents with rights of parental authority are the legal representatives of their non-emancipated minor children' (Article 162). The Code goes on to list a number of exceptions where this provision does not apply, including one that is of particular interest here: acts relating to personality rights or other rights that the child, in accordance with the law and his or her level of maturity, may exercise on his or her own behalf. In other words, parents (with rights of parental authority) are the legal representatives of their non-emancipated children, except with respect to acts relating to personality rights if the children concerned are capable of acting on their own behalf. Clearly, if a child is to undergo medical treatment, these rights are affected, and thus, to determine whether the child is able to decide for him- or herself, it is necessary to take into account what is known as his or her natural capacity for judgment, regardless of biological age. Put another way, what counts is the child's actual capacity to understand the nature and effects of the treatment about to be administered.

In addition to this general rule established in the CC, Article 9.3(c) and Article 4 of Law 41/2002 also stipulate that consent by representation cannot be granted in the case of minors unless they are not intellectually or emotionally capable of understanding the medical act, and only if they are not emancipated or if they are under 16 years of age. Nevertheless, in interventions that involve serious risks to the patient's health or life – according to the judgment of the physician – the minor's legal representatives must give consent, although the minor must be heard and his or her opinion taken into account.

Where, according to law, a minor does not have the capacity to consent to an intervention, such intervention may only be carried out with the authorization of his or her legal representative or an authority, person, or body provided for by law. The opinion of the minor shall be taken into consideration as an increasingly determining factor in proportion to his or her age and degree of maturity.

In accordance with Article 9.6 of Law 41/2002, the granting of consent by representation will be appropriate to the circumstances and proportionate to the needs to be addressed, always in favour of the patient and with respect for his or her personal dignity. The patient will participate in decision-making as far as possible throughout the healthcare process (Article 9.7 of Law 41/2002).

Admittedly, there are practical difficulties in ascertaining the degree of maturity of a minor patient, although this will only be necessary when the minor and his or her parents disagree with respect to acceptance of the physician's orders. In such cases, as mentioned above, parents are obliged to act in the best interests of their children (as the CC states, they must '*at all times aim to benefit their children, in accordance with their personality*'), although they are afforded support in that, in the exercise of their parental authority, they may seek the help of the authorities (Article 154 of the CC).

In case of disagreement between the parents and the physician, and if the latter considers that the parents' attitude is clearly harmful to the child – as occurs, for example, when parents reject treatment without good cause – the physician may intervene directly, based on the grounds of justification by necessity or duty fulfilment (Articles 20.5 and 7 of the Penal Code and Article 9.6 of Law 41/2002), provided that the situation is urgent and the patient's life is under threat. If the treatment is not urgent, any decision contrary to the best interests of the underage patient must be brought to the attention of the judicial authority, either directly or through the Public Prosecutor's Office, so that an appropriate resolution can be adopted. Paediatricians have a special role when treating children who have clearly been physically abused by their parents. In addition to the aforementioned option available to the paediatrician, he is legally obliged to notify the judicial authorities so that the necessary criminal proceedings may be initiated (Article 262 of the Criminal Procedure Code).

153. Parental duties, including the duty to provide religious education, oblige parents or guardians to do all that is necessary to benefit the health and life of their children or minors under their responsibility until they come of age and can exercise their religious freedom and take personal responsibility for their decisions. Refusal to allow a minor to be treated on religious grounds (e.g., refusing permission for a blood transfusion) constitutes an abuse of parental authority insofar as it reflects the parents' exercise of freedom to choose between different values and is not admissible in this case since it affects the children and serves not the children's interests but rather those of the parents. In such circumstances, the physician is obliged to act to protect the life of his or her patient, and any intervention will be supported by the legal authorities.

Spanish Constitutional Court Judgment 154/2002, of 18 July,[270] deals with a situation in which the minor himself refuses life-sustaining treatment because it contravenes his or her religious beliefs (e.g., blood transfusion). The Constitutional Court has held that 'the exceptional recognition of the minor's capacity as regards certain legal acts (…) is not sufficient in order, by way of comparison, to recognize

270. The full text of the Judgment in English can be consulted in: https://www.tribunalconstitucional.es/ResolucionesTraducidas/154-2002,%20of%20July%2018.pdf.

the legal effectiveness of an act – such as the one being considered here – which, as it negatively affects life, must be definitive and therefore irreparable'. Some legal scholars, however, tend to consider that the patient's wishes should be accepted.

With regard to the behaviour of the parents in these scenarios, the same Judgment also states that they are not required to act (whether by asking for or approving the transfusion or convincing their son to accept it) in a manner that contradicts their conscience or religious convictions and 'the teachings which, in the regular, normal, and ordinary exercise of their religious freedom, have been transmitted to their son for a long time before the accident took place or the first symptoms of the illness became evident'.

II. Minor's Lack of Capacity to Consent to Treatment

154. The physician must follow the rules mentioned above regarding the natural capacity for judgment. Where this capacity does not exist, the minor must be assisted by his or her parents or legal representatives. If, for any reason, the minor cannot be assisted by these individuals – and if the situation is urgent – the physician may intervene immediately; in other cases, consent will be provided by persons connected to the family for factual or familial reasons (Article 9.3(a) of Law 41/2002).

Spain's legal order explicitly stipulates that the actions of a minor's legal representatives, when exercising their authority, shall '*at all times aim to benefit their children, in accordance with their personality*' (CC, Article 154, paragraph 2). This means that parents or guardians must always act in the interests of the minor child under their care rather than in their own interests. The CC also provides that where a conflict of interest arises between parents and child, the former may not exercise legal representation of the latter in situations or acts related to that conflict. Needless to say, this is directly applicable to decisions concerning medical treatment provided to a minor. Let us now briefly consider some of the most salient aspects involved.

Article 156 of the CC states that parental authority shall be exercised jointly by both parents or by one alone with the express or tacit consent of the other. The acts performed by one parent will be valid in accordance with social customs, circumstances, or situations of urgent necessity. In the event of disagreement in the exercise of parental authority, either parent may request the intervention of the judicial authority, which, after hearing both parties and the child (if the child is sufficiently mature and, in any case, over twelve years old), shall grant decision-making power to one of the parents. If disagreements persist or if another cause seriously hinders the exercise of parental authority, the court may grant it wholly or partially to one parent or distribute its functions between them. If the parents live separately, parental authority shall be exercised by the parent with whom the child resides. However, upon a well-founded request from the other parent and in the interest of the child, the judicial authority may grant parental authority to the applicant so that it may be exercised jointly with the other parent or may distribute the functions inherent to its exercise between both parents.

A good example of these potential disagreements is when one parent refuses to vaccinate his or her child. Taking into account the voluntary nature of vaccinations in Spain, if both parents oppose vaccinating a healthy child, their decision will generally be respected. However, when the parents disagree on whether to authorize their child's vaccination, the judicial authority will decide which parent is granted decision-making power regarding the vaccination. In cases that have reached the courts, judges have usually ruled in favour of the parent supporting vaccination. These conflicts have even reached the Constitutional Court.

In effect, the Spanish Constitutional Court has approved the vaccination of a minor against COVID-19 despite a disagreement between the child's parents. This decision came after the Court unanimously dismissed an amparo appeal filed by one parent, who opposed the vaccination – citing concerns about potential side effects and the fact that the vaccine was still in an experimental phase.

The landmark judgment on this topic is the Judgment of the Spanish Constitutional Court No. 38/2023, which emphasizes the importance of respecting constitutional guarantees when making decisions that affect fundamental rights, including the right to physical integrity. The Court acknowledged that while vaccination does impact the person's physical integrity, the judicial decisions leading to its authorization were made with due regard for these constitutional protections.

Thus, the Court supported the parent's request to vaccinate the child, relying on recommendations from credible national and international health organizations. These included the Spanish Agency for Medicines and Health Products, the European Medicines Agency, and the American CDC, all of which concluded that the benefits of vaccination outweighed any associated risks, particularly for the minor age group.

The Court concluded that authorizing the vaccination effectively safeguarded the minor's best interests, particularly regarding the child's physical and mental health, through the protection offered by the vaccine against COVID-19.

155. A different issue is the question of the possible liability of doctors who decide not to initiate medical treatments or who withdraw existing medical measures that are sustaining the lives of severely disabled newborns (or neonates). In these cases, all the legal measures in Spanish legislation to protect the individual become relevant – namely, the offences of homicide, causing injuries, and omission of a medical duty to rescue. That is to say, a doctor who deliberately causes or hastens a child's death – whether by withdrawing or withholding treatment or by administering excessive doses of pain-killing drugs – is liable to criminal prosecution for homicide. Moreover, if the parents participate in the decision, they can also be prosecuted.

A very different scenario arises when medical treatment is omitted for a human being who is alive and viable but severely disabled, when it is thought that such a condition will result in a very poor quality of life – a life that will, on many occasions, be full of suffering. In the Spanish legal system, a person can only be considered guilty of the offence of homicide by omission if the individual who omitted the conduct had an obligation to act to prevent the result, which in this case would be the death of the newborn (Articles 11 and 138 of the Criminal Code). Consequently, it is necessary to determine whether doctors truly have an obligation to treat a newborn in every case – even if they know that, as a result, the infant will survive with a very poor quality of life. In this respect, legal scholarship has concluded that, in the case of newborns, not all measures aimed at saving lives are justified. It has been argued that doctors do not have a legal duty to save the life of a newborn in every case, particularly when, as a result of the intervention, the newborn will survive with a very poor quality of life. However, the decision to withhold treatment must be based on reasonable and well-founded medical criteria, and it is necessary to obtain the consent of the newborn's parents. Thus, if the decision to withhold treatment meets these two requirements – namely, objective medical and scientific criteria and the consent of the parents – this conduct can be considered acceptable from a medical point of view. Consequently, no legal obligation to provide treatment exists, and the absence of medical intervention will not be penalized despite the death of the child.[271]

156. Another complex scenario involving a lack of competence arises when a psychiatric hospitalization of minors is requested. The general procedure is contained in Article 763 of Law 1/2000, of 7 January, on Civil Procedure. This article also applies to the hospitalization of minors for reasons of a mental disorder. However, in such cases, Article 763.2 states that commitment shall take place at a mental health institution appropriate for the minor's age, subject to a report on the minor from healthcare services. Hospitalization requires court authorization, which must be obtained prior to commitment unless urgent circumstances necessitate immediate action before authorization is received. Should this occur, the head of the centre must report to the competent Court within twenty-four hours, and the Court must ratify the measure within seventy-two hours of being notified of the commitment.

III. Specific Cases

157. (a) The above exposition constitutes the general rules. However, consideration should also be given to exceptional or specific cases which, generally speaking, do not involve curative actions per se. In effect, Article 9.5 of Law 41/2002 provides that the practice of clinical trials and assisted human reproduction techniques is subject to specific regulation as well as to the general regime of legal age. According to Articles 5.6 and 6.1 of Law 14/2006, of 26 May, on Assisted Reproduction Techniques, gamete donors must be over the age of 18, as must any woman on whom the techniques are to be used. In addition, Articles 4.3 and 5 of Royal Decree 1090/2015, of 4 December – governing clinical trials with medicines, the Research Ethics Committees with medicines and the Spanish Registry of Clinical Studies (in compliance with Article 32 of Regulation (EU) No. 536/2014 of the European Parliament and of the Council of 16 April 2014, on clinical trials on medicinal products for human use, and repealing Directive 2001/20/EC) – set out the requirements for undertaking clinical trials on minors, namely: the informed

271. *See* S. Romeo-Malanda, 'Non-treatment of Severely Disabled Newborns and Criminal Liability under Spanish Law', in Charles Erin/Suzanne Ost (eds), *The Criminal Justice System and Health Care* (Oxford University Press 2007), pp. 207–224.

consent of the parents or legal representatives; that the minor has received information in accordance with his or her capacity for understanding; that the clinical trial provides some direct benefit for the group of patients and is conducted only when such research is essential to validate data obtained in clinical trials on persons capable of giving informed consent or through other research methods; and that the Ethics Committee, with paediatric expertise or after obtaining advice on clinical, ethical, and psychosocial issues in the field of paediatrics, has endorsed the protocol, etc.

(b) The voluntary interruption of pregnancy remains an issue that, even today, generates significant social controversy. Although several aspects of the subject have been – and continue to be – the object of discussion, one of the most controversial issues is the ability of underage women to consent to the interruption of pregnancy for themselves without the intervention of their parents or guardians. This debate has been addressed in legislation through successive legal modifications that have granted more or less autonomy to underage women depending on the political ideology of the governing party.[272]

Article 13 bis of Organic Law 2/2010, of 3 March, on Sexual and Reproductive Health and Voluntary Termination of Pregnancy (as amended by Organic Law 1/2023 and declared in accordance with the Spanish Constitution by the Spanish Constitutional Court – Judgment No. 92/2024) states that women may voluntarily terminate their pregnancy from the age of 16 without the need for the consent of their legal representatives. In the case of minors under 16 years of age, the provisions of Article 9.3(c) of Law 41/2002 shall apply. In the event of a disagreement between the minor and those responsible for giving representative consent, conflicts shall be resolved in accordance with civil law by the judicial authority.

(c) It should be noted that certain age restrictions also apply to the so-called prior medical instructions or advanced directives. Article 11.1 of Law 41/2002 provides that only persons who are of legal age are allowed to express their wishes through a document of prior instructions. Thus, although a minor who has attained the age of 16 can make actual healthcare decisions autonomously, he or she cannot make advanced healthcare decisions before reaching the age of 18.

158. (a) Moreover, a minor under the age of 18, or his or her legal representatives on his or her behalf, cannot consent to become a living donor of a transplant organ (Article 4(a) and (b) of Law 30/1979, of 27 October, on the Removal and Transplantation of Organs). There is, however, one exception which covers bone marrow donations: given that bone marrow is a tissue capable of regenerating, donation poses no – or should pose no – major risks for the donor and is extremely suitable for use between siblings, although the exception is not expressly limited to such relationships (Article 7.1 of Royal Decree-Law 9/2014, of 4 July, on setting standards of quality and safety for the donation, procurement, testing, processing, preservation, storage, and distribution of human cells and tissues, and on approving the

---

272. *See* S. Romeo-Malanda, 'Minoría de edad y aborto en España: pasado, presente y futuro', *Cuadernos Ibero-Americanos de Direito Sanitario,* nº. 12(1), 2023, pp. 1–16.

coordination and operation rules for their use in humans). Furthermore, minors cannot donate blood (Royal Decree 2005, of 16 September, which regulates the technical requirements and minimum conditions for blood donation and transfusion centres and services).

(b) A person under the age of 18, or that person's legal representatives, cannot consent to sex reassignment surgery and sterilization (Article 156 of the Spanish Penal Code), except when it is for strictly therapeutic reasons, in which case the general regulations governing curative actions are applicable. Hormone treatment is available for minors following the general rules on informed consent.

§2. The Mental Patient and Involuntary Placement

159. Treatment of mental patients or mentally deficient persons poses several legal problems,[273] ranging from admission to a hospital to (informed) consent to treatment. One question which must be decided beforehand is whether or not, for the purpose of consent (or authorization), these two aspects are linked or are entirely separate.

Spanish legislation has a set of legal provisions that aim to protect the rights of patients who are incapable of giving their personal consent to receive medical treatment, including fundamental rights and freedoms.[274] The Kingdom of Spain signed and ratified the Convention on the Rights of Persons with Disabilities.[275] This Convention has been in force in Spain since 3 May 2008.

We shall examine briefly the conditions of admission to and treatment in a hospital according to the different potential situations with respect to the validity of the mental patient's consent, namely, whether or not he has been declared incompetent by a judge, whether internment is urgent and whether he is to be treated for an organic or mental illness.

I. Voluntary Admission and Treatment

160. There can be no denying that psychiatric patients who are admitted of their own accord to a mental health institution are entitled to receive information, give informed consent and also to refuse treatment. It is quite possible that the extent or the nature of the patient's illness does not prevent him/her (i.e., he/she is not incompetent) from taking decisions such as contacting his/her own accord a mental health institution or other centres with such facilities and ask to be admitted for treatment.

273. For a more detailed study *see* C.M. Romeo Casabona, 'El tratamiento jurídico del enfermo mental en el Consejo de Europa y sistemas de garantías en el derecho español', in *Actualidad Penal*, 1991, pp. 329 ff.

274. *See* on this M. Aznar López, *Internamientos civiles y derechos fundamentales de los usuarios de centros sanitarios, sociales y sociosanitarios* (Comares, Granada 2000), pp. 94 ff.

275. As adopted in New York on 13 Dec. of 2006, and its Optional Protocol (Instrument of Ratification published in the Spanish Official State Bulletin of 21 Apr. 2008).

His/her decision must be accepted and residential treatment provided if it is indicated medically, given that in such cases, the principles of consent bases on the person's natural capacity for judgment and his/her grasp of the importance of his/her decision are applicable.[276]

Where the patient's condition and mental health worsen, or where his/her pathological picture on admission was already serious even though no significant deterioration is observed, the question arises as to what should be done if he refuses to continue treatment and wishes to be released from care but from the medical point of view continuation is advisable and his/her mental condition causes his/her fitness to take the appropriate decisions to be doubted. He would then be in the same position as an incompetent patient and the same criteria would therefore apply: if the patient decides he wishes to leave hospital but is prevented from doing so by the medical practitioner or the hospital management, notification must be given to a judge, who shall decide as appropriate. The situation is exactly the same as that of the involuntary internment (or, to be more accurate, extending internment)[277] of an allegedly incompetent person for reasons of emergency. It should be stressed that the hospital's decision to prevent the patient from leaving should not be based on the need for treatment but on any potential risks which his/her release might entail for his/her own or others' health or life.

II. Involuntary Admission and Emergency Treatment

A. Treatment of Physical or Mental Illnesses

161. If admission is urgent and the physician considers that treatment is urgently required because the patient's life is in danger but the latter is unable to give valid consent or he/she is legally unfit, this consent for the treatment shall be given by the patient's legal representatives. If the patient has no legal representative, consent shall be given by those persons having family or de facto links to him or her.[278] Finally, if the patient's family or guardian are unavailable, the physician must admit the patient and may intervene to treat a health-related problem. In this regard, he will be protected by the provisions governing exemption from liability in situations of urgent necessity; this possibility is catered for expressly by the Law on Basic Regulation of Patient Autonomy, which authorizes the physician to intervene without the required consent of the persons mentioned as above when there is an immediate and serious risk for physical or mental health (Article 9.2, b). The procedure is fully justified to avoid irreparable health consequences to the patient as a result of the increasing risk caused by the delay in obtaining prior consent. To sum up, the

276. Circular No. 2/1984 from the Attorney General's Office acknowledges the validity of these voluntary admissions, although it expresses considerable reservations and urges caution concerning the persistent use thereof and the possibility that they conceal admissions made under duress.

277. S. García Zarandieta, 'Internamientos psiquiátricos', in *Privaciones de libertad y derechos humanos* (Ed. Hacer, Barcelona 1987), p. 50.

278. *See* Art. 9.3a) and b) of LAP (Law 41/2002, of 14 November, basic law regulating Patient Autonomy and the Rights and Obligations regarding clinical information and documentation).

physician should act as he would with any other patient in a similar emergency situation, and in this case, the patient's mental illness has no bearing on the decision.

162. If, in the situation described just now, the mental patient or mentally deficient person is conscious and refuses admission and treatment, but his/her mental capacity does not permit him/her to take decisions because he/she is incapable of grasping the importance of his/her refusal and of his/her situation, intervention is possible under Article 9.2, b of the LAP, provided that, as in the previous case above, no next-of-kin or guardian is available (Article 9.3, a).

Nevertheless, Organic Law 6/1984 on the habeas corpus procedure (Article 1b) does not exclude the possibility of a patient or his/her representative seeking a judge's ruling on the legality of the confinement, both in this case and in others mentioned below.

The procedure established in Law on Civil Procedure (*see* below) should also be used in cases where confinement of a mental patient is necessary for the treatment of somatic illnesses which have no bearing on his/her supposed mental incompetence. This would certainly safeguard the patient's interests better because treatment would not be subject to prior authorization of the judge and medical intervention should thus not be delayed, as being an emergency situation.

B. Involuntary Admittance of a Person Due to His/Her Mental Disorder[279]

163. The Law on Civil Procedure[280] contains the premises and requirements for an involuntary admittance of a person due to his/her mental illness. Thus, the former regulation of this matter in CC (Article 211) has been changed.

The premises for admittance are as follows: Prior judicial authorization is required in all cases where the patient is unable to give his/her valid legal consent to the admittance or his/her valid legal refusal of admittance. While it is not expressly stated in Law, the admittance must be motivated by the need to treat the patient's serious mental illness or to prevent him/her from harming himself or others.

In emergency situations, the patient may be involuntarily admitted without prior judicial authorization. Under these circumstances, the medical manager of the centre where the patient has been admitted shall make a request to the judge to ratify

---

279. Aznar López, *Internamientos civiles y derechos fundamentales de los usuarios de centros sanitarios, sociales y sociosanitarios*, *supra*, pp. 83 ff.

280. Act 1/2000, of 7 January, on Civil Procedure (CPA), Art. 763. For a proper contextualization of this precept, Constitutional Court Rulings 132/2010 of 2 Dec. 2010 and 141/2012 of 2 Jul. 2012 are fundamental. *See* J.C. Cabañas García, 'Internamiento involuntario urgente por razones de trastorno psíquico y tutela del derecho fundamental a la libertad personal', in *Anuario de Derecho Civil*, 2012, pp. 1883 ff.; M.C. Berenguer Albaladejo, 'Los internamientos no voluntarios por razón de trastorno psíquico: especial consideración al procedimiento a seguir en los casos de urgencia médica', in *Derecho privado y Constitución*, 2014, núm. 28, pp. 263 ff.; F. Barrios Flores, 'El ingreso psiquiátrico involuntario de carácter urgente: una revisión, tras la STC 141/2012, de 2 de julio', in *Revista de la Asociación Española de Neuropsiquiatría*, 2012, n.º 116, pp. 829 ff.; C. Vega Vega/R.M. Bañón González/S.A. Fajardo Augustín, 'Internamientos psiquiátricos. Aspectos medicolegales', in *Atención Primaria*, vol. 42, núm. 3, 2010, pp. 176 ff.

the authorization for their admittance, within a period of twenty-four hours. Notification must include details of the interned patient, the circumstances surrounding and leading to the decision, and the reasons substantiating the request for confirmation by the judge of the measure taken. It must also include an estimation of the foreseeable length of stay, where this can be predicted in the short or medium term.

The court must give its decision within a seventy-two-hour period from when it was informed of the admittance. The judge shall authorize or refuse authorization in accordance with the procedure of voluntary jurisdiction provided for in the Civil Procedure Code.

There is a *legal procedure for authorizing or ratifying the admittance* established by law:

1. The court shall undertake the following activities before authorizing or ratifying the admittance: (a) consider the opinion on the admittance of the party affected by the decision, the Public Prosecution Service and any other person whose appearance is deemed appropriate or is requested by the party affected by the measure. (b) Examine the person whose admittance is in question.[281] (c) Receive the patient's medical report. (d) Undertake any other checks that shall be deemed appropriate.
2. The party affected by the measure shall be entitled to representation and defence.
3. There shall be recourse to appeal against the decision adopted by the court regarding the admittance.

Admittance conditions and duration. Physicians caring for the patient shall send periodic reports (every six months or more frequently on the court's request) to the court regarding the need for the measure to remain in place. The court may request these or other reports at other times. Every time the court receives these reports it shall decide whether the patient should continue to be admitted or not. The doctors caring for the patient may request the court to cease the admittance when they consider that it is no longer necessary.

Once confinement has been authorized, the judge is obliged by law to *review the situation of the internee*. This is one of the most important guarantees laid down in current legislation. He/she shall gather information regarding the need to extend the period of confinement when he/she considers it appropriate, but at least every six months, he/she will receive the reports mentioned above, and he/she shall then give a ruling on whether internment should be continued or ended (Article 763.4, 3 LEC).

Clearly, the *ending of confinement* must be authorized by the judge after his/her (at least) six-monthly review of the situation, at which time he/she is legally obliged to take the appropriate decisions regarding the continuation or not of internment.

281. *See* Rulings of Supreme Court (1st Chamber) of 2 Feb. 1988 and 12 Jun. 1989 (commented upon by R. Bercovitz Rodríguez-Cano, 'El examen por el Juez del presunto incapaz en el procedimiento de incapacitación', in *Poder Judicial*, No. 15, 1989, pp. 141 ff.) for references to details of the examination used to determine incompetence; to a large extent the criteria may be extended to cases of compulsory confinement.

Notwithstanding this, when physicians who are caring for the internee assume that it is no longer necessary to maintain the placement, the patient will be discharged and shall immediately inform the competent court (Article 763.4, 4 LEC).

The admittance of minors will always be performed in a health facility appropriate to their age, having before a report of child welfare services. To meet the appropriate decision in this field of mental illnesses in relation to consent to treatment by minors themselves or their legal representatives is a complex matter for which legal provisions of LAP will be followed.[282]

In the case of a mental patient who has been tried by a court *relating to the commission of an offence,*[283] the court may decide on placement in a psychiatric facility for treatment for a maximum period not exceeding the time it would have taken in prison by the ruling if the person prosecuted had been found responsible of the offence (Article 101.1 of Penal Code in relation to Articles 20.1 and 95). The court can, however, under Article 97 of PC, review its decision and order to stop further confinement and replace it with other preventive measures or to cease the imposition of any of them.[284] When a person is declared exempt from criminal liability due to the existence of any of the causes provided for in numbers 1 and 3 of Article 20 PC (mental illness and anomalies in perception since birth or infancy), the Public Prosecutor's Office shall assess, according to the circumstances of the case, the appropriateness of promoting proceedings for the judicial adoption of support measures for the person with disabilities or, in the event that such measures have already been previously agreed, for their review (First additional provision of PC).

C. Intervention by Next-of-Kin and Guardians

164. Still, in the hypothetical cases outlined above, if the next-of-kin or persons close to the patient are available (as indicated by Article 9.2, b of the LAP), they shall give consent on behalf of an unconscious patient, save where he/she has already been certified as being incompetent and has a guardian, in which case consent should preferably be given by the latter.[285] However, the preference of the guardian is not exclusive, or, put another way, if the guardian is not available, next-of-kin or other persons *in facto* close to the patient may decide. If the patient is conscious but (legally or de facto) 'incompetent' to take decisions, the same procedure shall be used for organic illnesses, both for admission (clearly, the guardian does not need a judge's permission to intern the patient in anything other than a psychiatric unit or special training or education centre) and for treatment. Lastly, where

282. *See* further on this above, Ch. 1, §2.

283. *See* on this A. Urruela Mora, *Imputabilidad penal y anomalía o alteración psíquica* (Comares, Bilbao-Granada 2004), pp. 218 ff.

284. *See* on this A. Urruela Mora, *Las medidas de seguridad y reinserción social en la actualidad,* (Comares, Granada 2009), pp. 91–102 and 130 ff.

285. A similar opinion is held by F. Bueno Arús, 'El consentimiento del paciente en el tratamiento médico-quirúrgico y la Ley General de Sanidad', in *Estudios de Derecho Penal y Criminología,* (UNED, Madrid 1989), p. 170.

involuntary confinement is necessary to treat mental illness, the procedure to be followed shall be that laid down by LEC for involuntary internment of a (conscious or unconscious) patient, as described above.

III. Involuntary, Non-urgent Admission and Treatment

A. Treatment of Organic Illnesses

165. In non-urgent situations where treatment is necessary, and if the patient is not competent to take decisions, the physician should seek consent from the guardian, next-of-kin or persons close to the patient (Article 9.3, a and b of the LAP). This should be understood as referring both to unconscious patients and also supposedly incompetent persons or ones who have already been certified as being incompetent (judicially modified capacity established in Sentence). As was stated above, these rules are valid for general interventions or medical treatment where confinement is not related to the cause of incompetence, that is, cases not involving persistent physical or mental deficiencies or illnesses which prevent the person from acting on his/her own behalf and avoid making harm to himself or to another.

B. Treatment of Mental Illnesses

166. Where the aim is to detain a supposedly incompetent person against his/her will (in a psychiatric hospital or other healthcare institution in order to treat the illness which has caused the incompetence) and the case is not of urgent necessity, the patient's next-of-kin should apply beforehand to the judge for authorization for confinement, in accordance with the conditions and procedures laid down in the Civil Procedure Act (Article 763 referred to above).

167. To sum up, consent to treatment need not always be given by the person who takes the decision regarding admission or confinement. Under normal circumstances, treatment decisions shall be taken by the next-of-kin or persons close to the patient or by the guardian where appropriate, while decisions concerning confinement shall be the responsibility of the judge. This separation of powers might well place the physician in a curious position if, for example, a judge authorizes detention, but the next-to-kin does not give the go-ahead to the treatment proposed by the physician.[286] However, doubts surround who should consent to treatment when a judge has ordered the detention in a psychiatric institution of a deranged person who has committed an offence; in principle, consent would be given by the next-of-kin or the guardian because the rights recognized by the Patient's Autonomy Act (LAP) apply to 'both public and private health-care services' (Article 1).

In any case, the legal authorities may intervene in treatment-related disputes or conflicts concerning respect for the wishes of the patient when, in spite of his/her

286. In this regard *see* J.J. Carrasco Gómez, *Responsabilidad médica y Psiquiatría* (2nd ed., Colex, Madrid, 1998), pp. 181 ff.

illness, he/she is competent to give consent. A similar situation may arise also where a judge orders detention (which presupposes that the internee cannot act on his/her own behalf), but the patient refuses the proposed treatment, if at that time he has sufficient capacity to understand the nature of his/her decision.

§3. The Dying Patient

168. When a patient is terminally ill – that is, approaching the end of life – the physician faces two critical questions. First, to what extent should curative or symptom-relieving measures be pursued without violating professional duties or hastening death in a legally punishable manner? Second, how should the physician assess and respect the patient's wishes, particularly when the patient, if capable, chooses to refuse all forms of treatment, including life-sustaining interventions?

I. Treating a Dying Patient

169. When caring for terminally ill patients who are near death, the primary responsibilities of healthcare professionals and medical institutions are to provide moral support and ensure that the patient experiences a dignified death. Treatment should not be based on the potential for recovery, as this would constitute discrimination. In such circumstances, humane and compassionate care is imperative. Patients must be granted unrestricted access to family members and individuals who can provide spiritual support in accordance with their religious beliefs. Additionally, they must be allowed to make decisions regarding their material interests, including matters related to work, property, and their last will and testament. If the patient wishes to be discharged, and if their condition and family situation permit it, they should have the option to return home to spend their final moments surrounded by loved ones. These measures stem from the patient's fundamental rights. When no treatment can offer improvement or recovery, alleviating the patient's suffering through medication or other means is not only lawful[287] but also an essential duty of the physician. Some legal scholars argue that a failure to fulfil this duty could even constitute an offence. In this regard, Article 196 of the Spanish Penal Code states: 'A medical practitioner who, while under obligation to do so, were to refuse health assistance or abandon the provision of health services, when refusal or abandonment were to cause serious risk to personal health, shall be punished with the

287. M. Bajo Fernández, *Derecho Penal (Parte Especial). Delitos contra las personas* (2nd ed., Ceura, Madrid, 1991), p. 96; J. Bustos Ramírez, *Manual de Derecho Penal, Parte Especial* (Ariel, Barcelona 1986), p. 50; C.M. Romeo Casabona, 'El marco jurídico-penal en la eutanasia en el Derecho español', in *Revista de la Facultad de Derecho de la Universidad de Granada*, No. 13, 1987, p. 191. More recently, C.M. Romeo Casabona/A. Perin, 'Capítulo 1. El homicidio y sus formas', in C.M. Romeo Casabona/E. Sola Reche/M.A. Boldova Pasamar (Coords), *Derecho Penal. Parte Especial* (3ª edición, Comares, Granada 2023), pp. 52–61.

penalties of the preceding Article, in the upper half, and with that of special barring from public employment and office, profession, or trade, for a term of six months to three years.'[288]

170. In general, administering drugs or other pain-relieving measures that may result in a negligible and unintended shortening of the patient's life – commonly referred to as indirect euthanasia – is considered lawful. Likewise, gradually increasing the dosage of certain painkillers, such as morphine, when the patient develops a tolerance to them is permitted, even if this increases the risk of respiratory depression leading to failure.[289] In such cases, there is no criminal liability for intentional homicide, as the physician's primary aim is not to hasten death but to relieve suffering. Although some would argue here in favour of possible intentional homicide,[290] i.e., that the physician foresees that the result – bringing forward of death – may occur but continues anyway, we consider that it should be ruled out given that in truth, the physician is not really allowing for that eventuality but is taking the necessary steps to relieve pain, without at the same time shortening the patient's life in a manner which might be determined causally.[291] Indeed, the most conflictive case of a treatment shortening the patient's life – terminal sedation – has been considered acceptable by the current Code of Medical Deontology (2022), Article 38.5.

171. A potential case of negligent homicide – where the outcome was either foreseen or at least foreseeable – depends on whether the physician has adhered to his duty of objective care and remained within the bounds of permissible risk, as would be expected of a prudent medical professional in similar circumstances.[292] This standard is assessed by considering whether the physician's actions align with the appropriate medical indication for the treatment and the principles of lex artis. Pain management is undeniably a fundamental function of medicine, as evidenced by the existence of specialized pain units in some hospitals that are dedicated to treating severe pain, as well as the establishment of hospices. Therefore, the careful

288. F. Flores Mendoza, 'Capítulo 11. Omisión del deber de socorro', en C.M. Romeo Casabona/E. Sola Reche/M.A. Boldova Pasamar (Coords), *Derecho Penal. Parte Especial* (3ª edición, Comares, Granada 2023), pp. 290–294.
289. I. De Miguel Beriain, 'Capítulo 26. El Derecho al final de la vida: rechazo al tratamiento, limitación del esfuerzo terapéutico, sedación en la agonía, auxilio al suicidio y eutanasia', in A. Palomar Olmeda y J. Cantero Martínez (Dirs), *Tratado de Derecho Sanitario. Volumen I, supra*, pp. 887–918.
290. Cf. E. Gimbernat Ordeig, 'Eutanasia, Constitución y Derecho Penal', in *Jano*, nº. 920, 1990, pp. 987 f.
291. G. Arruego Rodríguez, 'La naturaleza constitucional de la asistencia sanitaria no consentida y los denominados supuestos de "urgencia vital"', *REDC*, nº. 82, 2008.
292. A. Torío López, 'Instigación y auxilio al suicidio, homicidio consentido y eutanasia como problemas legislativos', A. Fernández Albor (ed.), *Estudios Penales y Criminológicos, IV* (Santiago de Compostela, 1981), pp. 191 f.

administration of medication or the use of medical equipment to manage pain in terminally ill patients does not constitute a breach of the duty of care, nor does any incidental shortening of life amount to a punishable act of negligence.[293]

It is also important to recognize that, although theoretically possible, it is extremely difficult in practice to determine the precise extent to which life may have been shortened in such cases. The most viable legal and ethical approach, in our view, is to consider that the physician should be exonerated on the grounds of a state of justifiable necessity. In this context, the potential risk of shortening the patient's life is of lesser significance than the essential and effective relief of their suffering. This perspective is fully endorsed by the Code of Medical Deontology (2022), which explicitly states: 'The physician has a duty to try to cure or improve the patient whenever possible. When this is not possible, the obligation remains to take appropriate measures to ensure the greatest possible well-being and dignity of the patient, even if this may result in a shortening of life' (Article 38.1).

II. Respecting a Patient's Wishes Regarding the Cessation of Treatment

172. Both the European Convention for the Protection of Human Rights and Dignity of the Human Being with regard to the Application of Biology and Medicine, ratified by Spain in 2000 and Law 41/2002, basic law regulating Patient Autonomy and the Rights and Obligations regarding clinical information and documentation, establish as a general principle that all healthcare interventions may only be carried out with the consent of the affected individual, following the provision of appropriate information. Moreover, both legal instruments explicitly state that any medical intervention can only proceed once the patient has given their free and unequivocal consent. Thus, it can be affirmed that the bioethical principle of autonomy of will – understood as the prohibition of medical intervention without a person's consent – is enshrined in an international legal document that has become part of the Spanish legal framework. Consequently, if a patient requests the suspension or discontinuation of treatment, their wishes should be respected, particularly in cases where recovery has been definitively ruled out.

This raises the question of whether a physician may be held liable for failing to administer treatment, a concern that has arisen in discussions regarding so-called passive euthanasia or the withdrawal of life-sustaining measures. When there is no possibility of recovery, the patient's wishes pose no legal or ethical dilemma. However, in situations where treatment is essential to sustaining life during the (pre)terminal phase of an illness, where death is not imminent, and where withholding or

293. C.M. Romeo Casabona/A. Perin, 'Capítulo 1. El homicidio y sus formas', in C.M. Romeo Casabona/E. Sola Reche/M.A. Boldova Pasamar (Coords), *Derecho Penal. Parte Especial* (3ª edición, Comares, Granada 2023), pp. 52–61; Bajo Fernández, *Derecho Penal (Parte Especial). Delitos contra las personas*, *supra*, p. 96; Torío López, 'Instigación y auxilio al suicido, homicidio consentido y eutanasia como problemas legislativos', *supra*, p. 193.

discontinuing life support would accelerate the dying process, the issue becomes significantly more complex.

According to Law 41/2002, basic law basic law regulating Patient Autonomy and the Rights and Obligations regarding clinical information and documentation, patients have the right to refuse treatment. However, Spanish law imposes certain restrictions on the exercise of this right in specific cases where it is deemed unenforceable – for instance, when refusal of treatment poses a risk to public health, when the patient lacks the capacity to make decisions, or when treatment is so urgently required that any delay could lead to irreversible harm or a life-threatening situation (Article 9.2). While the first two exceptions are relatively straightforward, the third is more ambiguous, potentially implying that life-saving treatment cannot be refused. This raises additional concerns regarding the duty to protect a patient's life in particular circumstances, some of which have already been examined[294] and will be further explored below.

173. Article 15 of the Spanish Constitution plays a crucial role in addressing this issue. It states: 'Everyone has the right to life and to moral and physical integrity; under no circumstances can any person be subjected to torture or to inhuman or degrading punishment or treatment (…)' Clearly, life serves as the foundation for the exercise and enjoyment of all other fundamental rights, which justifies the special legal protection afforded to it. It follows that such protection extends to all individuals, particularly those in vulnerable or critical conditions, including terminally ill patients, persons with disabilities, the elderly, and individuals suffering from mental illness or cognitive impairments. However, this constitutional provision raises interpretative challenges, some of which were addressed in a Constitutional Court ruling[295] concerning an appeal filed by prisoners on an indefinite hunger strike. Of particular relevance here is the question of whether individuals possess a constitutional right to dispose of their own lives as they see fit – a question that directly impacts the legality of euthanasia, as well as the right to refuse medical treatment on religious, conscientious, or personal grounds. This is a highly complex and controversial area of law, requiring an analysis of the Constitution as a whole to arrive at a sound conclusion.

To begin with, Article 15 alone does not establish an individual's right to dispose of their own life as they choose, as its primary function is to safeguard the right to life. Nor does it grant third parties the authority to intervene in another person's decision regarding their life.[296] However, precisely as a result of this role of guarantor (*vis à vis* the State and third persons), it cannot be inferred either that there is a duty to live against one's wishes, that is, that the State's obligations allow it to intervene when someone has expressed his desire not to carry on living.[297] A more

294. *See above*, Ch. 1, §1.

295. Constitutional Court Ruling of 27 Jun. 1990.

296. In this regard, *see* Constitutional Court Rulings of 27 Jun. 1990 (n. 7) and 19 Jul. 1990 (n. 5); *see also*, prior to these rulings, C.M. Romeo Casabona, 'Los derechos del enfermo a la luz de la Constitución española', in *Todo Hospital*, nº. 62, 1989, p. 29.

297. *See* G. Mendes De Carvalho, *Suicidio, eutanasia y Derecho Penal. Estudio del art. 143 del Código penal español y propuesta de lege ferenda* (Comares, Granada 2009).

comprehensive reading of Article 15, in conjunction with the overarching constitutional principles of personal freedom (Article 1.1) and respect for human dignity (Article 10.1), suggests that while there may not be an explicit right to dispose of one's own life, there is at least the recognized freedom to do so. Consequently, a physician cannot continue administering treatment against a patient's will, even if this means that death will be hastened as a result.

174. Thus, discontinuing or interrupting treatment for a person who has no objectively determinable prospects of survival does not contradict the principle of human dignity. On the contrary, prolonging medical intervention under such circumstances could amount to using the patient as an instrument to serve the physician's own professional interests or, worse, engaging in unnecessary and aggressive treatment – commonly referred to as acharnement thérapeutique or therapeutic obstinacy. Such practices may constitute a violation of the constitutional prohibition against inhuman and degrading treatment (Article 15), which in turn infringes upon the fundamental right to human dignity.[298] The Spanish Constitutional Court, in a ruling dated 27 June 1990 (Legal Principle No. 9), addressed this issue in the context of force-feeding hunger-striking prisoners. The Court held that no violation of the prohibition against inhuman or degrading treatment existed in that case because the medical intervention in question was not intended to inflict harm, punishment, or suffering but rather to prevent the irreversible effects of voluntary starvation and mitigate physical harm. However, the ruling also clarified that while force-feeding undertaken to prevent death does not inherently constitute inhuman or degrading treatment, it could be considered such depending on the means used to carry it out or if it merely prolongs suffering without ultimately preventing death. From this, it can be deduced that while providing appropriate medical care to sustain life is not inherently inhuman or degrading, the same cannot be said when such measures serve only to needlessly extend suffering without altering the inevitable outcome of death.

175. In light of the above considerations, Law 41/2002, of 14 November, basic law regulating Patient Autonomy and the Rights and Obligations regarding clinical information and documentation, should be interpreted restrictively in cases when it allows practitioners to carry out clinical interventions essential to the patient's health without the patient's consent when there is an immediate serious risk to the patient's physical or mental integrity and it is not possible to obtain his consent, consulting, when circumstances permit, his relatives or persons with whom he has de facto ties (Article 9.2.b). This means that medical intervention by a third party may be ruled out if the patient has expressed a clear and unequivocal desire not to

298. *See* C. Álvarez-Linera, 'El derecho a la vida y a la integridad. Prohibición de la tortura', in *La Ley*, nº. 1763, 1987, pp. 1 ff.; F. Bueno Arús, 'Límites del consentimiento en la disposición del propio cuerpo desde la perspectiva del Derecho Penal', in *Poder Judicial*, 1985, p. 14; C.M. Romeo Casabona, 'Los derechos del enfermo a la luz de la Constitución española', in *Todo Hospital*, nº. 62, 1989, p. 29.

continue living.[299] The Spanish Constitutional Court appears to support this interpretation, stating that: 'One thing is the decision of a person who assumes the risk of dying through an act of their own volition, affecting only themselves. In such a case, it could be argued that compulsory medical assistance or any other means of preventing the fulfilment of this wish is unlawful. However, an entirely different situation arises in the case of individuals in a special context, such as imprisonment ...' The Court further clarifies that: 'This constitutional right [to physical and moral integrity] is affected when medical assistance is imposed upon a person against their will, regardless of the reasons behind their refusal, which may extend beyond a mere desire to die. Coercive medical assistance, therefore, constitutes a restriction that infringes upon this fundamental right unless a constitutional justification for the intervention exists.'[300] A revised constitutional interpretation of the aforementioned law would suggest that, even in emergency situations, a patient has the right to refuse treatment. The exception contained in the law should thus be understood as applying only to cases in which the patient is unable to provide consent (e.g., due to unconsciousness) and where no next of kin or close associates are available to give consent on their behalf. In such situations, given the immediate risk of death or irreversible harm, medical intervention may proceed without awaiting consent. In criminal law terms, this means that the physician may act under the legal protection of a state of necessity.

176. The refusal of life support measures presents a distinct legal and ethical issue, as it raises the question of whether these measures constitute a form of medical treatment and whether their withdrawal should be considered an act or a mere omission. Some Spanish legal scholars have argued that life support measures qualify as medical treatment and, therefore, their withdrawal – regardless of whether the patient has requested it – constitutes an active intervention rather than an omission. Under this reasoning, the act of withdrawing life support could be classified as euthanasia and punished accordingly under Spanish criminal law. However, the prevailing legal doctrine holds that life support measures, including hydration and artificial nutrition, are indeed a form of medical treatment.[301] Consequently, the decision to withdraw such measures should rest with the patient, in accordance with Law 41/2002, and healthcare professionals cannot impose their own criteria against the patient's expressed wishes. This interpretation has been upheld by the Spanish judiciary in landmark cases such as those of Ramona Estévez and Inmaculada Echevarría, both of whom refused life support measures (although, in the case of Ramona Estévez, the decision was made by her family rather than by the patient herself).

---

299. R. Junquera De Estéfani (Dir.), *Bioética y bioderecho: reflexiones jurídicas ante los retos bioéticos* (Comares, Granada 2008), pp. 129–154.
300. Constitutional Court Ruling of 27 Jun. 1990, legal principles 7 and 8, respectively.
301. A. Couceiro, 'El enfermo terminal y las decisiones en torno al final de la vida', en A. Couceiro (Ed.), Ética en cuidados paliativos (Tricastela, Madrid 2004), pp. 263–304.

III. Euthanasia

A. Lawful Conduct in Relation to Euthanasia

177. Earlier, in discussing the terminally ill, we outlined the requirements governing the actions of physicians in such situations. These may include the administration of drugs that may, as a side effect, reduce the lifespan of the patient (indirect euthanasia). This would not constitute an offence so long as the physician acts in accordance with lex artis. It was even argued that the doctor should respect the patient's decision to discontinue treatment, a situation that brings us into the realm of what is known as passive euthanasia.

178. Passive euthanasia. Passive euthanasia raises extremely complex issues. What is crucial from the criminal law perspective is the prior establishment of the different 'acts' (omissions) which entail passive euthanasia. Unfortunately, there is disagreement in the literature as to where these limits lie.

179. In the first place, we must identify, delimit and legally appraise the concept of orthothanasia, which, while similar in certain respects to passive euthanasia, has a completely different meaning. The word orthothanasia means 'justified death in the sense of death that occurs at the right moment'.[302] Orthothanasia, therefore, consists in the 'cessation of special treatments intended to revive the incurably ill when in a state of profound irreversible coma, in the terminal phases of an illness, those whose lives are being maintained artificially or who are on the point of death' (Roskam). Orthothanasia is clearly lawful in the situation where the patient has died, though some bodily functions continue because they are artificially maintained by machines that control respiration and circulation. These are patients who have suffered brain death (irreversible lack of all functions from the brain stem) and can remain in the same condition almost indefinitely. Disconnecting machines or mechanisms or discontinuing treatment (medication, intravenous feeding) does not constitute homicide in the eyes of the law, given that the subject is clinically and *actually* dead.

180. Disthanasia is another neologism with the opposite meaning to orthothanasia.[303] It means (from the Greek *dys*, bad, anomalous and *thanatos*, death) 'bad death', that is to say, prolonging the natural course of death – rather than life – by all available means despite the fact that death is inevitable in the circumstances. This is something that arises chiefly in hospitals as one of the negative consequences of the constant progress made in the biomedical sciences. At the same time as achieving spectacular results with patients who would have been considered

302. De Miguel Beriain, 'Capítulo 26. El Derecho en el final de la vida: Rechazo al tratamiento, limitación del esfuerzo terapéutico, sedación en la agonía, auxilio al suicidio y eutanasia', *Tratado de Derecho Sanitario. Volumen I, supra*, pp. 897–902; J.F. Higuera, 'Eutanasia: precisiones terminológicas', in *Dilemas éticos de la Medicina actual* (Public. Univ. Comillas, Madrid 1986), p. 149.

303. De Miguel Beriain, 'Capítulo 26. El Derecho en el final de la vida: Rechazo al tratamiento, limitación del esfuerzo terapéutico, sedación en la agonía, auxilio al suicidio y eutanasia', *supra*, pp. 909–910.

beyond help in the not-too-distant past and thus improving considerably the life expectancy of the population as a whole, the biomedical sciences have made it possible to delay death, which can imply prolonging the pain and suffering of the patient. This is a clear instance of how the advantages and disadvantages of technical progress are not always under our control. Awareness of these situations, with the enormous economic burden they imply for the families concerned and for the community, and the unlikely prospect of a change in the patient's condition or prognosis, has led to justifiable anxiety at the risks of medicine becoming excessively technical and of *unnecessary therapeutic cruelty* to the patient. This awareness, in turn, has led to greater sensitivity towards what is often termed 'the right to die with dignity' or 'the dignity of death'.

Beginning or continuing treatment when it is no longer called for because there is no realistic hope of the patient's regaining consciousness demonstrates at the very least a serious lack of respect for the dignity of the human being, since it amounts to simply delaying death. It is also, therefore, a serious violation of a basic legal principle and limitation of positive law[304] which is explicitly recognized in our Constitution Article 10.1.[305] For this reason it has been rightly contended that such actions constitute 'inhuman and degrading treatment', explicitly prohibited by the Spanish Constitution in Article 15.[306] Respect for human dignity is also applicable to the death of the individual, although it can often prove somewhat complex. It might be deemed indignant (subjectively-speaking) to subject the patient to artificial means or machinery which serve an objectively therapeutic purpose, although such an approach, if adopted, would considerably lessen knowledge of the ways and means that medicine can combat disease and death. If there is something that identifies the science of medicine and sets it apart, it is precisely this capacity to alter the course of nature in our favour. However, dying with dignity can also be understood in the sense of an individual who withstands physical pain and moral suffering and is able to rely on others (the doctor, the family) to do everything possible to fight death, even in hopeless situations where the prognosis is grim. This positive view of life should also be respected. Nevertheless, prolonging the life of the person when it is not in his interests to do so or assisting him to die would amount to an offence in cases where the decision is not based on ethical principles but for the economic benefit of the family, the healthcare system or for political or other reasons.[307]

The primary purpose of medicine continues to be healthcare, which implies preserving and prolonging human life, but this does not mean that suffering should not be alleviated or eliminated, as we said above.[308] Nevertheless, the doctor's duty of

---

304. J. Cerezo Mir, 'La regulación del estado de necesidad en el Código Penal español', in *Estudios Penales y Criminológicos*, X, 1987, pp. 87 and f.
305. Article 10.1 of the Spanish Constitution can be translated as follows: 'The dignity of the individual, the independent development of personality, respect for the law and the rights of others are fundamental to public order and peace in society.'
306. Bueno Arús, 'Límites del consentimiento en la disposición del propio cuerpo desde la perspectiva del Derecho Penal', *supra*, p. 14.
307. A. Eser, 'Límites del deber del tratamiento médico desde el punto de vista jurídico', in *Nuevo Foro Penal*, 1985, p. 447.
308. *Ibid.*, p. 446; Romeo Casabona, *El Médico ante el Derecho*, *supra*, pp. 4 and ff.

care is limited to the obligations imposed by *lex artis; lex artis* in fact demands that all treatment and any artificial measures to prolong biological life that are unnecessarily cruel should be discontinued where there is no rational reason to believe that the patient might recover (excluded from this of course are palliative measures to alleviate pain that are appropriate in the circumstances). Meeting these demands would not, therefore, constitute a punishable omission. This is worth clarifying and underlining.

In accordance with this function, fulfilment of the duty of care for the doctor is limited, (*limitations of the duty of care*) as are all legal duties to act, to circumstances in which effectively prolonging life – not death – is practicable from the outset. The treatment must imply objective and rational possibilities of recovery. This is not the case, for example, of individuals in irreversible comas who will not regain consciousness because the reactivation of cerebral function is not possible, even when the situation arises as a result of a substantial deterioration in the patient's condition. The same goes for newborn infants with incurable abnormalities that will inevitably result in death in the short term. It is even less the case if there is some other pathological condition that occurs jointly with the abnormality or illness in question. Once the situation has been recognized, it is irrelevant for the criminal law that the decision involves the cessation of treatment with drugs, non-performance of a surgical operation or the switching off of any machines that are maintaining vital functions.

B. Juridico-penal Evaluation of Strictly Passive Euthanasia

181. What remains therefore of passive euthanasia in the strict sense of the term and what is its legal position in the eyes of our positive Law? It is from this point onwards that the wishes of the individual concerned become relevant (and the issue more disputed). If the patient himself refuses life-saving treatment, however, the law recognizes his right to do so, as we said above.

Withdrawing treatment from a seriously ill patient where the *possibility of survival* still exists, even though the quality of life will be worse than prior to the illness or accident that has led to the condition (e.g., hemiplegic patients, non-terminal cancers, non-terminal kidney failure) constitutes legally punishable passive euthanasia if the patient has not given his consent, even where death is foreseeable in the long term. In such cases, it does not matter if the person's life is being maintained by means of machines (respirators, pacemakers, kidney machines, etc.). The criminal law's response is to consider such cases as unlawful homicide (or murder, depending on the circumstances) committed by omission, since the physician is in a position to guarantee life in such cases, as we shall *see* below, and has not been relieved of this responsibility by the patient giving his consent. This position as guarantor is a necessary condition for homicide by omission to exist. However, accurate appraisal by the criminal law requires further consideration of the nature of the physician's duty of care in such cases. If the physician has breached his duty, liability may arise, but not otherwise.

The legal duty of care occurs (*source of duty of care*), in principle, when the person who treats the individual in need of treatment has a special relationship with this person, a relationship known literally as 'a position of guarantor'.[309] This is to be understood as the situation of vulnerability that arises in relation to the legally protected interest (in this case, the patient's life) as a result of the special relationship created between the physician and the legal interest. The vulnerability of the life or health of the patient is the result of his submitting to treatment, from the point when the patient or his representatives cease to avail themselves of the services of all other doctors apart from the one treating the patient. Once the position of guarantor has been established, it follows that a duty of care exists. To establish the limits of this duty of care, the wishes of the patient must be taken into account. If the doctor wishes to begin or continue a treatment but the patient is opposed to this, the doctor is not obliged to act in all cases, according to Law 41/2002, of 14 November, basic law regulating Patient Autonomy and the Rights and Obligations regarding clinical information and documentation and the Oviedo Convention.

182. There are two objective criteria that may help those concerned to decide how to act in such circumstances. The first of these is from the patient's point of view (as can be seen, it is in reality an objective-subjective criterion), and the second is from the point of view of the doctor.

1. The appropriateness or lack of appropriateness of a treatment or operation depends primarily on whether or not it is necessary from a therapeutic perspective, that is to say, once the possible risks and advantages that the treatment involves have been weighed up. The more delicate the patient's health, the greater the risks entailed and the lack of certainty with regard to outcome. This means that its therapeutic indication is reduced accordingly, and the treatment becomes elective. The weighing up of the therapeutic indication of the treatment corresponds to the physician who shall base his decision on his scientific and technical knowledge; however, the actual taking on of the risk must always rest with the patient regardless of the seriousness of the illness (all the more so when the illness is serious and prognosis uncertain). The patient is entitled to refuse treatment, even vital treatment, if the risks are very high and there is no guarantee of improvement. The physician's decision is an objective evaluation, which should be arrived at without taking the patient's ulterior motives into account, since these may influence the objective considerations. For example, the patient may wish to die so as to put an end to the suffering caused by the illness or to refuse a blood transfusion for religious reasons (however, let us just suppose that there is good reason to believe that the blood is contaminated by some pathogen: the hepatitis virus or HIV. This would constitute an objective fact with regard to the indication, in this case, a contraindication), etc. In a wider context, and as has been recalled above, the doctor must not use professional regulations or superior knowledge (principle of paternalism) as grounds to decide what is best for the well-being of the patient.

---

309. *See* on this issue J.M. Silva Sánchez, 'La responsabilidad penal del médico por omisión', in *La Ley*, nº. 1632, 1987, pp. 1 and f.

It is the patient who is best able to decide with respect to the risks he is willing to take (principle of autonomy or self-determination).[310]

183. Beginning, continuing and extending treatment is obligatory only when there is a possibility that the physician (or, to be more accurate, medical science) can bring about a cure. In the light of the patient's condition, if this is not possible and it has been established thus, in accordance with the criteria of *lex artis*, there is no duty to treat the patient (aside from palliative measures to counteract pain and suffering). This would be the case in the terminal phases of an illness for which, by medical standards, no effective treatment exists. If, on the other hand, there is some chance of improvement or of the patient's regaining consciousness (or of this occurring at a later stage of development in the case of newborn babies), the obligation to treat the patient holds good, and if it is not fulfilled the physician risks prosecution for homicide by omission, provided that the position of guarantor exists. All these considerations are particularly relevant in cases where the patient cannot express his wishes for whatever reason (comatose state, newborn, etc.), although similar criteria also apply when the family and legal representatives act on the patient's behalf, in accordance with the terms of Law 41/2002, of 14 November, basic law regulating Patient Autonomy and the Rights and Obligations regarding clinical information and documentation (Article 9).

184. The living will. The living will was introduced into the Spanish Legal Framework by the Convention for the Protection of Human Rights and Dignity of the Human Being with regard to the Application of Biology and Medicine: Convention on Human Rights and Biomedicine, and came into effect in Spain on 1 January 2000, following its ratification by Parliament. As Article 9 (Previously expressed wishes) stated, 'The previously expressed wishes relating to a medical intervention by a patient who is not, at the time of the intervention, in a state to express his or her wishes shall be taken into account.' It is important to highlight that according to this law, the implementation of the living will is delegated to the different health services directors, one in each region. Accordingly, some of the Spanish regions passed their own legislation on this topic. In practice, this meant that some differences (for instance, regarding the possibility of minors gaining access to a living will) could occur in Spain. The registers of the living would also depend on the Regional Governments, but in order to ensure their coordination, a central register, depending on the Ministry of Health, was created (Central living will Register).

This task was addressed by Law 41/2002, of 14 November, basic law regulating Patient Autonomy and the Rights and Obligations regarding clinical information and documentation, which dedicated its Article 11 to tackle the living will tool. According to it, all Spaniards who have reached the age of majority, that is, 18 years of age (in some Regions also emancipated minors), with sufficient legal capacity

310. A. Eser, 'Problemas de justificación y exculpación en la actividad médica', in S. Mir Puig (ed.), *Avances de la Medicina y Derecho Penal* (PPU, Barcelona 1988), p. 46.

and freely,[311] may communicate their instructions about actions that should be taken into account should they reach a situation in which they can no longer freely express their wishes. If the person maintains the ability to let their wishes be known, this will always prevail over the contents of the living will document. Thus, as long as the patients keep sufficient capacity to communicate their preferences, healthcare professionals will take into account what they decide at each moment, not what is written in their living will. In other words, it will only be implemented in those situations in which the patients are unable to make decisions regarding their own healthcare or treatments, for example, if they are unconscious, in a coma or just incapable of deciding.[312]

The contents of the Living Will will be private and thus only available to the doctor attending the patient during a time of crisis. The Living Will can also be revoked, changed or replaced at any time by the interested party. The Living Will Document, which must not include any dispositions contrary to law and/or 'lex artis' (Article 11.3), may include:

a. An expression of life goals and personal values. This provides guidance for the interpretation of the remainder of the document and serves to help the medical team before they take decisions.
b. Instructions about medical treatment. It can refer both to an illness or injury that is being suffered at the time of granting the document or to any future situation. With the only limitation being good clinical practice and respect for the law, the medical interventions that the person wishes to receive or not to receive may be indicated. This means that people can choose the treatment they want to receive, but certain treatments will only begin when medical professionals consider them to be clinically indicated.

Living will can be formalized in different ways: (1) By public deed executed before a Notary. (2) By a declaration before three witnesses, adults with full capacity to act, two of which must not have any direct relationship with the grantor. (3) By a declaration made in the correspondent Register.

The registration of the living will document is not compulsory. However, if it is not registered, the obligation of letting people know of its existence will fall on the patients, who must deliver a copy to the healthcare Centre so that it is included in their clinical records, or the patients must carry it with them. Once the living will is redacted, access to it is incorporated into the medical history. This means that health professionals can consult it if necessary and guarantees that the patient's wishes and preferences are respected. The law also allows people to choose a person of trust as their representative or healthcare proxy for making decisions on their behalf if they

---

311. People declared legally incapacitated, providing there is no impediment in the legal sentence itself, and who, when deciding to make one, are capable of formalizing their declaration and are also allowed to redact a valid Living Will.
312. *See* M.I. Tamayo Velázquez et al., *A Guide to Making an Advance Health Care Directive* (Junta de Andalucía, 2013), at: https://juntadeandalucia.es/export/drupaljda/GuiaVVA_En.pdf.

are in such a situation. In some regions, a second representative can also be appointed as a substitute if, for some reason, the first one is unable to make these decisions.

It is important to highlight that according to this Law, the implementation of the living will is delegated to the different health services directorates, one in each Region. Accordingly, some of the Spanish Regions have passed their own legislation on this topic. In practice, this means that some differences (for instance, regarding the possibility of minors gaining access to living will) might be found in Spain. The Registers of the living will also depend on the Regional Governments, but in order to ensure the coordination of them all, a Central Register depending on the Ministry of Health was created (Central living will Register).

C. *Active Euthanasia*

185. Until 2021, direct active euthanasia was always punishable under the previous version of the Spanish Criminal Code. However, the approval of Organic Law 3/2021, of 24 March, on the Regulation of Euthanasia has brought about a radical change in the Spanish legal system regarding the treatment of euthanasia by recognizing the legality of certain acts of active euthanasia.[313] Organic Law 3/2021 designates these acts as 'assisted dying' and defines this as the act of providing the necessary means to a person who meets the requirements set out in the law and has expressed his wish to die. This 'assistance' has two variants, consisting of acts of executive cooperation and necessary cooperation, respectively, which are classified under the Spanish Penal Code (initially, Article 143.4 of the Penal Code) but are not punishable if the requirements established in Organic Law 3/2021 are met. The two variants in question are: (a) The direct administration of a substance to the patient by a competent healthcare professional. (b) The prescription or supply of a substance by a healthcare professional to the patient so that they can self-administer it in order to cause their own death. As can be seen, the new law has opted for a 'medicalization of euthanasia': only doctors are authorized to provide assisted dying (even to individuals who are not hospitalized and are in their own homes). Family members, even though they may be deeply emotionally involved and under significant pressure, can at most avail themselves of the penal mitigation offered by Article 143.4 of the Penal Code, without prejudice to the possibility of further reducing or even eliminating the penalty if mitigating or exculpatory circumstances are recognized (temporary mental disturbance, incomplete exculpation, or a mitigating factor by analogy, under Articles 20.1, 21.1, and 21.7 of the Penal Code, respectively). Article 5 of Organic Law 3/2021 enumerates the requirements that must be met in order to receive assisted dying: (a) Having Spanish nationality, legal residence in

313. *See* a critical analysis of the draft law presented in 2020 for the regulation of euthanasia in Spain in: Marcos del Cano, 'Capítulo 2. La eutanasia: cuestiones ético-jurídicas', Serrano Maíllo/ Sánchez Sánchez (eds), *Una introducción criminológica a la Medicina Legal y Forense*, *supra*, pp. 72–79. On the legislative initiatives that culminated in the text of the law currently in force in Spain, *see* P. Nicolás Jiménez/S. Romeo Malanda/A. Urruela Mora, 'Toma de decisiones al final de la vida: situación actual y perspectiva de futuro en el Derecho español', *Revista da Faculdade Mineira de Dirito*, Vol. 23, nº. 46, 2020, pp. 108–140.

Spain, or a registration certificate proving residence in Spain for more than twelve months; being of legal age; and being capable and conscious at the time of the request. (b) Having received written information about their medical condition, the available alternatives, and possible courses of action, including access to comprehensive palliative care covered by the common services portfolio and any benefits they are entitled to under dependency care regulations. (c) Having voluntarily submitted two requests in writing or through another means that allows for documentation, ensuring that these are not the result of external pressure, with a minimum of fifteen calendar days between them (if the responsible physician determines that the patient's loss of capacity to give informed consent is imminent, they may accept a shorter period based on the clinical circumstances, which must be recorded in the medical history). (d) Suffering from a serious and incurable illness or a severe, chronic, and disabling condition as defined by this Law, certified by the responsible physician. (e) Providing informed consent prior to receiving assisted dying. This consent must be included in the patient's medical records. Compliance with requirements (b), (c), and (e) is not necessary in cases where the responsible physician certifies that the patient is not in full possession of their faculties and cannot freely, voluntarily, and consciously provide consent. However, requirement d) must still be met, and the patient must have previously signed an advance directive, living will, advance healthcare directive, or other legally recognized equivalent document, in which case assisted dying may be provided according to the provisions of that document.[314]

Naturally, Organic Law 3/2021 regulates other important aspects, such as: The requirements for requesting assisted dying (Article 6). The denial of assisted dying (Article 7). The procedure to be followed by the responsible physician when there is a request for assisted dying (Article 8). The procedure to be followed when a situation of factual incapacity is identified (Article 9). The prior verification by the Commission for Guarantee and Evaluation (Article 10). The execution of assisted dying (Article 11). The notification to the Commission for Guarantee and Evaluation after assisted dying has been carried out (Article 12), among others.

186. If, on the other hand, the patient did not consent because he was unable to as a result of his condition (unconsciousness due to a somatic illness, mental illness or deficiency, age) or was opposed to the act (a situation in which it would be difficult to imagine anyone committing homicidal euthanasia) or simply 'allowed it to happen' (a completely passive attitude), the act falls within the bounds of wilful homicide or, most probably, murder, because it is considered that there is premeditation – one of the necessary conditions for murder – when one takes the life of a helpless and defenceless person. The Criminal law responds to such cases with uncompromising force, and the Penal Code imposes its maximum punishment for the crime of murder.

---

314. *See* Romeo Casabona/Perin, 'Capítulo 1. El homicidio y sus formas', *supra,* pp. 52–61.

D. Premature or Neonatal Euthanasia

187. There should be no difference between paediatric medical practice and medicine applied to adults and, as a result, the legal responses (or lacunae) should not differ greatly. The life of a child is worth just as much as that of an adult. Nevertheless, when the patient is a child or newborn infant there are specific aspects of such complexity that they make it difficult for the law to provide a clear-cut response. One of these is that in some cases it is not possible to know the child's wishes or preferences, since the child simply lacks wishes or preferences, which develop with age.

What we must clarify first of all is what is meant by the expression 'premature euthanasia'. In fact, the expression itself is inappropriate as it does not refer to euthanasia in the strict sense of the word, which is what we have been discussing up until now. It does not concern helping someone who is suffering to die, but the elimination, by action or omission, of newborn infants (hence the term 'premature') who are viable but who are seen to have deformities or serious brain damage. Such actions are in all probability eugenic, involving the elimination of beings who are devoid of 'valuable life', against whom the law does not discriminate (it could not do so), as we shall *see* further on. Furthermore, the right to life most definitely comes into play here, but not (for obvious reasons) the right to do as one pleases with one's life – or death – given that at the end of the day, third parties and not the newborn baby take the decisions.

188. In Spanish criminal law, direct active euthanasia of a newborn is always punishable. It is crucial to recognize that, in these cases, consent is not considered an attenuating factor in crimes such as murder of a newborn infant.

189. When it comes to the failure to provide treatment to a newborn infant with serious abnormalities, the same situation arises and the same problem occurs as with adults, particularly those who are in a comatose state. Once again, it is necessary to establish the limits of a duty of care or a duty not to treat. The abnormality itself must not constitute the main reason for making the decision, as it is irrelevant as an excuse before the law. A duty of care is maintained in principle and what should influence the doctor's decision is the child's life expectancy. Clearly, this is where disagreement may arise.

190. We can distinguish a body of proposals that emphasize the child's future capacity to relate to others. Those who hold this view ask whether it should be demanded that the child be kept alive when the abnormality is irreversible and so serious that there is no chance of him being able to perceive and communicate.[315] The German Society for Medical Law (DGMR) proposed some years ago a series of Recommendations (*Einbecker Empfehlung*) being the following cases in which the doctor should not continue treatment:

315. A. Kaufmann, 'Relativización de la protección jurídica del la vida', in S. Mir Puig (ed.), *Avances de la Medicina y Derecho Penal* (PPU, Barcelona 1988), p. 46.

1. when lasting life cannot be maintained and it is simply a question of delaying certain death;
2. despite treatment, any possibility of the newborn child ever communicating with its environment has been discounted; and
3. when the child's vital bodily functions can only be maintained in intensive care facilities.[316]

Other experts focus only on the child's chances of improvement while also considering the disproportionate nature of the relationship between the effort involved and the suffering caused. This perspective has the advantage of reducing to reasonable dimensions the question of evaluating quality of life and therefore seems more manageable. We have emphasized throughout that children and adults should be treated equally, and in the case of children, the risk of causing additional suffering should be weighed up against the possible results of the treatment. It is thus held that there should be no intervention when there are multiple injuries and where the treatment will only cause suffering without actually stabilizing the health of the child. The Department of Health and Human Services in the United States (DHHS) set out the following circumstances as being situations in which feeding or medical or surgical treatment should not be provided:

1. if the newborn infant is in a chronic or irreversible coma;
2. when the treatment would only prolong the inevitable process of dying, would not be effective or would not overcome or correct the life-threatening situation and plays no role in the survival of the foetus; and
3. when, apart from the other two sets of circumstances, the treatment would be inhumane.[317]

E. Attenuation of or Exemption from Criminal Liability in Punishable Euthanasia

191. Apart from the lawful cases of direct active euthanasia outlined in Organic Law 3/2021 (as analysed above), it is necessary to examine whether there is a possibility to mitigate or exempt from criminal liability a person who participates as a perpetrator or cooperator in active euthanasia.

First and foremost, we can conclude that the consent of the individual concerned is not a sufficient basis on which to justify the lawfulness of direct active euthanasia. However, it is sufficient for the patient to refuse treatment, even life-sustaining treatment, in which case the treatment may be discontinued. This is especially true

316. For the full text of the Deutsche Gesellschaft für Medizinrecht recommendations *see* 'Einbecker Empfehlung', in H.D. Hiersche/G. Hirsch/T. Graf-Baumann (eds), *Grenzen der ärztlichen Behandlungspflicht bei schwerstgeschädigten Neugeborenen* (Springer, Berlin 1987), pp. 183 and ff.
317. M. Bueno Sánchez, 'Bioética y Pediatría', in *Anales Esp. de Pediatría*, 1991; N. King, 'Federal and State Regulation of Neonatal Decision-Making', in R.C. McMillan/H.T. Engelhardt, JR./S.P. Spicker (eds), *Euthanasia and the Newborn* (Reidel Publ. Co., Boston 1987), pp. 90 and ff.

when discontinuing the treatment does not pose an immediate risk to the patient's life or when the treatment itself carries additional risks that the patient is unwilling to accept.

Nevertheless, consent does have certain attenuating effects on the unlawfulness (or wrongfulness) of the act, given that without consent, the act would, in some cases (active euthanasia, for instance), constitute manslaughter or murder. Let us consider the case, for example, when euthanasia is practised by the mother of the newborn infant. In fact, in this case, the courts would convict the mother of murder. On the basis of the altruistic motive of compassion – not, it should be said, merely the desire to dispense with the economic and emotional burden of having an abnormal or seriously ill child – this family relationship can be seen in this case as an attenuating circumstance as Article 23 Penal Code (On the mixed circumstance of kinship) states that 'a circumstance that may mitigate or aggavate accountability, according to the nature, motives and effects of the crime, is when the victim is or has been the spouse or person with whom the convict has had a stable emotional relationship, or being the ascendant, descendant or biological or adoptive sibling of the offender or spouse or cohabiting partner thereof'.

192. Regarding the possibility of acknowledging the presence of a general ground for *justification*, it should be noted that the current legal framework does not allow for the application of such general justifications – such as, for example, the justifying state of necessity provided for in Article 20, paragraph 5, of the Spanish Criminal Code. This conclusion stems from the fact that the legislature has opted: (a) to decriminalize euthanasia when performed by a physician and when the formal and material requirements established in 'Organic Law 3/2021, of March 24, on the Regulation of Euthanasia' are met, and (b) to expressly maintain certain mitigated criminal offences in order to more leniently sanction punishable conduct related to the consensual suicide of another person.[318]

193. That said, with regard to the potential application of an excuse or mitigating circumstance operating within the scope of the offender's culpability, it should be noted that in exceptional situations – such as those that may arise within the victim's family environment – the complete exemption from criminal liability on the grounds of mental disorder (provided for in Article 20, paragraph 1, of the Spanish Criminal Code) could be applicable only if the necessary psychiatric and psychological conditions for its recognition are met. Furthermore, nothing precludes, under similarly exceptional circumstances, the application of an incomplete exemption from criminal liability based on mental disorder (Article 21, paragraph 1, of the Spanish Criminal Code, in connection with Article 20, paragraph 1 of the same Code), or even the application of a complete exemption, an incomplete exemption, or a mitigating circumstance based on perceptual disturbances experienced by the offender since birth or childhood (Article 20, paragraph 3, of the Spanish Criminal

318. *See* Romeo Casabona/Perin, 'Capítulo 1. El homicidio y sus formas', *supra,* p. 57.

Code).[319] Far more problematic, however, is the potential recognition of a mitigating circumstance grounded in humanitarian or compassionate motives. It could be argued that, in such cases, the mitigating circumstance provided for in Article 21, paragraph 3,[320] of the Spanish Criminal Code, or the analogous mitigating circumstance established in paragraph 7[321] of the same article, could be invoked. The basis for the mitigating circumstance set forth in paragraph 3 lies in the temporary impairment of the mental faculties of the person acting under the emotional strain and distress caused by witnessing another's suffering – particularly when the person affected is a family member, a friend, or a close acquaintance. The same rationale may also apply to altruistic motives, even in the absence of significant emotional distress (e.g., in the case of a doctor or nurse), in which case it could be argued that the mitigating circumstance is applicable by analogy, pursuant to paragraph 7 of Article 21. However, as previously noted, it appears that the current legal framework does not permit the application of such mitigating circumstances, given that the article criminalizing euthanasia in the Spanish Criminal Code (Article 143, paragraph 4) expressly provides for a mitigated penalty in cases where the conduct is motivated by humanitarian or compassionate reasons.[322]

319. It should be clarified that the exemption from criminal liability grounded in perceptual disturbances affecting the offender since birth or early childhood (Art. 20, para. 3, of the Spanish Criminal Code) has seen very limited application in judicial practice.
320. Article 21. The following are mitigating circumstances: (…) 3. Acting under causes or stimuli so powerful as to produce a state of violent emotional upheaval, mental obfuscation, or another passionate condition of similar magnitude.
321. Article 21. The following are mitigating circumstances: (…) 7. Any other circumstance of analogous significance to those previously mentioned.
322. *See* Romeo Casabona/Perin, 'Capítulo 1. El homicidio y sus formas', *supra,* p. 57.

Chapter 3. Specific Activities

§1. Termination of Pregnancy (Abortion)

I. The Offence of Abortion in Spanish Law

194. A fuller understanding of the complex question of abortion in Spanish law can only be achieved through a discussion of the legal rules relating to abortion and the cases in which it is punishable.[323]

195. The legal interest protected by the abortion law. As a general rule, it can be said that from a criminal law perspective, abortion consists of causing the death of the embryo or human foetus either in the womb or through causing its premature expulsion from the womb.[324] In the case of the latter, some argue in favour of a lack of viability and maturity in the expelled foetus.[325]

The legal interest protected by the offence of abortion is the life of the conceived (embryo or foetus). This conclusion is reinforced in so much as the life of the conceived is a legally protected interest under the terms of the Spanish Constitution (Article 15), as was upheld by the Constitutional Court on 11 April 1985, and the Penal Code granted this protection under the Criminal Law in view of the vital interests of the individual and the community. It is normally accepted that alongside this primordial and basic interest, there are also other secondary interests, such as the freedom of the pregnant woman, as can be seen in the longer sentences applied if the freedom of the pregnant woman is also impinged upon. Accordingly, the *material object* of the aggressive conduct is the embryo or the live human foetus implanted in the woman's uterus. Therefore, the offence is deemed to have been committed regardless of whether at the moment of termination, the conceived is viable or non-viable outside the uterus, whether the action is performed inside or outside the womb, whether it occurs after expulsion or in fact involves provoking expulsion with the aim of terminating the pregnancy; beyond the parameters of the law are spontaneous abortion of non-viable foetuses (the embryo is always deemed

323. For a more complete account *see* C.M. Romeo Casabona, 'La reforma penal del aborto: límite mínimo, figuras delictivas y sistema de las indicaciones', in *Propuestas para la reforma penal* (Centro de Estudios Criminológicos, Universidad de La Laguna, Santa Cruz de Tenerife 1992), pp. 143 and ff.

324. *See* Bustos Ramírez, *Manual de Derecho Penal. Parte Especial*, *supra*, p. 59; G. Landrove Díaz, *Política Criminal del aborto* (Bosch, Barcelona 1976), p. 15; F. Muñoz Conde, *Derecho Penal. Parte Especial* (25ª ed. Tirant Lo Blanch, Valencia 2023), p. 91; A. Serrano Gómez/A. Serrano Maíllo, *Derecho Penal Español. Parte Especial* (15ª ed. Dykinson, Madrid 2010), p. 79; Javier Cigüela Sola/Mirentxu Corcoy Bidasolo (Dir.) et al., *Manual de Derecho Penal. Parte Especial (Tomo I)* (3ª edic., Tirant lo Blanch, Valencia 2023), p. 82; Juan Carlos Carbonell Mateu/J.L. González Cussac (Coord.) et al., *Derecho Penal. Parte Especial* (7ª edición, Tirant lo Blanch, Valencia 2022), p. 99; A. Urruela Mora, 'El aborto', in C.M. Romeo Casabona/E. Sola Reche/M.A. Boldova Pasamar (Coords) et al., *Derecho Penal. Parte Especial* (3ª edición, Comares, Granada, 2023), p. 66.

325. *See* references in E. Farre Trepat, 'Sobre el concepto de aborto y su delimitación de los delitos contra la vida humana independiente', in *Anuario de Derecho Penal y Ciencias Penales*, 1990, pp. 337 and f.

non-viable) as well as ectopic pregnancies, since these are non-viable inside the uterus; neither is the destruction of an embryo that is the result of 'in vitro' fertilization deemed to constitute abortion, so long as the embryo has not been implanted and nested in the uterus. The offence may be committed at any time between the moment of nesting (although the Penal Code does not define this explicitly) and the moment of birth. Up to this former point, no interest exists to which effective protection may be given under the Penal Code, whereas, after birth, there is an independent human life that deserves protection of a different type; deformed foetuses or monsters are also covered by the offence, provided that they are viable inside the uterus.

196. Abortions performed outside Spain on Spanish citizens. In accordance with the provisions of the 'Ley Orgánica del Poder Judicial' of 1985, which is concerned with, among other things, the territorial jurisdiction of Spanish criminal law, abortion is only punishable when committed in Spain (Article 23.1), except where, under the complementary principle of personality (Article 23.2), it is also punishable in the country where it was performed (principle of double incrimination), apart from other requirements. As a result, Spanish women who travel to neighbouring countries where voluntary abortion is legal may not be prosecuted in Spain, notwithstanding the fact that the Spanish Penal Code would consider this an offence, since the Spanish courts do not have jurisdiction over an act which is not an offence in the other country. This interpretation has been confirmed both by the Supreme Court[326] and the Constitutional Court.[327]

II. Voluntary Abortion

A. System Adopted Between 1985 and 2010

197. Since the reform of the Penal Code under *Organic Law* 9/1985 of 5 July – once the hurdle posed by an appeal on the grounds of alleged unconstitutionality had been overcome and the Bill amended in line with the Constitutional Court ruling of 11 April 1985 – and until the approval of Organic Law 2/2010, of 3 March, of sexual and reproductive health and of voluntary interruption of pregnancy, abortion was legally permitted under Spanish law in any of the circumstances established by Article 417 bis of the former Penal Code, which did not include indication for socio-economic reasons.[328] Clearly, the Legislature followed the criterion of

326. Supreme Court Ruling (2nd Chamber) of 5 Dec. 1986, in the opposite sense to earlier decisions: 20 Dec. 1980, 15 Oct. 1983.

327. *See* Constitutional Court 75/1984, 27 June.

328. Article 417 bis could be translated thus: '*Abortion performed by a doctor, or under his/her supervision, in an accredited health-care centre or institution, be it public or private, with the explicit consent of the pregnant woman is not punishable in the following circumstances: 1st When it is necessary to avoid grave danger to the life or physical or psychiatric health of the woman and that this is stated in a certificate issued prior to the operation by an appropriate specialist physician other than the doctor who is to perform the abortion or under whose supervision the abortion is to be performed. In emergency conditions where there is a life-threatening risk to the woman, the*

rule-exception in this regard. The rule was that wilful abortion was banned in all cases and was punished accordingly under the criminal law, even when the pregnant woman herself agreed to the abortion. The exception was that under certain circumstances authorized by the Law, abortion was lawful, when specific conflicts of interest occurred, in which case specific principles applied. The Spanish Legislature opted for a system of indications, as opposed to one of time limits (which also responds to an assumption of conflict) or to an across-the-board right to abortion. To sum up, the situation in Spain between 1985 and 2010 was as follows: if the life or physical or mental health of the mother were seriously endangered (therapeutic or medical indication) or if the woman had become pregnant following rape (ethical or criminological indication) or, finally, if through prenatal diagnosis or some other procedure, evidence emerged that the foetus was likely to be born with significant abnormalities (eugenic or embriopathic indication), an abortion may be performed.

The reform of the regulation in the field of abortion was demanded by many sectors of society who felt that under the Penal Code provisions in the version in force until 2010, no conditions apart from therapeutic considerations rendered abortion lawful.

B. *In Force Regulation: Time Limits System of Abortion (Organic Law 2/2010, of 3 March, of Sexual and Reproductive Health and of Voluntary Interruption of Pregnancy)*[329]

198. The regulatory framework on abortion is established in the Organic Law 2/2010 (whose current version is the one established after the modification produced by Organic Law 1/2023, of 28 February), as well as in two Royal Decrees which develop certain particular aspects of the previous one: Royal Decree 825/ 2010, of 25 June, on partial development of Organic Law 2/2010 (whose content has partly lost its validity following the entry into force of Organic Law 1/2023) and Royal Decree 831/2010, of 25 June, of guarantee of healthcare quality of the system of voluntary interruption of pregnancy aimed at assuring access to abortion in conditions of equality throughout the national territory.

Organic Law 2/2010 includes in its title the key concepts in order to understand the problem of abortion: the importance of sexual and reproductive health that the

requirements for explicit consent and a written certificate are waived. 2nd When the pregnancy is the result of an act that constitutes the crime of rape under Article 429, so long as the abortion is performed in the first 12 weeks of pregnancy and the aforementioned act has been reported to the authorities. 3rd When it is assumed that the foetus will be born with grave physical or psychiatric abnormalities so long as the abortion is performed in the first 22 weeks of pregnancy and the written statement is issued by two specialists from a public or private accredited health-care centre or establishment, neither of whom shall perform or supervise the abortion. 2. In the cases envisaged in the previous clause the pregnant woman's actions will not be punishable even if the abortion is not performed in a public or private accredited centre or health-care establishment or if the medical certificates not been issued.'

329. Modified by Organic Law 1/2023, of 28 February.

Organic Law 2/2010 directly connects with abortion. An aspect that seems undeniable is that advances in sexual culture will give rise to greater control by women in the reproductive process and therefore will cause a decrease in the rate of voluntary abortions.

The special connection between women's rights and sexual and reproductive health is noted by many international instruments. Within the United Nations (UN) system, Article 12 of the Convention on the Elimination of All Forms of Discrimination Against Women adopted by General Assembly Resolution 34/180 of 18 December 1979 establishes that 'States Parties shall take all appropriate measures to eliminate discrimination against women in the field of health care in order to ensure, on a basis of equality of men and women, access to health care services, including those related to family planning.' The Beijing Platform for Action, adopted at the Fourth World Conference on Women held in 1995, recognizes that 'The human rights of women include their right to have control over and decide freely and responsibly on matters related to their sexuality, including sexual and reproductive health, free of coercion, discrimination and violence.' Within the EU, European Parliament Resolution 2001/2128(INI) on sexual and reproductive health and associated rights makes several recommendations to Member States on issues of contraception, unwanted pregnancy, and sex education. These recommendations were based, *inter alia*, on the huge inequalities experienced by European women in terms of access to reproductive health services, contraception and abortion according to their income or country of residence.

The Convention on the Rights of Persons with Disabilities of 13 December 2006, ratified by Spain, requires States Parties to ensure that 'The rights of persons with disabilities to decide freely and responsibly on the number and spacing of their children and to have access to age-appropriate information, reproductive and family planning education are recognized, and the means necessary to enable them to exercise these rights are provided' and to ensure that these persons 'retain their fertility on an equal basis with others.'

Organic Law 2/2010 takes an especially careful account of the constitutional doctrine laid out in the decisions of the Constitutional Court. In Decision 53/1985, the Tribunal, though often divided on substantive questions, did lay out certain principles that were subsequently validated by jurisprudence and which served as benchmarks for this law. One of these principles is that the competing rights and interests involved in regulating voluntary termination of pregnancy are not absolute. As such, the legislature must 'balance the protected legal interests and rights at hand and attempt to harmonize them if possible, or if not, spell out the conditions and requirements for one of them to prevail' (Constitutional Court Decision 53/1985). Although 'the system of laws does not consider the unborn as citizens entitled to the fundamental right to life guaranteed under article 15 of the Constitution', this is not meant to deprive them of all constitutional protection (Constitutional Court Decision 116/1999). Prenatal life is a legal interest deserving of protection. While it is the role of legislators to extend such protection, they must not overlook the fact that the manner in which protection is configured and implemented is always contingent on guaranteeing the fundamental rights of pregnant women.

Organic Law 2/2010 recognizes the right to freely decide whether and when to have children. This implies, *inter alia*, ensuring that women can make conscious, responsible decisions as to whether to carry a pregnancy to term and that these decisions are respected. Based on expert opinion and comparative law, legislators considered it reasonable to allow a period of fourteen weeks to guarantee the right of women to make an informed decision about termination of pregnancy, free from interference. This concept, referred to in Constitutional Court Decision 53/1985 as 'conscious selfdetermination', considers that decisive third-party intervention to shape a pregnant woman's will provides no significant guarantees to the foetus while needlessly restricting the right to personal growth and development protected under Article 10.1 of the Constitution.

According to the preamble of Organic Law 2/2020, experience shows that prenatal life is best protected by policies that actively support motherhood and pregnant women. In the early stages of pregnancy, protection of a legal right is best achieved by working with the pregnant woman rather than against her.

As noted in Constitutional Court Decision 53/1985, a crucial milestone of the pregnancy process 'is the moment when the nasciturus becomes viable outside the womb'. Foetal viability, in the general consensus of the scientific community based on neonatology research, begins at approximately the twenty-second week. Until then, the Law allows termination of pregnancy, provided that the life or health of the pregnant woman is at serious risk or that the foetus is seriously malformed. These health grounds for voluntary termination of pregnancy are complemented by steps designed to ascertain with complete accuracy that this is indeed the case. On top of that, Organic Law 2/2010 imposes a clear time limit on application of the so-called therapeutic indication. If a woman's life or health is at risk beyond the twenty-second week of pregnancy, the appropriate course of action is to induce labour, which fully balances her right to life and physical integrity and protection of the life in formation.

Beyond the twenty-second week, the law contemplates two exceptions for termination of pregnancy. The first refers to cases of 'fetal anomalies incompatible with life', an exception to considering prenatal life a protected legal interest under Article 15 of the Constitution (Constitutional Tribunal Decision 212/1996). The second exception applies when 'the fetus has an extremely serious and incurable condition, as confirmed by a Medical Committee'. Confirmation defers to the expert opinion of medical practitioners based on current scientific knowledge.

From the point of view of the regulation of voluntary abortion, Organic Law 2/2010 establishes in its Article 14 that pregnancies may be terminated within the first fourteen weeks of gestation at the request of the pregnant woman.

In the light of Organic Law 2/2010, the time limit solution is adopted in Spain in the field of abortion. Women can take a free and informed choice on the termination of pregnancy without interference from third parties during the first fourteen weeks of gestation.

According to Article 17 Organic Law 2/2010, all women who express their intention to undergo a voluntary termination of pregnancy shall receive information from health personnel on the different methods of surgical and pharmacological termination of pregnancy, the conditions for termination provided for in the law, the public and accredited centres to which they may go and the procedures for accessing the service, as well as the conditions for its coverage by the corresponding public health service. In the case of voluntary termination of pregnancy after fourteen weeks of gestation for medical reasons, all the information on the different possible procedures must be provided to enable the woman to choose the most appropriate option for her case. In cases where women so require, and never as a requirement for access to the service, they may receive information on one or more of the following issues: details of centres available to receive appropriate information on contraception and safe sex, information on facilities offering pre- and post-abortion counselling, public assistance available to pregnant women and health coverage during pregnancy, childbirth and employment rights linked to pregnancy and maternity, public benefits and aid for the care and attention of children, tax benefits and other relevant information on incentives and aid for childbirth. In the case of termination of pregnancy provided for in Article 15.b (risk of severe foetal abnormalities), the woman who expressly requests it, although never as a requirement for accessing the service, may receive information on the rights, benefits and existing public aid relating to support for the autonomy of persons with disabilities, as well as the network of social organiZations providing social assistance to these persons.

The Organic Law 2/2010 completes the time limit system with the inclusion of two indications – the second one with two submodalities – (therapeutic indication – Article 15.a Organic Law 2/2010 – and embriopathic indication – Article 15.b and c Organic Law 2/2010) that allow abortion beyond the time period referred of fourteen weeks. According to Article 15 Ley Orgánica (LO) 2/2010 (*termination on Health Grounds*), exceptionally, a pregnancy may be terminated for medical reasons in any one of the following circumstances:

a. Prior to the twenty-second week of pregnancy, if the woman's life or health is at serious risk, as confirmed in advance by a medical specialist not performing or supervising the procedure. Confirmation will not be required in emergency cases of immediate life-threatening risk. Specific requisites of this indication:
   - *Certificate of opinion issued by a specialist.* It is essential that a specialist issues the relevant certificate of opinion vouching not only that the danger to the life or physical or mental health of the pregnant woman actually exists but also that abortion is necessary to prevent the danger. The responsibility which rests with the physician is obvious, and the law also demands that he has to be a specialist in the relevant field, that is to say, in the type of illness from which the woman is suffering or from which she is probably suffering. In order to ensure the independence of the certificate of opinion, the specialist who issues it must not be the physician who is to perform or supervise the abortion. The requirement of the certificate may be waived in emergency cases of mortal danger to the life of the pregnant woman, that is when her life is under threat.
   - *Woman's life or health is at serious risk.* It must be a 'serious risk'. This alludes to the concrete and specific risk that in the relatively near future, the pregnant woman will die or her health will be seriously damaged. It is no easy matter to establish the required degree of probability that such an event might occur; nevertheless, the degree required should be reduced in inverse proportion to the gravity of the threat, particularly where, for example, the

woman's life is in danger.[330] Serious risk excludes from the indication all the usual discomforts and risks entailed in a normal pregnancy and birth. Serious risk to life may be of both organic and psychological origin. Extreme depression with suicidal tendencies would be classified as the second of these types of serious risks.

b. Prior to the twenty-second week of pregnancy, provided that there is a risk of serious foetal anomalies, as confirmed in advance by two medical specialists not performing or supervising the procedure.
c. In case of foetal anomalies incompatible with life as confirmed in advance by a medical specialist not performing or supervising the procedure, or when the foetus is found to suffer from an extremely serious condition that is incurable at the time of diagnosis, as confirmed by a Medical Committee.

In any case, a number of mandatory common requirements have to be met in order to practice an abortion under the Spanish legal framework (assessed under Article 13 Organic Law 2/2010):

– *The abortion must be performed by a medical specialist, preferably in obstetrics and gynaecology, or performed under his/her supervision.* The Legislature has deemed the participation of a qualified person necessary to safeguard the life and health of the pregnant woman in view of the risks entailed in the performance of an abortion. Furthermore, the Legislature has rightly emphasized[331] that the participation of the physician provides an additional guarantee and professional supervision to ensure that the process of abortion is carried out in accordance with the law, first by ensuring that the legal time limit is respected or that the indication which the woman claims to be applicable does in fact exist, as it is the physician who will be the first to benefit from the exemption from liability established by the law (i.e., physician who is to carry out or supervise the abortion). He should simply verify that the case does conform to the law (and its requirements).

  The physician's participation, whether direct or indirect, that is, an abortion under his/her supervision, must conform to *lex artis* in all cases. Clearly, the most appropriate physician is a specialist in Obstetrics and Gynaecology,[332] but the participation of any other properly qualified physician capable of performing the abortion is equally lawful.[333] Supervision by a qualified physician, which the law

330. J. De Vicente Remesal, 'El grave peligro para la salud psíquica de la madre en la nueva ley del aborto', *La Ley*, 1985, p. 8.
331. Díez Ripollés, 'Análisis de los elementos de la causa de justificación del art. 417*bis* del Código Penal', *supra.*, p. 216.
332. R.D. 831/2010, of 25 June, on guarantee of healthcare quality of the system of voluntary interruption of pregnancy. Its Annex states that the healthcare establishments in order to perform high risk abortions or in case of pregnancies of more than fourteen weeks must provide at least (among other conditions) a Unit of Obstetrics and Gynaecology as well as Unit of Nursery and a corresponding blood bank.
333. A. Cuerda Riezu, 'El delito de aborto ante la Propuesta de Anteproyecto del Nuevo Código Penal', in *Documentación Jurídica. Monográfico dedicado a la propuesta de Anteproyecto del Nuevo Código Penal (vol. I)*, 37/40, 1983, pp. 376 and f.; J.L. Díez Ripollés, 'Análisis de los elementos de la causa de justificación del art. 417*bis* del Código Penal', in *Comentarios a la legislación penal.*

offers as an alternative procedure, refers to the sharing out of functions among members of a team working together,[334] which implies that when the physician acts as supervisor, he is still subject to *lex artis* as are all those who are physically involved. However, for the physician in this case *lex artis* primarily implies the evaluation of the capacity of the individual who performs the abortion under his/her supervision. As is discussed below, the complementary regulations distinguish between high-risk pregnancies and abortions and those that do not entail such risks. Therefore, the physician's analysis of this situation is one of the most crucial elements in any consideration of the possibility of delegating (supervising) to another healthcare professional (GP or specialist, intern or resident, midwife). This decision to delegate also depends on the intensity of subsequent treatment which may be required and the extent to which functions are delegated. These reservations are not sustainable, however, when the physician directs the pregnant woman herself by instructing her as to pharmaceutical preparations that she should then administer herself or any other action that she should take (including performing the abortion herself under the physician's supervision). The same applies to members of the woman's family or her representatives (in the broad sense of the term): in such circumstances, as lay persons, they would not be prosecuted for illegal practice of medicine.

- *Abortions may be performed only in approved public or private health centres or healthcare establishments.* This requirement stems also from the previous one in that it seeks to lessen the risks which abortion entails for the woman.[335] At the same time, it provides a means of controlling and monitoring the number of abortions performed in Spain (by preventing clandestine abortions). As regards requirements concerning approval of centres or establishments, reference should be made to the regulations of the Royal Decree 831/2010, which distinguishes between centres for the performance of abortions that do not imply high risk to the pregnant woman and performed within fourteen weeks of conception and those centres which carry out abortions involving high risk and or after completion of the aforementioned fourteen-week period (Annex Royal Decree 831/2010). The approval of public centres is automatic once they satisfy the established requirements. Accreditation of private centres is the responsibility of the Autonomous Communities (Article 4 of the Royal Decree 831/2010).
- *Abortion must be performed with the express written consent of the pregnant woman or her duly authorized representative*, as the case may be, pursuant to the provisions in Law 41/2002. Express consent may be dispensed within the cases

---

Tomo IX (Edersa, Madrid 1989), pp. 219 and f.; D.M. Luzón Peña, 'Indicaciones y causas de justificación en el aborto', in *Poder Judicial*, 13, 1989, p. 644.

334. *See* the fuller account in Jorge Barreiro, *La imprudencia punible en la actividad médico-quirúrgica*, (Tecnos, Madrid 1990), pp. 113 and ff. (with some interesting decisions on medical negligence for unjustified delegation of responsibility to nurses in obstetrics cases, p. 154); Romeo Casabona, *El Médico y el Derecho Penal, I, supra.*, pp. 247 and ff. On the impact of the principle of trust in the criminal sphere, in particular, in the field of medical-surgical activity, *see* C.M. Romeo Casabona, 'El tipo del delito de acción imprudente', in C.M. Romeo Casabona/E. Sola Reche/M.A. Boldova Pasamar (Coords) et al., *Derecho Penal. Parte General* (2ª ed. Comares, Granada, 2016), pp. 141–142.

335. As for the previous requirement, the ruling of the Constitutional Court of 11 Apr. 1985 was to this effect, which led to its inclusion in the definitive version of the text of the law.

contemplated in Article 9.2.(b) of the said Law. In the case of women with support measures for the exercise of their legal capacity, the provisions of Article 9.7 of Law 41/2002 shall be taken into account.

Time limit system of abortion adopted by Organic Law 2/2010 has been expressly admitted by Constitutional Court Ruling 44/2023, of 9 May, which states that 'we consider that this regulatory option is in accordance with our constitutional text and with the doctrine of this court, as it satisfies the state's duty to protect prenatal life – with preventive and punitive measures, the weight of which varies as the gestation process progresses – and does so without infringing women's rights. It must be reiterated that the time-limit model is not only a mechanism for the protection of prenatal life, but also, and reciprocally, a measure restricting women's rights. This court considers, however, that this restriction – which translates into the requirement that, after the fourteenth week of gestation, circumstances additional to the woman's free will for the legal termination of pregnancy, connected with other essential aspects of her fundamental rights, must be met – is constitutional because (i) it obeys the legitimate aim of protecting prenatal life; (ii) it is appropriate and necessary for the achievement of that aim; (iii) its gradual configuration in the light, on the one hand, of the progress of gestation and the physiological and vital development of the conceived, and, on the other, of the additional or extraordinary affectation of the woman's constitutional rights, is in accordance with the canon of proportionality required by this court for the constitutionality of any limitation of fundamental rights, as well as with the gradual model of protection of prenatal life accepted by STC 53/1985 itself; and (iv) it is carried out respecting, in any case, the possibility of a 'reasonable' exercise of the woman's rights, through the recognition of a timeframe in which she can decide, in a free and informed manner, whether to continue with the pregnancy or to terminate it, assuming, in a conscious and voluntary manner, all the consequences derived from one or the other decision'.

199. Finally, it should be recalled that the termination of a pregnancy must never be for the purposes of donation or subsequent use of embryos or foetuses or their biological structures. Moreover, the medical team that carries out the abortion may not be involved in any subsequent use made of the foetus or embryo.[336]

C. Criminal Law Regulation

200. The introduction of the Organic Law 2/2010 has also led to the corresponding reform of the Penal Code on punishment of abortion, adapting the criminal sphere (and, basically, the scope of the prohibitions that it embodies) in these areas to the legislative model introduced in 2010. Abortion is regulated in the Spanish Penal Code in its Title II (*On Abortion*) Book II (Articles 144–146 CP). The following crimes do exist in Spain related to abortion:

336. According to Art. 28.2 of Law 14/2007, of 3 July, on Biomedical Research.

1. *Intentional abortion without the consent of the pregnant.* According to Article 144 Spanish Penal Code, whoever perpetrates an abortion on a woman without her consent shall be punished with a sentence of imprisonment from four to eight years and a special barring from practising any health profession or from providing services of any kind at public or private gynaecological clinics, institutions or surgeries, for a term of three to ten years. The same penalties shall be applied to whoever perpetrates an abortion, having obtained the consent of the woman through violence, intimidation or deceit.

   Active subject of this figure can only be a third party (not, therefore, the pregnant herself) acting without the consent of the woman. In this case, a double attack does occur: first, not only to the life of the unborn child but also to the freedom of the pregnant woman. The penalties apply not only in case of absence of consent but also when consent by the woman has been obtained through violence, intimidation or deceit.

   In order to determine when a woman is competent to issue consent in the light of Article 144 Spanish Penal Code, the reference standard is established by Law 41/2002, of 14 November, basic law regulating Patient Autonomy and the Rights and Obligations regarding clinical information and documentation.
2. *Intentional abortion with consent of the pregnant.* According to Article 145 Penal Code:

> 1. Whoever perpetrates an abortion on a woman, with her consent, outside the cases allowed by Law shall be punished with a sentence of imprisonment from one to three years and special barring from practising any health profession and from providing services of any kind at public or private gynaecological clinics, institutions or surgeries, for a term of one to six years. The Judge may hand down the sentence in its higher half when the acts described in this Section are perpetrated outside an authorised public or private centre or institution. 2. The woman who causes herself an abortion or allows another person to cause it, outside the cases allowed by Law, shall be punished with a fine from six to twenty-four months. 3. In all cases, the Judge or Court of Law shall impose the penalties respectively foreseen in this Article in the upper half when perpetrated after the twenty-second week of gestation.

First, it must be pointed out that Article 145 Penal Code incriminates abortions perpetrated on a woman *with her consent.* The cases established in Article 145.1 and 145.2 Penal Code imply that the abortion is perpetrated 'outside the cases permitted by law' which is a de facto referral to the Organic Law 2/2010, concretely to its Articles 14 (time limit system) and 15 (abortion for medical reasons).

Article 145.1 Penal Code foresees an optional aggravation for the acts described in this Section (*The Judge may hand down the sentence in its higher half when the acts described in this Section are perpetrated outside an authorised public or private centre or institution).* On the other hand, and related to both Article 145.1 and 145.2, the Penal Code provides for a mandatory aggravation (*'In all cases, the Judge or Court of Law shall impose the penalties respectively foreseen in this Article in the upper half when perpetrated after the twenty- second week of gestation').*

3. *Abortion within the cases admitted by Organic Law 2/2010 but omitting certain requirements.* Article 145 bis CP: '*1. Punishment with a fine from six to twelve months and special barring from providing services of any kind at public or private gynaecological clinics, institutions or surgeries shall be applied, for a term of six months to two years, to whoever, within the cases admitted by the Law, perpetrates an abortion: a) Without having obtained the required prior reports; b) Outside an authorised public or private centre or institution. In this case, the judge may impose the punishment in its upper half. 2. In all cases, the Judge or Court of Law shall impose the penalties foreseen in this Article in the upper half, when the abortion is perpetrated as of the twenty-second week of gestation. 3. The pregnant woman shall not be penalised under this provision*'.

   Article 145 bis Penal Code punishes cases of intentional abortions with the woman's consent within the cases admitted by Organic Law 2/2010 but omitting any of the requirements set out in points (a) to (b) of Article 145 bis 1 Penal Code.

4. *Abortion by serious negligence.* According to 146 Penal Code, '*whoever causes an abortion due to serious negligence shall be punished with a sentence of imprisonment of three to five months, or a fine from six to ten months. When an abortion is perpetrated due to professional negligence, the punishment of special barring from practising the profession trade or holding office shall also be imposed for a term from one to three years. The pregnant woman shall not be penalised under this provision*'.

Under Article 146 Penal Code, abortion is exclusively punishable by gross negligence, being unpunished; therefore, if the abortion is caused by minor negligence.[337]

§2. Sterilization

I. Concept and Penal Scope

201. The legal framework for sterilization in Spain has undergone a changing trajectory over the last two centuries.[338] For example, between 1962 and 1983, sterilization was considered a serious crime, even with the consent of the person concerned. The penalty, in fact, was twelve to twenty years' imprisonment, similar to

337. *See* A. Urruela Mora, 'Sobre el delito de aborto imprudente a la luz del anterior y del actual Código Penal', in *Actualidad Penal*, nº. 6, 2000, pp. 119 ff.
338. *See* C.D. Medina Castellano, 'Lección 10. Esterilización e interrupción voluntaria del embarazo', in C.M. Romeo Casabona/P. Nicolás Jiménez/S. Romeo Malanda (Dirs), *Manual de Bioderecho* (2ª edición, Dykinson, Madrid 2025), pp. 253 ff. https://bioderecho.eu/manual-bioderecho/; *see also* J. Vizueta Fernández, 'Las lesiones', in C.M. Romeo Casabona/E. Sola Reche/M.A. Boldova Pasamar (Coords) et al., *Derecho Penal. Parte Especial* (3ª ed. Comares, Granada, 2023), p. 95.

homicide. The 1983 reform of the Penal Code introduced a fundamental modification in our law, allowing the freely and expressly given consent of the person to exempt the practitioners from criminal liability for 'procedures carried out in cases of organ transplants conducted in accordance with the law, sterilizations, and transsexual surgery performed by a practitioner [...]'; in this way, voluntary sterilization is given legal status.

Currently, the situation has followed this general guideline. It is important to acknowledge that sterilization is strictly penalized under our Criminal Code. According to its Article 149.1,[339] '*whoever causes to another person, by any means or procedure, to forfeit or lose the use of a major organ or limb, or a sense, or sexual impotence, sterility, serious deformity or to suffer a serious physical or mental illness, shall be punished with a sentence of imprisonment from six to twelve years*'.

In terms of the Spanish legal framework, sterilization consists of the permanent or lasting removal of the reproductive capacity of a fertile man or woman by whatever procedure, be it surgical (suture of the deferent ducts or tubal ligation), or by means of biochemical or hormonal substances (though contraceptive pharmaceutical products do not fall within this definition), or by exposure to so-called absorbable radiation.[340] Sterilization is distinguished from castration on the basis that the latter implies the violent removal of the genital organs and has as a consequence not only the permanent loss of the ability to reproduce, as in sterilization, but also of other hormonal and endocrinal functions that affect the general behaviour of the individual, such as, in the sexual domain, diminished or total lack of libido and the specific case of the male the very high accompanying risk of *coeundi* impotence or the inability to perform the sexual act.

The offence of sterilization includes reversible sterilizations, which require surgical operation or similar procedures to restore fertility to the person.[341] It goes without saying that this would not be the case, for example, of the removal of a diaphragm or intrauterine device (IUD), even where a physician has had to intervene.

202. There is, moreover, an aggravated case, which is mentioned in the second section of the same Article 149: '2. Whoever causes to another person a genital mutilation in any form shall be punished with a sentence of imprisonment from six to twelve years. Should the victim be a minor or person requiring special protection, the punishment of special barring from exercise of parental rights, guardianship, care, safekeeping or fostership shall be applicable for a term from four to ten years, should the Judge deem it appropriate in the interest of the minor or of the person requiring special protection.' As can be seen, this aggravated formula is

339. In fact, the Spanish Penal Code does not actually define what sterilization consists of Art. 149 stipulates that whoever causes another, by any means or procedure, the loss or disablement of a major organ or limb, or of a sense, impotence, sterility, a serious deformity, or a serious somatic or mental illness, shall be punished with imprisonment of six to twelve years.

340. *See* E.J. Armaza Armaza/E. Atienza Macías, 'El tratamiento jurídico de las intervenciones en el aparato reproductor humano: esterilización, castración química y cirugía de reasignación sexual', *Tratado de Derecho Sanitario, Volumen II*, *supra*, p. 740.

341. On this issue *see* A. Guallart de Viala, *La nueva protección penal de la integridad corporal y la salud* (Ed. Ceura, Madrid 1992), pp. 73 and f.

intended to specifically target non-consensual sterilizations of minors or those that cause special harm, such as those affecting the genital organs. However, not all sterilizations are penalized in Spain, as we will *see* below.

II. Therapeutic Sterilization

A. *Scope of the Lawfulness of Voluntary Sterilization*

203. The Spanish regulation adopted a position of clear liberalization in terms of the power to dispose of the legal interest, since it affords a wider implicit recognition of the individual right to non-reproduction than can be deduced in practice from the depenalization of the use of other contraceptive methods.

As a result, sterilization of the individual who has given consent is lawful under Spanish law, provided that the requirements stipulated in Article 156 of the Penal Code for non-therapeutic sterilization are met. Indeed, according to such article:

> Notwithstanding the provisions of the previous article [referring to the reduction of the penalty in cases of bodily harm when consent is given], valid, free, conscious, and expressly given consent exempts from criminal liability in cases of organ transplants carried out in accordance with the law, sterilizations, and transsexual surgery performed by a physician, unless the consent was obtained through deceit, or for a price or reward, or the grantor is a minor or lacks absolute capacity to give it, in which case the consent given by them or their legal representatives will not be valid.

204. With Article 156 of the Penal Code, a position of clear liberalization is adopted in terms of the power to dispose of the legal interest, since it affords a wider implicit recognition of the individual right to non-reproduction than can be deduced in practice from the depenalization of the use of other contraceptive methods. For this reason, the introduction of the legal provision discussed here was appropriate precisely in relation to non-therapeutic sterilization. Under this umbrella, first and foremost, the performance of surgical interventions carried out by competent personnel, in accordance with lex artis and with the prior consent of the person to be operated on, even if they involve sterilization, is covered. Also, however, all those other procedures that are not merely reparative but that produce some kind of anatomical alteration or change the original nature of the affected organ or system, as happens in cases of voluntary sterilization or sex reassignment, provided they are effectively performed by a competent physician for that purpose. Instead, sterilization by imposition or coercion, that is, against the will of the individual concerned (e.g., for State demographic policy reasons), is not permitted since it is clearly unconstitutional and is considered a crime.

B. Requirements

205. In the first place, sterilization must be performed *by a qualified physician* and not by any other kind of person; frequently, this physician will be a surgeon (for the removal of the fallopian tubes in the woman), but any other medical doctor capable of performing minor surgery is also appropriate (vasectomy in the male). The physician acts in the legitimate exercise of his profession and is authorized for this specific circumstance by the Penal Code itself. Nevertheless, for the physician's performance of the operation to be lawful, consent must be given by the individual who is to be operated on.

206. All *other requirements* included in Article 156 for sterilization to be valid centre on the conditions that must be satisfied with regard to the interested party's consent. It must be freely given (without coercion and not obtained under threat) and explicit (verbal or written),[342] furnished without foul play (not obtained by means of deception or erroneous belief), without payment or reward and the consenting party must be an adult with full use of his mental faculties, i.e., must not be a minor or incompetent.

C. Sterilization of Minors

207. Article 156 stipulates that when the person who is to be sterilized for whatever reason is a minor, he may not give valid consent, nor can such consent be given by the legal representatives; in other words, the individual cannot undergo sterilization. The *legal representatives* are not empowered to give their consent on behalf of the minor. Neither may the *judicial authority* substitute for the will of the minor and authorize sterilization. Therefore, we may not arrive at the lawful sterilization of the minor by this route.

208. Thus, only those 18 years or more who are not legally incompetent can give valid consent, and from this age onwards, no restrictions may be imposed. In general, this does not create a major issue, since minors do not generally present specific circumstances in terms of sterilization, such as socio-economic or eugenic indications, but the case of the couple who has married before attaining their majority is of practical interest.

D. Sterilization of Judicially Incapacitated Persons

209. For a long time, the sterilization of judicially incapacitated persons was possible in Spain under certain conditions. In fact, the second paragraph of Article 156 of the Penal Code stated the following: '*Sterilization agreed upon by a judicial body shall not be punishable in the case of persons who are permanently unable to*

342. *See* LGS, Arts 10.5 and 6.

give any form of consent referred to in the previous paragraph, provided that it is an exceptional case where there is a serious conflict of protected legal rights, in order to safeguard the greater interest of the affected person, all in accordance with the provisions of civil legislation.'

210. However, Organic Law 2/2020, of 16 December, repealed this provision, eliminating from Spanish law any possibility of forced or non-consensual sterilization, with prior judicial authorization, of disabled persons who are judicially incapacitated. The Explanatory Memorandum of the analysed regulation explained the reason for adopting such a measure. It was adopted in order to 'improve the protection of the rights of girls and women with disabilities and to defend the basic rights of people with disabilities, it is necessary that forced or non-consensual sterilization cease to be practiced in Spain'. Thus, the provisions of the Convention for the Protection of the Rights of Persons with Disabilities and the Council of Europe Convention on Preventing and Combating Violence against Women and Domestic Violence were introduced in our country.

211. This same orientation has been brought by the reform of LO 2/2010, of 3 March, on sexual and reproductive health and voluntary interruption of pregnancy (modified by LO 1/2023), in which it now states that forced sterilization is a form of 'violence against women in the reproductive field that consists of the practice of a surgical intervention aimed at or resulting in ending a woman's ability to reproduce naturally without her prior and informed consent or without her understanding of the procedure' (Article 2.8). Finally, its Article 31.1 establishes the obligation of public authorities to ensure, among other actions, the prevention of forced sterilization, 'with special attention to women with disabilities'. Regarding these, paragraph 2 of the same article obliges the authorities to promote sexual and reproductive health programmes aimed at women with disabilities, 'which include measures for the prevention and detection of forms of reproductive violence (...)' in the terms that the article itself specifies.

§3. Medically Assisted Reproduction

I. Social Context and Legal Background

212. The Spanish socio-political debate on medically assisted reproduction began in the 1980s. During this period, a Parliamentary Select Committee was established to study human *in vitro* fertilization (IVF) and artificial insemination. The committee conducted extensive research, culminating in a comprehensive report known as the *Informe Palacios*. This report included a total of 155 recommendations, along with a series of suggestions from parliamentary groups regarding areas of disagreement. Shortly thereafter, the Spanish Parliament approved the country's first law on this matter: Law 35/1988, of 22 November, on Assisted Reproduction Techniques. This landmark legislation was swiftly followed by the enactment of Law 42/1988, of 28 December, on the Donation and Use of Human

Embryos and Foetuses or Their Cells, further regulating the ethical and legal framework surrounding assisted reproduction in Spain.

213. Law 35/1988 consisted of seven chapters, preceded by an extensive and well-documented preamble that introduced the definition of the pre-embryo, an entity that played a fundamental role in the regulation. Overall, the law was a highly liberal document that permitted most of the assisted human reproduction techniques available at the time. These included artificial insemination using the husband's semen (*ex* Articles 5.8 and 8), the semen of a partner in an unmarried couple (*ex* Article 9.3), or donor semen (*ex* Article 5). The law also allowed an infertile woman to receive a donated egg and carry the pregnancy to term, as well as the reception of a pre-implanted embryo (also referred to as a pre-embryo) originating from donors, from the couple's own gametes, or from a combination of the woman's egg and either her partner's semen or that of a third-party donor (*ex* Article 5.1). The only notable restrictions in this otherwise permissive framework concerned sex selection, which was strictly prohibited except for therapeutic purposes, and a general ban on surrogacy and pregnancy substitution, both of which were explicitly forbidden under Article 10.

Despite its overall liberal stance, the 1988 legal framework was rather conservative regarding the use of embryos for research. The law prohibited research on viable embryos except when aimed at diagnosing, treating, or preventing diseases in the embryo itself. In doing so, it anticipated the later ruling of the Spanish Constitutional Court,[343] which affirmed that 'Law 42/1988 of 28 December on the Donation and Use of Human Embryos and Fetuses or their Cells' was based on the fundamental principle that biomedical research could only be conducted on non-viable human embryos and foetuses. This principle was reaffirmed in Constitutional Court Judgment 116/1999 of 17 June.[344]

214. Law 35/1988 was never widely accepted without controversy. Three vetoes were lodged against the bill in its entirety, including one from the main opposition party, 'Partido Popular (PP)'. From legal, civil, and legislative perspectives, the law was heavily criticized on both technical and substantive grounds.[345] It was therefore unsurprising that, when 'Partido Popular' won the 2000 general election with an absolute majority, it pursued a significant overhaul of Spain's legislation on assisted reproduction. This led to the approval of Law 45/2003, of 21 November, which amended Law 35/1988 on Assisted Reproduction Techniques.

The most significant change introduced by Law 45/2003 concerned the regulation of surplus embryos. The new law imposed a general ban on the creation of surplus embryos by limiting the number of fertilized ova to three – the same number of embryos typically transferred into the uterus according to IVF protocols at the

343. Constitutional Court Judgment 212/1996, of 19 December.

344. A. Cabanillas Sánchez/J. Zavala, 'Ethics and Legal Keys To Biomedical Research In Spain', *The Age of Human Rights Journal*, 2 (June 2014) pp. 51–67 (62–63).

345. *See* for example, F. Pantaleón Prieto, 'Contra la Ley sobre Técnicas de Reproducción Asistida', *Jueces para la Democracia*, 1998, p. 5.

V. Issues Related to Surrogacy

226. As previously mentioned, the current Act (Law 14/2006) retained the previously existing ban on surrogate motherhood.[354] Indeed, it declares null and void the contract by which a surrogate pregnancy is agreed, with or without financial compensation, where a woman would then formally renounce her right to maternal filiation in favour of the party who ordered the child or another third party (Article 10.1 Law 14/2006). Indeed, the affiliation of any children born out of surrogacy is determined by birth (Article 10.2 Law 14/2006); that is to say, maternity lies with the woman who gave birth to the child regardless of whether the ovum was hers or that of another woman or the semen that of the male partner of the couple concerned. If the male partner has provided the semen (or if it has been provided by a third-party donor unconnected with an authorized centre or by a donor in collusion with the centre), the biological father can claim paternity (Article 10.3 Law 14/2006).

However, in recent years, a lot of Spanish couples decided to overpass this ban by travelling abroad to make use of this technique in countries where it is not regulated or has been legally accepted, such as the USA, Mexico, India, Ukraine, and Russia, among others. Therefore, a complicated legal issue arose when those couples intended to register the filiation of their children in Spain in their own name, as far as it involved an obvious contradiction with our legal framework. Indeed, some of these couples' claims were refused by the Spanish Registrees and Provincial Courts.[355]

Finally, one conflictive surrogate pregnancy reached the Supreme Court as a result of an appeal filed to the Provincial Court of Valencia in 2011 by a couple whose registration was refused. The Supreme Court resolved this issue in its ruling dated 6 February 2014. It considered that in order to recognize the foreign certificate where the filiation is stated, it is necessary to conduct a thorough check of said certificate of the Registry that wants to be accepted, verifying that it is ordinary and authentic, so as to make sure that it offers similar guarantees to those required for the registration of the same deed in Spain, complying with the Spanish Law. As a consequence, this statement supported the refutation, that is, the recognition of filiation asked by the couples paying for surrogate motherhood abroad. However, it provided the appellants with an alternative way to solve the problem by highlighting the possibility of claiming the paternity regarding the biological father – if he actually provided the gamete remains available according to the general rules – (Article 10.3).

The rationality supporting this solution was challenged by a vote authorized by one of the Judges, to which the other three joined, stating that *'what counts is the recognition of the filiation resulting from the American legislation in relation to the protection given to children of Spanish nationals, regardless of a contract, in whose creation the underage did not intervene, whereby the contractual instrument cannot*

354. A. Ruiz Sáenz, 'Capítulo 64. Gestación por sustitución: Problemática jurídica de los vientres de alquiler', *Tratado de Derecho Sanitario. Volumen II*, *supra*, pp. 800–805.

355. *See* A. Urruela Mora, 'El derecho y la bioética ante el fenómeno de la maternidad subrogada', in *Derecho y Salud*, Vol. 29, nº. 1, 2019, pp. 113–144.

be the reason for the refusal of this recognition. The solving of the issue should be focused on deciding whether this decision is contrary to the international public order or not and see whether it can introduced within the Spanish legal framework to fill the corresponding legal purposes'. Besides, to these four magistrates, the international public order must guarantee the prevailing interest of the underage, which requires the recognition of the filiation.

Indeed, the appellants did not accept the ruling and the proposed alternative. Soon afterwards, they filed a motion for dismissal of proceedings of the tribunal, arguing that its ruling breached some fundamental rules of the appellants: the right to legal protection, the right to equality and the privacy of the family. The appeal was dealt with by the Chamber of Civil Cases of the Supreme Court in its Ruling, of 2 February 2015, which reasoned that the Ruling did not breach the invoked rights of the appellants. Therefore, the Chamber considered that *'there are no grounds to dismiss the proceedings of the ruling num: 835/2013, from February the 6th, issued by the Plenary Board of this Chamber'*.

Therefore, it could be stated that the Spanish Court has somehow decided that it is in the interest of the children to integrate them into their family de facto, as far as children cannot find themselves unprotected in a juridical limbo but avoiding any breach of Article 10 of the Law on Assisted Reproduction Techniques (Law 14/2006). For this purpose, they have suggested the couples an alternative way to obtain a satisfactory ending – that of the claim of paternity on the basis of the biological link with the child. Notwithstanding the foregoing, it is important to highlight that, in general, there have been several rulings by the Supreme Court which have made it clear that surrogacy agreements are contrary to public policy. Among such rulings are the most recent judgments issued by the Supreme Court (First Chamber) on 31 March 2022 and 4 December 2024. Taking into consideration this scenario, it should be a matter of priority to undertake a change in legislation which regulates the practice of surrogate pregnancy in order to provide for legal certainty for all subjects involved.[356]

§4. Preimplantation Genetic Diagnosis and Human Genetics

I. Purpose and Legal Framework of Preimplantation Genetic Diagnosis

227. In 1988, preimplantation genetic diagnosis (PGD) was still an experimental technique, whose potential for improving IVF outcomes and preventing genetic diseases had yet to be fully confirmed. Despite its experimental status, Law 35/1988, of 22 November, on Assisted Reproduction Techniques, permitted preimplantation genetic testing not only as a tool to support assisted reproduction techniques in cases of infertility or sterility but also as a diagnostic and therapeutic

356. A. Emaldi Cirión, 'Una respuesta jurídica necesaria a un problema urgente', *Perspectivas en Derecho y Genoma Humano*, Núm. 25, Junio 2025, Cátedra Interuniversitaria – Diputación Foral de Bizkaia de Derecho y Genoma Humano Universidad de Deusto – Universidad del País Vasco UPV/EHU (ed.), p. 2. Available at: https://bioderecho.eu/perspectivas/

instrument for detecting hereditary diseases. The goal was either to facilitate treatment, where possible or to advise against transferring an affected embryo into the womb. Given the technique's experimental nature, its regulation was deferred to future legislative developments. As a result, the Spanish legal framework for IVF lacked specific provisions governing PGD at the time.[357]

228. It should be noted that a comprehensive legal framework for preimplantation diagnosis was only established in 2006 with the enactment of Law 14/2006, of 26 May, on Assisted Human Reproduction Techniques.

229. Under this law, the authorization for PGD can be granted in two situations: (a) for the detection of serious hereditary diseases with early onset and no available postnatal curative treatment, according to current scientific knowledge, to allow the selection of unaffected pre-embryos for transfer; and (b) for the detection of other genetic abnormalities that may compromise embryo viability (Article 12.1). Thus, under Spanish law, the use of PGD to detect severe early-onset diseases that significantly impact a person's future development is legally authorized. For all cases meeting these criteria, IVF clinics and hospitals are merely required to notify the regional authority, which in turn informs the *Comisión Nacional de Reproducción Humana Asistida* (National Assisted Human Reproduction Committee (CNRHA)), without the need for further authorization.[358]

It is also worth mentioning that, beyond these two scenarios, Law 14/2006 allows the use of PGD for additional purposes, such as the selection of embryos for Human Leukocyte Antigen (HLA) matching. In such cases, the clinical request for PGD involves not only the detection of a hereditary disease but also the determination of HLA compatibility. This situation typically arises when a couple with an affected child – e.g., suffering from acute myeloid leukaemia – seeks to have another child who can serve as a compatible donor. This use of PGD is legal in Spain, but Law 14/2006 requires express authorization from the relevant health authority. Such authorization is granted on a case-by-case basis, provided that the CNRHA issues a favourable report after evaluating the clinical, therapeutic, and social aspects of each case (Article 12.2).

In these situations, the role of the ONT must be taken into account, as it serves as the coordinating and advisory body for the Ministry of Health in matters related to organ and tissue donation and transplantation (Additional Clause 3).

---

357. Indeed, *'The 1988 Act introduced a regulatory framework for the use of assisted reproduction techniques based on three measures: the licensing and the monitoring of authorized assisted reproduction centres; the setting-up of a consultative body to inform the government and to elaborate appropriate legislative measures on the advances of assisted reproduction techniques, and the creation of a National Registry, in which assisted reproduction activities and gametes and embryo donation could be recorded and stored. Although these three measures were all introduced to ensure both the safety and the transparency of assisted reproduction activities, their actual implementation and evolution followed very different trajectories.'* V. Pavone/F. Arias, *Pre-Implantation Genetic Testing in Spain: Beyond the Geneticization Thesis* (Instituto de Políticas y Bienes Públicos (IPP), CCHS-CSIC, Working Paper, Number 12, Madrid 2010), pp. 9–10.

358. Pavone/Arias, *Pre-Implantation Genetic Testing in Spain: Beyond the Geneticization Thesis*, *supra*, pp. 10–11.

II. Embryonic and Foetal Therapy and Research

230. Advances in embryonic and foetal research and therapy open new possibilities, including a reduction in the number of abortions performed for eugenic reasons, as certain foetal abnormalities can now be corrected.[359] It is worth recalling, in this context, the relevance of the 1959 Declaration of the Rights of the Child, which, despite its limited jurisdiction, recognizes the right to treatment even before birth (Article 4).

In this scenario, physicians face the unique challenge of treating a 'patient' – the foetus – whose situation differs from that of an ordinary patient, as it exists within another person, the mother. All foetal therapies must necessarily be conducted through the mother's body.[360] As a result, the concept of 'patient' as applied to the foetus carries distinct legal implications. These include issues related to potential bodily harm to the mother (e.g., performing a caesarean section or administering certain drugs to reach the foetus), the risks that the treatment poses to her health and life, and the fact that her consent is required for a procedure that benefits the foetus rather than herself (although in some cases, the mother may also experience related symptoms). It should also be noted that foetal therapy can sometimes result in injuries to the foetus that only become evident after birth. In certain cases, foetal therapy may even cause the death of the foetus, either before birth or shortly afterwards.

As previously mentioned, Spanish law recognizes the life of the unborn child as a legally protected interest independent of the mother. For this reason, the law criminalizes intentional abortion – and, in some cases, negligent abortion (Article 146 of the Penal Code) – while allowing for specific exceptions, mainly within the first trimester of pregnancy. Furthermore, the Spanish Penal Code contains two provisions aimed at protecting the foetus from harm.

Article 157 states: *'Whoever, by any means or procedure, causes an injury or disease to a foetus that seriously harms its normal development or results in a severe physical or mental disability shall be punished with a prison sentence of one to four years and special disqualification from practicing any health profession or providing services in public or private gynecological clinics, institutions, or offices for a period of two to eight years.'*

Article 158 adds: *'Whoever, through serious negligence, commits the acts described in the preceding article shall be punished with a prison sentence of three to five months or a fine of six to ten months. If the acts result from professional negligence, the punishment shall also include disqualification from practicing the profession, trade, or position for a period of six months to two years. The pregnant woman shall not be penalized under this provision.'*

It can thus be concluded that the Spanish legal framework primarily targets physicians, requiring them to provide proper care to the foetus and avoid any practice that may cause harm to the foetus or the human being it may become.

---

359. Some authors consider that in future all the current indications for abortion will cease to exist because treatment will be possible outside the woman's body. This will even be the case when the pregnancy endangers the woman's life as the foetus would be removed and placed in an artificial placenta. Interrupting a pregnancy will not therefore involve terminating the life of the conceived child. V.L. Lombardi Vallauri, 'Bioetica, potere, diritto', in *Giustitia*, 1984, p. 21.

360. *See* W. Kapp, 'Der Fötus als Patient?', in *Medizinrecht*, 1986, p. 276.

B. The Use of Human Gametes, Embryos, and Foetuses for Genetic Research or Other Therapeutic and Non-therapeutic Purposes

1. Introductory Considerations

234. Doctors, researchers, and legal experts are fully aware of the ethical and legal dilemmas raised by scientific advances that have proven effective in certain treatments and have contributed significantly to reducing child mortality and morbidity (e.g., conditions related to Rh incompatibility and respiratory diseases). These advancements have also deepened our understanding of nutrition, foetal endocrinology, pharmacology, prenatal diagnosis, improved delivery techniques, human fertility, and abortion procedures.

Despite the undeniable benefits of these practices, many have emphasized the need for regulation and oversight to prevent risks and manipulations involving live foetuses during pregnancy. Such actions could result in malformations that become evident after birth. Furthermore, regulation seeks to mitigate the risk of pregnancies and abortions being deliberately induced for research purposes or to harvest foetal tissues, with the consent of the mother – potentially in exchange for financial or other compensation.

Another crucial legal question concerns how to address experiments performed on live human foetuses extracted during legal abortions. Similarly, embryos created in vitro, whether intended for implantation or not, are valuable research material that is relatively easy to obtain. These biological components can also be used, and in some cases have been used, in the development of pharmacological and cosmetic products.

The ethical and legal debate on foetal research reflects divergent views. While the freedom to conduct research – recognized as a fundamental right in the Spanish Constitution (Article 20.1(b)) – promotes scientific progress for the benefit of current and future generations, it must be balanced against the need to protect embryos and foetuses, regardless of their status or ultimate fate (alive or deceased, viable or non-viable, conceived naturally or in vitro, terminated or otherwise, presenting serious or minor risks, or used for the benefit of science or the foetus itself).

2. Embryos, Pre-embryos, and Foetuses

235. The Spanish legal framework concerning the early stages of human life makes a somewhat controversial distinction between pre-embryos, embryos, and foetuses. According to Law 14/2007, a *pre-embryo* is defined as an in vitro embryo comprising a group of cells resulting from the progressive division of the fertilized ovum up to fourteen days after fertilization. An *embryo* refers to the phase of embryonic development from the moment the fertilized ovum is implanted in the uterus until the beginning of organogenesis, which occurs fifty-six days after fertilization, excluding periods when development may have been temporarily halted. A *foetus* is defined as an embryo with human appearance and fully formed organs, developing from the 57th day after fertilization until birth, again excluding any periods when development may have been paused.

3. Donation of Human Oocytes, Pre-embryos, Embryos, and Foetuses

236. The donation of human oocytes, pre-embryos, embryos, and foetuses is governed by Law 14/2006 (on Assisted Human Reproduction Techniques) and Law 14/2007 (on Biomedical Research).[363] According to Article 5 of Law 14/2006, the donation of gametes and pre-embryos for authorized purposes must be non-remunerative, formal, confidential, and based on mutual agreement between the donor and the authorized centre. Such donations must never be considered a commercial process or promoted with financial incentives.

Nevertheless, donors are entitled to financial compensation for physical inconvenience and travel expenses. The Ministry of Health and Consumer Affairs periodically sets the criteria and financial limits for this compensation to ensure that it does not become the sole incentive for donation.

The Ministry of Health, with authorization from the CNRHA, establishes the essential conditions to ensure that donations remain non-lucrative. Donations must be anonymous, and gamete banks must guarantee donor confidentiality. Individuals born through assisted reproduction have the right to obtain general information about donors but not their identities, except in extraordinary circumstances where disclosure is necessary for health reasons.

Law 14/2007 also establishes that in the case of oocytes, the donor's consent must explicitly authorize the use of specific techniques to be applied to the donated oocytes. Healthcare professionals responsible for collecting the oocytes must provide donors with appropriate information before obtaining their consent, which must be documented in writing (Article 32.2).

237. The donation of human embryos and foetuses is regulated by Law 14/2007. According to Article 29, such donations must meet the following requirements:

a. The donor(s) must provide prior written consent. If the donor is a non-emancipated minor or a person with a disability, consent must also be obtained from their legal representatives.
b. The donor(s) or their legal representatives must receive written information before providing consent. This information must explain the potential purposes of the donation, its consequences, the interventions required to extract embryonic or foetal cells or structures (including from the placenta or membranes), and the risks associated with these interventions.
c. The embryos or foetuses must have been expelled – either spontaneously or through induced termination – without the possibility of maintaining their vital autonomy, as specified in Article 28.3.2.

The law also clarifies that if the individual from whom the embryos or foetuses originate is deceased, the donation can proceed only if there is no record of their

363. *See* S. Romeo Malanda/F. Arias Aparicio/P. Nicolás Jiménez, 'Aspectos jurídicos de la obtención, utilización y circulación de los gametos humanos', *InDret. Revista para el Análisis del Derecho*, nº. 3, julio 2018, pp. 1–64.

express opposition. If the deceased is a minor or a person with a disability, the donation is permitted unless their legal representatives have recorded an explicit objection during the person's lifetime.

4. Research with Gametes, Pre-embryos, and Embryos Resulting from Artificial Reproduction Techniques ('In Vitro'): A General Approach

238. Law 14/2006 authorizes the use of gametes for basic or experimental research, provided that they are not subsequently used for reproduction (Article 14.1 and 14.2). The law also imposes limitations on diagnostic or therapeutic procedures involving pre-embryos (i.e., those that have not yet been implanted in a woman). Such procedures are only permitted for diagnostic or therapeutic purposes when there is a tangible benefit.

For diagnostic purposes, intervention is allowed exclusively to assess the viability or non-viability of the pre-embryo, detect hereditary diseases for treatment when possible, or recommend against transfer for procreation (Article 12.1).

For therapeutic purposes, intervention is permitted to treat a disease or prevent its transmission, provided there are reasonable and proven guarantees of success (Article 13.1).

In both cases, informed consent must be obtained from the couple or the woman providing the embryos, and the intervention must not alter the non-pathological genetic heritage (Article 13.2). Additionally, prior authorization from the corresponding HealthCare Division is mandatory (Article 13.3).

It is also important to note that Law 14/2007 explicitly states that intervention on a live embryo or foetus in utero is only permitted when the primary purpose is diagnostic or therapeutic, notwithstanding the legal provisions regarding the voluntary interruption of pregnancy (Article 30). Moreover, the law strictly prohibits the termination of pregnancy for the purpose of donation and later use of embryos, foetuses, or their biological structures (Article 28.2).

239. When the purpose of intervention is not the well-being of the embryo – particularly for research or experimental purposes – Spanish regulation combines the provisions of both Law 14/2006 and Law 14/2007. According to Law 14/2007, human embryos that have lost their capacity for biological development, as well as dead embryos or foetuses, may be donated for biomedical research or other diagnostic, therapeutic, pharmacological, clinical, or surgical purposes (Article 28).

However, the use of embryos and foetuses for research is only permitted under the following conditions (Article 31.1, Law 14/2007):

1. They must be deceased or have lost their capacity for biological development.
2. They must have been donated in accordance with the procedures established in Article 29 of Law 14/2007.
3. An application detailing the expected use must have been submitted and approved by the Guarantees Commission for the Donation and Use of Human Cells and Tissues.

4. Authorization must be granted by the corresponding autonomous or State authority.

Once the project has been authorized, the responsible research team must report the results to both the entity that authorized the project and the Guarantees Commission for the Donation and Use of Human Cells and Tissues (Article 31.2, Law 14/2007).

5. Research with Gametes, Pre-embryos, and Embryos Resulting from Artificial Reproduction Techniques ('In Vitro'): Guarantees and Procedures

240. Law 14/2007 establishes a series of requirements and guarantees for research involving human gametes, pre-embryos, embryos, and foetuses (Article 34). According to this law, research or experimentation with surplus oocytes or pre-embryos from assisted reproduction techniques – or their biological structures – for purposes such as obtaining, developing, and using embryonic stem cell lines or for other purposes unrelated to assisted reproduction techniques must meet the following requirements:

a. The research must adhere to ethical principles and the applicable legal framework, particularly the provisions of this law and its implementing regulations. It must follow the principles of relevance, feasibility, and suitability, with specific obligations placed on the principal investigator, the research team, and the facilities where the research is conducted.
b. The research must be based on a project that has been authorized by the State or an autonomous authority after obtaining approval from the Guarantees Commission for the Donation and Use of Human Cells and Tissues for projects involving matters specified in Article 35.2.

The authorization of research projects is subject to the inclusion of at least the following elements:

1. Authorization from the management of the research centre and approval from the corresponding CEI.
2. Disclosure of any relationships or interests – of any nature – or confirmation of their absence between the research team and the centre involved in the assisted reproduction process that generated the pre-embryos or obtained the oocytes.
3. A written agreement to provide the relevant public authority with data enabling the identification and tracking of the conservation status of cell lines obtained from the research.
4. An agreement to freely transfer cell lines obtained from the research to other researchers for their use.

5. When oocytes or pre-embryos are used, an indication and justification of their number and origin, along with a signed informed consent document from the donor(s) or progenitors, as applicable.

Furthermore, most research involving human pre-embryos, embryos, or foetuses requires prior approval from the Guarantees Commission for the Donation and Use of Human Cells and Tissues. This commission, composed of multiple experts and affiliated with the Instituto de Salud Carlos III, is a permanent consultative body that provides counsel and guidance on research and experimentation involving human embryonic biological samples. It also contributes to the dissemination and updating of scientific and technical knowledge in this field.

The most relevant examples of research requiring such approval include:

a. Research with human pre-embryos for the derivation of cell lines, embryological research, and other purposes unrelated to assisted reproduction techniques.
b. Research with human embryonic stem cells.
c. Activation of oocytes through nuclear transfer for therapeutic or research purposes.
d. Any technique that uses human biological samples – partially or wholly – to obtain stem cells.
e. Research with embryonic cells or tissues obtained through procedures mentioned in Article 33.2 (somatic cell nuclear transfer).
f. Any research line involving human embryonic cell material or other functionally similar material.
g. Research involving embryonic stem cell lines obtained from other countries, whether within or outside the EU. The project submitted for authorization must specify the origin of these cell lines.

6. Genetic Engineering and Human/Animal Chimeras and Hybrids

241. Gene therapy in Spain is regulated by Legislative Royal Decree 1/2015, of 24 July, which approves the revised text of the Law on Guarantees and Rational Use of Medicines and Health Products, further developed by Royal Decree 477/2014, of 13 June, regulating the authorization of non-industrially manufactured advanced therapy drugs.

However, any intervention aimed at introducing modifications to the genome of descendants – genetic engineering affecting the germline – is classified as a 'very serious' breach under Law 14/2007 (Article 74). This law also prohibits the creation of interspecific hybrids that involve human genetic material, except for specific cases provided for under the Law on Assisted Human Reproduction Techniques, mainly the Golden Hamster test. Both actions are punishable with fines ranging from EUR 10,001 to EUR 1,000,000 and may result in the revocation of research or activity authorization.

242. The Spanish Penal Code also considers the manipulation of human genes for purposes other than correcting or reducing serious defects or diseases a criminal offence. Article 159 establishes that anyone committing such an offence '*shall be punished with a sentence of imprisonment from two to six years and special disqualification from public employment or office, profession, or trade for seven to ten years'*.

Section 2 of the same article specifies: '*If the alteration of the genome is committed due to serious negligence, the punishment shall be a fine from six to fifteen months and disqualification from public employment or office, profession, or trade from one to three years.*'

7. Cloning and Stem Cell Research

243. Reproductive cloning is strictly prohibited in Spain. The Spanish Penal Code (Article 160) states: 'Those who fertilize human oocytes for any purpose other than human procreation shall be punished with a sentence of imprisonment from one to five years and special disqualification from public employment or office, profession, or trade for six to ten years. (…) The same penalty shall apply to the creation of identical human beings through cloning or other procedures aimed at racial selection.' Although the wording of this article lacks clarity, it is generally understood that reproductive cloning is prohibited. However, the offence is only committed when the cloned cell is transferred into a woman's uterus.

Therapeutic cloning, however, presents a more complex legal situation. As previously mentioned, the Convention on Human Rights and Biomedicine – which came into effect in Spain on 1 January 2000 – prohibits the creation of human embryos for research purposes under Article 18.2, thereby seemingly banning therapeutic cloning in all signatory countries, including Spain.

However, the Spanish government sought to circumvent this restriction. Law 14/2007 explicitly stated that nuclear transfer does not result in the creation of a human embryo. According to Article 3.1, an embryo is defined as: '*a phase of embryonic development from the moment the fertilized oocyte is implanted in a woman's uterus until the beginning of organogenesis, which ends 56 days from fertilization, excluding periods when development may have been halted*'.

Since nuclear transfer does not involve fertilization, it cannot be considered a process that creates a human embryo. Consistent with this interpretation, Article 33 of Law 14/2007 provides the following:

> Article 33. Obtaining Embryonic Cells
>
> 1. The creation of human pre-embryos and embryos exclusively for experimentation purposes is prohibited.
> 2. The use of any technique to obtain human stem cells for therapeutic or research purposes is permitted, provided it does not involve the creation of pre-embryos or embryos exclusively for this purpose, including the activation of oocytes through nuclear transfer.

Based on this legal framework, Spanish legislators affirmed in the Preamble to Law 14/2007 that: *'In accordance with the gradualist perspective on the protection*

the implanting of artificial mechanisms or anatomical parts from animals raise specific legal issues to which the current legislation may not be able to provide clear and precise answers.

247. Objectives set out in the Law. From the above, the importance of a carefully thought-out body of law which balances all the interests that come into play in the long and complex process of a transplant is self-evident. The legislation addresses these important issues in line with current European and global trends and sets out three main objectives in an effort to clarify any potential technical and legal problems:

2. To facilitate the obtaining of viable – usable – organs for subsequent transplant operations performed on persons in medical need of such organs.
3. To adequately protect the rights and interests of the individuals concerned so as to balance any possible conflicting interests, chiefly those of the living donor, the deceased donor and the recipient.
4. To provide a legal framework for medical professionals and health authorities within which they may carry out such operations unhindered by difficulties and in accordance with guidelines which are, at least in theory, clear and easy to follow.

II. The Living Donor

248. Although the giving of organs by living persons for subsequent transplant to a person suffering from an illness who requires the organ affects the integrity of the body, which is in principle punishable by law (Articles 147 and ff. of the Penal Code on bodily harm offences), it is explicitly permitted by the 1979 Law and by the Penal Code itself (Article 156). It is not enough for the operation to be performed by qualified personnel (a surgeon) for this exemption to come into effect. The donor must also give his/her consent and all other requirements of the Law (Article 4) of Royal Decree 1723/2012 (Article 8) and of Royal Decree-Law 9/2014 (Article 7) must be strictly adhered to.

249. Age and legal capacity restrictions. The donor must have attained the age of legal majority (18 years), be in full possession of his/her mental faculties and be in sufficiently good health for the removal to be performed (Article 4 a and b of the Law). This means that minors may not give their organs (e.g., for use by a brother or sister who is suffering from an illness and who is also a minor), even where consent is given through the parents, as this is considered to exceed the scope of the rights and duties inherent in parental authority (Articles 154 and ff. and 162 and ff. of the CC). This is intended to safeguard the interests of the minor, who, without such protection from the Law, would find difficulty in not succumbing to the moral pressure brought to bear by the family or/and would be subject to the danger of the family consenting on his/her behalf (if he is unable to express his/her own consent) in the interests of the recipient and at his/her expense. The same principles underlie the exclusion of the intellectually disabled, those suffering psychiatric illness or persons who for any other reason are unable to give their explicit, free and conscious consent. However, the Royal Decree-Law 9/2014 (Article 7.1) makes an exception in the case of surgical residues or haematopoietic stem cells or other tissues or cell groups reproducible (*except in the case of surgical residues or haematopoietic stem cells or other tissues or cell groups reproducible whose therapeutic indication is or may be vital to the recipient*) because of its capacity for regeneration and because donation and transplant usually concern siblings.

250. Limitations related to the organ. The organ must be one whose removal is compatible with the continuing life of the donor and whose function can be compensated adequately and in a sufficiently safe way by the donor organism (Article 8 Royal Decree 1723/2012). As a result, the law allows the donation of organs or tissue provided that removal does not permanently affect the health or endanger the life of the donor. The donor's physical or psychological capacities should not be diminished by the removal of the organ, nor should it result in the loss of any important bodily function. For this reason, single vital organs may not be removed nor may single remaining organs from pairs (in cases of the prior damage to or loss of the second organ as a result of illness or injury). Limbs are also excluded as are any parts of the body the removal of which would involve diminished bodily functions. The removal of paired or double organs is permissible when the remaining organ can act as a functional substitute. The same is true of regenerative tissue (blood, bone marrow, bones, cartilage, etc.). A full and thorough medical examination of the donor is therefore needed to determine whether or not his/her current health would result in him being seriously affected by the removal of the organ. In the case of obtention of organs, if the donor's physical and mental health is good enough for the removal to go ahead, a physician other than the one(s) who will perform the operation must make a statement to that effect (Article 8.3 of the Royal Decree 1723/2012). This physician is also responsible for providing the donor with all necessary information. In the case of obtention of organs, it is compulsory to have a favourable report from the Ethics Committee concerned.

251. Donor information and consent. The donor must previously have been informed of all consequences stemming from his/her decision and must have freely, consciously and impartially given his/her express consent. This is the key to the donor consent requirement, which is fundamental. In the first place, for consent to be valid, it is essential that the donor has previously been fully informed as to the foreseeable somatic, emotional and psychological consequences involved and the long-term implications that donation may have in terms of his/her personal, family and professional life. At the same time, he should be provided with information about the benefits that the transplant might be expected to imply for the recipient (Article 8 of the RD 1723/2012 in the case of organs and Article 7 Royal Decree-Law 9/2014 in the case of cells and tissues). The relevant information must be given in an appropriate format. In the case of obtention of organs, consent must also be given in the presence of the judge (during the hearing in the course of the voluntary jurisdiction process opened for the transplantation), the physicians who provided the information and the doctor who is to perform the removal of the organ as well as the responsible person to give his/her conformity to the transplant.

Clearly, valid consent can only be given for the donation of the organs and tissues referred to above, in view of the fact that in Law, valid consent to endangering one's own life cannot be given (e.g., consent to donating a vital organ). Neither is consent valid if it has been obtained under pressure or through coercion (e.g., from members of the family of the would-be recipient of the organ) or where financial or material interests have influenced the decision to give the organ concerned, as we will *see* below. The possibility of the donor withdrawing consent is considered. Consent may be withdrawn at any time prior to the operation without any further formality being required (an exception arises in cases of collection of haematopoietic progenitor cells from peripheral blood or bone marrow where revocation can only occur before the start of the conditioning at the receiver). Withdrawal of consent cannot give rise to any kind of claim for compensation.

252. *Restrictions governing the subsequent use made of the organ.* The Law stipulates that the organ must be for transplant in a specific individual with the purpose of substantially improving the person's chances of survival or quality of life (Article 4d, 1979 Law). This requirement, which may seem obvious, implies that the whole process of donation must revolve around a specific potential recipient, in most cases, a member of the donor's family. The process, therefore, begins with histocompatibility studies of both parties, along with all other tests deemed necessary to guarantee the viability and success of the transplant operation. As a result, the process of donation by a living person may not commence until a candidate recipient has been selected, nor can the organ subsequently be donated to someone else, as this would mean beginning the process all over again in order to comply with all the requirements of the Law. The clearly therapeutic nature of the operation, as stipulated by the Law, rules out donations for primarily experimental or research purposes, although this does not mean that the operation may not involve a certain degree of uncertainty as regards a successful outcome.

253. *Anonymity of the recipient.* Finally, the law stipulates that the anonymity of the recipient must be guaranteed. Clearly, we are faced here with a *Tapsus Legislature* if this is also to be understood to apply to the donor, which would run counter to the other (and particularly the last of the) requirements noted above. Donations by living donors are usually made for members of their own family as a sign of solidarity and affection. This requirement, which is not adhered to in practice, does make sense in the case of donations after death as it would thus prevent members of the donor's family later taking advantage of the situation by demanding some kind of material or financial compensation from the recipient (alleging, for example, that the donor was the sole source of financial support for the family). It is, however, possible to arrive at a more satisfactory interpretation that eliminates this apparent incoherence, as we shall see shortly.

254. *Consequences of donation: the lawful removal of the organ, cells and tissues.* Adherence to all the above-mentioned requirements means that the attack on the physical integrity of the donor that the donation implied is lawful, as is the

operation performed by the surgeon. Failure to comply in any way with the regulations (regulations are understood to mean material and substantial requirements and not merely formal or procedural requirements which would only give rise to an administrative offence only) is equivalent to the offence of mutilation and is severely punished by the Penal Code (Articles 149 and 150).

These observations are endorsed by the Spanish Penal Code, which explicitly recognizes the possibility of consenting to attacks on one's physical integrity if this takes place in accordance with the provisions of the Law governing Organ Transplants. This provision is laid down in Article 156 of the Penal Code, which sets out the various conditions that must be fulfilled. These are essentially the same as those contained in the 1979 Law on removal and transplant, which can thus be regarded as being unaltered by the reform of the Penal Code.[368] Furthermore, the fact that the Penal Code makes explicit reference to this Law means that the other requirements continue to be applicable where the provisions of the Penal Code are not sufficient.

III. The Deceased Donor

255. The Law on transplants (Article 5 of the 1979 Law and Article 9 Royal Decree 1723/2012) and to an even greater extent the Penal Code[369] seek to guarantee effective medical assistance and protection of the life of a potential *post-mortem* donor while even the most minimal chance of recovery exists. Nevertheless, this very real protection is compatible with the possibility of obtaining organs for subsequent transplant in the case of the death of the potential donor. It is on this question that the Law has been particularly explicit as regards resolving potential legal problems. At the same time, it is here that most disagreement exists. There are two conflictive issues which we will examine now.

256. Definition, diagnosis and verification of death. Within the biological process of destruction entailed in the death of living beings, a precise moment at which the process is irreversible must be fixed. Once this point is reached, there is no possibility of saving the life of the individual in question (precisely because death has occurred). The moment must also be established early enough to ensure that organs and tissues may be removed and that they have not been affected by the process of destruction and are therefore suitable for transplant. A balance must, therefore, be struck through an early but faithful diagnosis of the moment of death, from which point on, it is possible to remove the organs in biological conditions consistent with

368. Article 156 reads as follows: '*Notwithstanding the provisions of the previous article, valid, explicit, conscious and freely given consent removes criminal liability in the case of organ transplants carried out in accordance with the Law, sterilizations and transsexual surgery performed by a physician, unless consent has been obtained under false pretences or through pressure or the promise of financial gain or if the person giving consent is a minor or is legally incompetent, in which neither this consent nor that of the legal representatives shall be valid.*'

369. *See* Arts 138, 139, 143, 195 and 196: the crimes of homicide, murder, assisting a suicide, failure to fulfil the duty to answer a call for help and refusal of giving medical healthcare, respectively.

transplant.[370] Any doubt as to determining the moment when death occurs must be resolved in favour of the potential *post-mortem* donor to the exclusion of all other interests, no matter how important and pressing they may seem.

In contrast to the previous legislation (of 1950), the current Law has rightly established the point of reference for determining death as not depending on the cessation of certain vital functions, such as circulation or breathing, which can now be maintained artificially almost indefinitely. The Law takes as an alternative point of departure permanent, irreversible brain damage, which is incompatible with life (Article 5.1). This starting point and the other guarantees that are required for the death certificate to be issued should be viewed as being highly positive, given that in current medical practice, an irreversible comatose state is considered to be sufficient basis for certifying that death has occurred. The Royal Decree 1723/2012 stipulates the conditions that must be fulfilled before such a diagnosis can be made (Article 9 and Annex I); namely, certain signs deemed to be incompatible with life.

257. The specific conditions that the diagnostic team must fulfil in transplant cases constitute additional guarantees for the potential donor: the team must comprise three physicians, at least one of whom should be a specialist in procedures for determining death.[371] All three physicians must agree to certify death and must not be involved in the removal and subsequent transplant of the organ.

258. Deceased donors; relevance of wishes. Major conflicts arise where there is a legal assumption that anyone who dies is a donor unless during his/her lifetime he has explicitly stated that he does not wish to be a donor: 'The removal of organs or other anatomical parts from deceased persons may be performed for therapeutic or scientific purposes so long as he has not explicitly expressed opposition to this.' (Article 5.2 of the Law).

Despite the somewhat striking nature of this sentence, it should be noted that it is not so striking as previous legislation, in which the notion of assumed willingness to act as a donor was included as a third subsidiary procedure in potential donor cases that were subject to legal intervention (instances of violent death, as is known, are usually the most suitable for organ donation from the medical point of view) and the lack of opposition referred not to the deceased but to his/her family. A criterion similar to that of the Spanish Law of 1979 was adopted by the Council of Europe and proposed to the Member States in Resolution 78 (Article 29). The World Health Organisation takes a similar approach in its Guiding Principles for the Transplant of Human Organs (1991).

Of the various alternative criteria which the Legislature could have opted for the following deserve mention:

1. express wishes of the deceased made known during his/her lifetime authorizing donation;

370. *See* C.M. Romeo Casabona, *Los trasplantes de órganos. Informe y documentación para la reforma de la legislación española sobre trasplantes de órganos* (Bosch, Barcelona 1979), pp. 61 and ff.
371. The team shall comprise a Neurologist or Neurosurgeon and the Chief Medical Officer of the unit or his/her substitute (Art. 5 of the Law and Art. 9 Royal Decree 1723/2012).

2. the same criterion with the addition of the subsidiary criterion (in the absence of consent on the part of the deceased) of consent by the deceased person's family;
3. absence of explicit opposition on the part of the deceased or his/her family;
4. lack of opposition on the part of the deceased alone; and
5. no consideration given to the wishes of the individual concerned.[372]

259. Independently of what has just been stated, it is necessary to analyse the drawbacks that the alternatives imply in an effort to better understand the Spanish Legislature's reasoning in rejecting them:

1. Positive act of personal donation. In the first place, we have the criterion of voluntary personal donation, that is to say, a positive declaration of the desire of the individual citizen to freely donate his/her organs, to take effect after death. This solution causes a variety of problems, particularly with regard to the fact that there is a very high potential demand for the organs of deceased persons and the difficulties involved in finding a donor and recipient who are biologically compatible. Furthermore, cadavers that fulfil the stringent medical conditions that provide minimum guarantees of transplant viability are rare. Only those killed in road accidents and a further small number from accidents in the workplace with very localized head injuries (haemorrhages, tumours, vascular accidents) or cardiac arrest are usually considered to be genuinely viable candidates for organ donation, with the additional provision that they die in a hospital equipped to remove organs. Public information campaigns designed to create a favourable attitude towards organ donations are costly and are slow to produce what are not particularly satisfactory results in the long term. They must reach the entire population and be repeated over and over again to maintain the desired level of awareness among the population. As we shall *see* below, the task of providing information is, nevertheless, extremely important and is dealt with in the Spanish regulations.
2. Irrelevance of the wishes of the individual. Neither does it seem appropriate to disregard altogether the wishes of the deceased, as made known during his/her lifetime. A series of cultural norms – of social and religious origin – in our society seek to maintain respect for the dead through a kind of spiritual bond between society – particularly family and friends – and the deceased. The Law has weighed up these collective sentiments and has regarded them as worthy of protection. For this reason, the Penal Code punishes profanation of cadavers when there is a lack of respect for the memory of the death (Article 526). Respect for the deceased's memory also implies observing whatever wishes he would have expressed in terms of his/her body during his/her lifetime (so long as these do not violate any other public order requirements), for example, as regards his/her willingness or opposition to having parts of the body removed

372. *See* a fuller account in Romeo Casabona, *Los trasplantes de órganos*, *supra*, pp. 71 and ff.

and transplanted to another person suffering from an illness. Transplant legislation seeks to respond to this concept by requiring the restoration and preservation of the cadaver.

260. The irrelevance of the deceased's family's wishes in the Spanish legislation. The Spanish Law does not require the consent of the family of the deceased except where minors or mentally deficient persons are concerned.[373] The reasoning given above is also valid here. It is a question of respecting the wishes of the deceased, not those of his/her family – whose wishes may be in conflict with those of the deceased – although at the same time, it is recognized that the family are most likely to know or be able to indicate the wishes of the deceased if they were made known during his/her lifetime. But this does not mean that they have property rights over the cadaver because no such right exists. Furthermore, from the humanitarian point of view, it woud seem ill-advised to subject the family to a further emotional burden after being informed of the sudden tragic death of a loved one – husband, son, daughter, etc. To do otherwise would be tantamount to burdening them with moral responsibility for deciding if another person should continue to live or have a better life as a result of their consent. They should not have to take on this responsibility in the first place, nor are they in the best position to do so. Because of this, the Law makes no mention of them, but the Royal Decree 1273/2012 indicates that the Hospital's Transplant coordinator, or the person to which he/she delegates, shall carry out the necessary checks on the will of the deceased person:

1) investigate whether the donor made clear its will to any of his/her relatives or to the professionals who have treated him at the hospital, through the notes that they have done in the clinical history, or by the means provided in the current legislation.[374] Nevertheless, it is customary for physicians (or tansplant coordinators) to seek the agreement of the family of the deceased, which is a sensible precaution as long as it is done tactfully.

Finally, it should be noted that even though no real conflict of interest arises in practice, the intangibility of the cadaver and the respect for related wishes in this regard (such as society values) are played off against the life and health of other persons. If any conflict were to occur, the criminal law would provide the appropriate answer and would normally come down in favour of the life and health of the recipient.

261. As a means of recording possible opposition to the removal of organs, procedures for the provision of information and a register of volunteers have been established in authorized hospitals. It is clear that recourse may be made to other means apart from those established by the Regulations (Article 9 Royal Decree

373. In fact, the Law does not establish exceptions for these last two circumstances. For organs, Royal Decree 1723/2012 states that 'where minors or mentally deficient patients are concerned, opposition may be expressed by their legal representatives according to the civil legislation' (Art. 9.1) while the same applies for cells and tissues according to Art. 8.1 Royal Decree-Law 9/2014.
374. Article 9.1 of the Royal Decree 1723/2012.

1723/2012) to ascertain any possible opposition on the part of a potential donor (written declarations, membership of religious or ideological groups that are clearly opposed to interference with the cadaver, information from the family of the deceased, etc.). Possession of a donor card – one which is compatible with legal requirements – such as those issued by Associations of Patients (Federación Nacional ALCER), some Autonomous Communities or the ONT or other such regional organizations makes the task of determining the wishes of the deceased very much easier.

IV. The Recipient

262. In contrast to the legislation of other countries, which do not concern themselves with this question, Spanish legislation includes guarantees to protect the recipient of the organ, as it is the recipient who is in fact subject to the main risks. These guarantees are as follows: that the operation is for therapeutic purposes; that the necessary medical tests have been performed prior to the operation and that all appropriate specific preparation has been undertaken and that the patient has been fully informed and has given his/her consent or that the family or legal representatives have consented in the case of minors and the mentally disabled (Article 6 of the Law). The Law has been particularly meticulous and scrupulous in its efforts to protect the legal interests of the recipient of an organ transplant and anticipate the rights established by Article 10 of the LGS (updated by Law 41/2002 nowadays in force – *see* Articles 4 ff.), which also apply here.

Given that decisions taken are always of the greatest importance to the recipient, it is essential that the information requirement is scrupulously fulfilled prior to the transplant. Information is normally provided on two occasions: when the need for the transplant becomes evident and the patient's name is put on the waiting list and again when an organ becomes available for the recipient. The 1979 Law (Articles 6.1 and 2) is unequivocal as regards this information requirement, as is Law 41/2002 on a more general level.

A problem arises in the selection of recipients and the criteria used to establish priority of one recipient over another. Clearly, only strictly objective medical criteria agreed upon by professionals can be considered in decisions concerning selection and priority. First and foremost, it must be established that the patient is not suffering from a serious illness, the risks of which would be greatly increased by surgery and, second, that he is in urgent need of the transplant. Optimum histocompatibility between the organ and recipient (and therefore the optimum chances of success) is also a prime consideration. A secondary criterion would be the length of time the patient has been waiting. On no account should social considerations be brought to bear,[375] or should a patient be rejected because he suffers from another (corregible) illness (e.g., an alcoholic recipient of a liver transplant).

375. *See* World Health Organisation, *Guiding Principles on Human Cell, Tissue and Organ Transplantation* (as endorsed by the sixty-two World Health Assembly in May 2010, Resolution WHA63.22),

V. Other General Guarantees

263. The guarantees described above refer to the requirements for transplants and are designed to protect the interests of donors and recipients alike. There are, however, further requirements that also protect these individuals, albeit less directly, and that in one way or another contribute significantly to the achievement of the objectives enumerated at the beginning of this section. The successful putting in place and functioning of the legal mechanisms designed to serve these objectives depend on these requirements. It should be said that many of these go beyond the limits of the purely legal framework, as they depend on the existence of the appropriate structure, organization and planning of health services and on funding.

264. Prohibition on the use of organs for commercial ends. Organs may not be bought or sold, nor may the donor or members of his/her family or third parties ('intermediaries', hospitals, pharmaceutical or research laboratories) receive money in exchange for organs. The costs of donation should not have to be met by the donor or his/her family (Article 2 of the Law). By this means, injustices that might easily occur both in the case of recipients and potential donors with limited financial resources or other limitations (e.g., prisoners seeking a reduction in their sentence) can be avoided. Even if in Spain, no instances of the sale of organs of living persons have actually occurred, despite occasional attempts, the possible damage that can be done by simply offering such organs for sale in the media should not be underestimated. Such offers would cause great confusion among the general public and could even lead people to withdraw their names from donor lists.

This issue has acquired great importance in recent years because of claims that a black market in organs in developing countries benefits patients in the developed world or in rich countries. In Spain, the buying and selling of organs from living or deceased persons is not only prohibited, as we have just seen, but severely punished by the Penal Code (Article 156 bis Penal Code).[376]

Article 156 bis CP:

1. Anyone who in any way promotes, favors, facilitates, publicises or executes the trafficking of human organs shall be punished with a prison sentence of six to twelve years in the case of the organ of a living person and a prison sentence of three to six years in the case of the organ of a deceased person.

Guiding Principle 9: 'The allocation of organs, cells and tissues should be guided by clinical criteria and ethical norms, not financial and other considerations. Allocations rules, defined by appropriately constituted committees, should be equitable, externally justified and transparent.'

376. *See* C. Moya Guillem, 'Consideraciones sobre el delito de tráfico de órganos', in *Anuario de la Facultad de Derecho de la Universidad Autónoma de Madrid*, 18, 2014, pp. 45–66; C. Alastuey Dobón, 'Aspectos problemáticos del delito de tráfico de órganos', in *Revista Penal*, núm. 32, 2013, pp. 3–22; C. Gómez Rivero, 'El delito de tráfico ilegal de órganos humanos', in *Revista Penal*, núm. 31, 2013, pp. 113–133; L.M. Puente Aba, 'La protección frente al tráfico de órganos: su reflejo en el Código penal', in *Revista Derecho y proceso penal*, núm. 26, 2011, pp. 135–151; C.M. Romeo Casabona, 'La prohibición del tráfico ilegal y la exclusión de la comercialización de los órganos y tejidos', in *Revista Aranzadi Doctrinal*, núm. 7, 2010, pp. 171–180.

For these purposes, trafficking in human organs shall be understood to mean:

(a) the unlawful removal or procurement of another person's human organs. Said removal or procurement shall be unlawful if it is carried out in any of the following circumstances:
   1. that it has been carried out without the free, informed and express consent of the living donor in the manner and with the requirements provided for by law;
   2. that it has been carried out without the necessary authorisation required by law in the case of the deceased donor,
   3. in exchange for the extraction or procurement, for the donor's own benefit or that of another, a gift or payment of any kind is requested or received by the donor or a third party, either personally or through an intermediary, or an offer or promise is accepted. A gift or payment shall not include the reimbursement of expenses or loss of income resulting from the donation.

(b) The preparation, preservation, storage, transportation, transport, transfer, receipt, import or export of illegally harvested organs.

(c) The use of illegally harvested organs for the purpose of transplantation or for other purposes.

2. The same shall apply to those who, for their own benefit or for the benefit of others:
   (a) solicit or receive, either personally or through an intermediary, a gift or payment of any kind, or accept an offer or promise for proposing or recruiting an organ donor or recipient;
   (b) they offer or give, themselves or through an intermediary, a gift or payment of any kind to medical personnel, public officials or private individuals in the exercise of their profession or position in public or private clinics, establishments or surgeries, for the purpose of carrying out or facilitating the unlawful removal or procurement or implantation of organs that have been unlawfully removed.
3. If the recipient of the organ consents to the transplant knowing of its illegal origin, he or she shall be punished with the same penalties provided for in section 1, which may be reduced by one or two degrees depending on the circumstances of the act and of the guilty party.
4. The penalties provided for in paragraph 1 shall be increased in degree when:
   (a) the life or physical or mental integrity of the victim of the offence has been seriously endangered.
   (b) the victim is a minor or is particularly vulnerable on account of his or her age, disability, illness or situation.

   If both circumstances are present, the penalty shall be imposed in the upper half.
5. Any practitioner, public official or private individual who, in the exercise of their profession or position, carries out the conduct described in paragraphs 1 and 2 in public or private centres, or requests or receives the gift or remuneration referred to in letter b) of the latter paragraph, or accepts

the offer or promise to receive it, shall be liable to the penalty indicated therein which is higher in degree and, in addition, to that of special disqualification from public employment or office, profession or trade, from exercising any health profession or from providing services of any kind in clinics, establishments or surgeries, whether public or private, for the duration of the sentence. If, in addition, any of the circumstances provided for in paragraph 4 apply, the penalties shall be imposed in the upper half of the sentence.

For the purposes of this Article, the term practitioner includes doctors, nursing staff and any other person who carries out a health or social-health activity.

6. The penalty higher in degree than that provided for in section 1 and special disqualification for profession, trade, industry or commerce shall be imposed for the duration of the sentence, when the offender belongs to a criminal organisation or group dedicated to carrying out such activities. If any of the circumstances provided for in paragraph 4 apply, the penalties shall be imposed in the upper half of the sentence. If the circumstance provided for in paragraph 5 applies, the penalties provided for in that paragraph shall be imposed in the upper half.

   In the case of the heads, administrators or persons in charge of such organisations or groups, the penalty shall be applied in the upper half of the sentence, which may be increased to the next higher degree. In any case, the penalty shall be increased to the next higher degree if any of the circumstances provided for in paragraph 4 or the circumstance provided for in paragraph 5 apply.
7. Where, in accordance with the provisions of Article 31 bis a legal person is liable for the offences referred to in this Article, it shall be liable to a fine of three to five times the amount of the benefit obtained.

   In accordance with the rules laid down in Article 66 bis, the judges and courts may also impose the penalties set out in Article 33(7)(b) to (g).
8. Provocation, conspiracy and proposition to commit the offences provided for in this Article shall be punishable by a penalty one to two degrees lower than that corresponding, respectively, to the acts provided for in the previous paragraphs.
9. In any case, the penalties provided for in this Article shall be imposed without prejudice to those corresponding, where appropriate, to the offence of Article 177 bis of this Code and other offences actually committed.

   Convictions by foreign judges or courts for offences of the same nature as those provided for in this Article shall produce the effects of recidivism, unless the criminal record has been cancelled or may be cancelled under Spanish law.

In 2019, the Spanish legislature proceeded to reform Article 156 bis of the Criminal Code (offence of organ trafficking) in order to adapt it to the provisions contained in the Council of Europe Convention on the fight against trafficking in human organs, opened for signature in Santiago de Compostela on 25 March 2015. This reform completed the system for the prevention and prosecution of the crime of trafficking in human organs, which constitutes a serious violation of the fundamental rights of individuals and seriously undermines legal assets such as life, physical integrity and human dignity, as well as poses a major threat to public health. Spain has been and continues to be a regulatory benchmark in Europe and Latin America in the field of human organ transplantation thanks to robust controls that impose the principles of voluntariness, altruism, confidentiality, non-profit and free-of-charge. Therefore, in order to preserve this state of affairs and in view of the growing risks, such as the proliferation of transnational organized crime groups that make use of violence, deception or threats or take advantage of situations of precariousness of the alleged donor to acquire high profits, the legislator proceeded to reform the offence of organ trafficking (adapting it to the 2015 Council of Europe Convention on the subject) in order to strengthen a system whose bankruptcy would ultimately undermine the confidence of the population as a whole in the system.

The World Health Organisation implemented various measures in an effort to stamp out these practices elsewhere: the World Health Assembly adopted resolution WHA 42.5 on the prevention of the buying and selling of organs on 15 May 1989, while its *Guiding Principles on Human Cell, Tissue and Organ Transplantation* (as endorsed by the 62 World Health Assembly in May 2010, Resolution WHA 63.22) devotes several principles to this prohibition: principle 5 ('Cells, tissues and organs should only be donated freely, without any monetary payment or other reward of monetary value. Purchasing, or offering to purchase, cells, tissues or organs for transplantation, or their sale by living persons or by the next of kin for deceased persons, should be banned. The prohibition on sale or purchase of cells, tissues and organs does not preclude reimbursing reasonable and verifiable expenses incurred by the donor, including loss of income, or paying the costs or recovering, processing, preserving and supplying human cells, tissues or organs for transplantation'), principle 6 ('promotion of altruistic donation of human cells, tissues or organs by means of advertisement or public appeal may be undertaken in accordance with domestic regulation. Advertising the need of or availabiltiy of cells, tissues or organs, with a view to offering or seeking payment to individuals for their cells, tissues or organs, or, to the next of kin, where the individual is deceased, should be prohibited. Brokering that involves payment to such individuals or to third parties should also be prohibited'), principle 7 ('physicians and other health professionals should not engage in transplantation procedures, and health insurers and other payers should not cover such procedures, if the cells, tissues or organs concerned have been obtained through exploitation or coercion of, or payment to, the donor or the next of kin of a deceased donor'), principle 8 ('all health care facilities and professionals involve in cell, tissue or organ procurement and transplantation procedures should be prohibited from receiving any payment that exceeds the justifiable fee for the services rendered') and principle 9 ('The allocation of organs, cells and tissues should be guided by clinical criteria and ethical norms, not financial and other considerations. Allocations rules, defined by appropriately constituted committees, should be equitable, externally justified and transparent'). Article 14 of the Council of Europe's Resolution (78) 29 and Articles 4.1(b) and (c) or 7 Council of Europe Convention on the fight against trafficking in human organs (2015) also prohibit profit making.

A significant preventive measure with regard to the trafficking of organs taken from cadavers is the use of all possible means to guarantee that the recipient should not know anything that would identify the donor or his/her family and, similarly, that the donor's family at the same time should have no information about the recipient and his/her family. Responsibility for maintaining this level of confidentiality lies with the staff of the healthcare centre, regardless of their professional status or the nature of their duties. This obligation is explicitly stated in the current regulations with regard to organ transplants.

265. Intervention by the legal authorities. The removal of organs from those who have died of unnatural causes (through accident or any other kind of violent death) requires prior authorization by the Judge responsible for the case. He shall give this authorization where removal does not present any obstacle to the pre-trial investigation, the cause of death being apparently clear (Article 5.3 of the 1979 Law). Strictly speaking, this is not a guarantee relevant to the transplant process but rather to the work of the Judge in that it prevents the removal of organs in situations where this would hinder the establishment of the causes of death in cases where death may give rise to liability (either civil or criminal) or an insurance claim etc.

266. Recognition of hospitals and medical teams. Authorization is only granted to those hospitals and teams that meet the stringent material, technical and professional conditions established by the law and that can provide evidence of adequate training and experience in these techniques and in associated treatments.[377] The health authorities take responsibility for supervising the work of these hospitals and teams and may even withdraw authorization if performance is unsatisfactory or falls below the standards for which authorization was initially granted.

267. Organizations for the exchange of organs from cadavers. The ONT and Autonomic Coordinations. In accordance with Law 30/1979 (Article 7), these organizations enable maximum benefit to be obtained from organs made available for transplant by means, for example, of locating the most suitable recipient – or even the recipient in most urgent need. Organs can be made available through the system to other centres in the same city or elsewhere in Spain and abroad. The system also controls the preservation of parts of bodies in 'organ banks' when this is scientifically feasible.

In order to achieve qualitative and quantitative improvement in transplant services, it is essential to strengthen the regional health organizations and the national coordination of organ exchanges so as to ensure that the maximum number of organs can be removed and transplanted, optimum compatibility between the organ and the recipient can be achieved and also that patients in urgent need (hyperimmunised patients, those who are terminally ill as the result of the failure of single vital organs or the remaining organ from a pair) can be given the fastest possible access to transplants. This will help redress regional imbalances and give fuller effect to the principle of equality of access to medical assistance (Article 3 of the

377. *See* Art. 3 of the Law of 1979 and Arts 10 and 11 of the Royal Decree 1723/2012.

Health General Law). Responsibility for these functions lies with the ONT and the Authonomic Coordinations, which must be coordinated and supervised by the National Organisation.

The creation of the position of Transplant Coordinator is a further important step in terms of the coordination and optimum use of organs or potential donors. Coordinators in each hospital involved in the removal and/or transplant of organs, regional coordinators for the Authonomic Coordinations mentioned above and a National Coordinator (who is also the director of the ONT) have been appointed.

The ONT not only was established under the Resolution of 27 June 1980 (being regulated at present by RD 1825/2009) but is also subject to the provisions of the Spanish Constitution of 1978 concerning the competences of the Autonomous Communities in the area of health and to the health system structure. Another more recent procedure that has contributed to an increase in the number of transplants and to increased organ mobility is the removal of several organs from a single donor.

268. Information and health education. Royal Decree 1723/2012 (Article 6) provides for the carrying out of frequent and extensive information and educational campaigns to increase awareness of the contents of the Law, particularly in relation to the obtaining of organs from cadavers, thereby reducing the difficulties entailed in informing the family of the deceased at the moment of death and eliminating the all too often need for medical staff to seek their approval in order to avoid complications.

§7. Research with Human Beings

I. Conflicting Interests

269. Research in Medicine and the Biological Sciences has gradually improved our well-being and indeed our life expectancy. In the final analysis, after the appropriate laboratory studies and experimentation on animals, research almost always requires the testing on human subjects of new techniques and substances to which beneficial or therapeutic effects are attributed. It is at this point that the question of certain individuals (healthy or otherwise) becoming subjects of experiments arises, with all the risks and dangers that experimentation entails, even though these risks need not necessarily affect the experimental subjects themselves. A potential conflict of interests or of crucial values arises: on the one hand, there is the need to carry out research with the obvious benefits that this brings to society and, on occasions, to the individual who has acted as an experimental subject; on the other, there is the right of these individuals not to sustain any damage to their health or to expose their lives to grave dangers, not to mention the protection of other individual interests that may be affected, such as freedom. The need for research is fully recognized in our legal order, but when it comes to experimentation on human subjects, a series of provisions directly or indirectly seek to prevent any injury or harm to the person, given that his/her most prized legal interests are at stake.[378]

270. Because of differing objectives, effects, limitations and possible legal consequences, it is usual to draw a distinction between therapeutic experimentation and pure experimentation. The former consists of the application to specific patients of treatments the efficacy of which has not yet been entirely established from the scientific point of view and which, therefore, have not been included among medically recognized treatments. Pure experimentation refers to research carried out on those suffering from diseases or on healthy individuals with a view to obtaining scientific results that do not imply any immediate benefit to the person who acted as an experimental subject. This second type of experimentation is, therefore, governed by more stringent conditions.

II. Relevant Legislation

271. The Spanish Constitution recognizes and protects the right to 'literary, artistic, scientific and technical production and invention' (Article 20.1b) as one of the fundamental public rights. It is obvious that scientific and technical production and invention inevitably involve research. At the same time, given its social significance, our Constitution also stipulates in the chapter devoted to guiding principles of social and economic policy that 'the public authorities shall promote science and scientific and technical research in the interests of the community' (Article 44.2). Having said that, the fundamental right to scientific and technical invention and production is limited by the Spanish Constitution itself when it alludes to *respect for the rights recognized under the same heading* as the one in which this right is set out, namely, fundamental rights and duties (Article 20.4).

In fact, the constitutional prohibition of inhuman or degrading treatment (Article 15) imposes limits on *research and experimentation on human beings* and is confirmed here because Spain has ratified and officially published the International Covenant on Civil and Political Rights of 1966 (13 April 1977, Official State Journal of 30 April) and it thus forms part of the domestic law (Article 96.1 of the Spanish Constitution). The Covenant groups both aspects together when it states that 'no-one shall be subjected to torture nor to cruel and degrading punishment or treatment. *In particular*, no-one shall be subjected to medical or scientific experiments without their freely given consent' (Article 7). The LGS provides for the minimum precautions and guarantees necessary when it requires that the patient be informed and that he gives his/her consent prior to the experiment, that the doctor and the administration of the healthcare centre agree to the experiment and, above all, that 'under no circumstances should it involve additional dangers to health [that of the patient]' (Article 10.4 of the LGS). These requirements, together with the principles of preservation of dignity and privacy and the avoidance of discrimination, underpin more specific legislation, namely, the Legislative Royal Decree 1/2015, of 24 July, which

378. C.M. Romeo Casabona, 'Aspectos jurídicos de la experimentación humana', in *Revista de la Facultad de Derecho de la Universidad Complutense de Madrid*, nº. 11, 1986, pp. 569 and ff.

approves the refunded text of the Law on guarantees and rational use of medicines and health products; the Royal Decree 1090/2015, of 4 December, which regulates clinical trials with medicines, the Research Ethics Committees with medicines and the Spanish register of clinical trials and Title II of Law 14/2007, of 3 July, on Biomedical Research (biomedical research that implies invasive procedures in human beings – excluding pharmaceutical research which is regulated under Legislative Royal Decree 1/2015).

272. In the field of clinical trials with medicines and clinical devices, the Legislative Royal Decree 1/2015, of 24 July, which approves the refunded text of the Law on guarantees and rational use of medicines and health products, establishes a number of basic principles regulating clinical trials (*Title III-On Research with medicines of human use and their guarantees*; Articles 58 to 62), which have been developed further and completed by the aforementioned Royal Decree 1090/2015. Aside from the relevant administrative controls governing the trials themselves, their funding and the publications that may result from the trials, the Law on guarantees and rational use of medicine and health products created CEICs – replaced in Law 14/2007 by the CEIs (whose functions in the field of clinical trials with medicines has been assumed after the entry into force of RD 1090/2015 by the CEIm) with important functions in terms of laying down guidelines for the methodology to be employed, ethical considerations and the risks and benefits that may be entailed in the trials. The Law (in the version according to Legislative Royal Decree 1/2015) also introduces measures to guarantee respect for ethical principles, with the specific requirement that trials 'must be undertaken in conditions which assure respect for the fundamental rights of the individual and the ethical considerations which apply to biomedical research involving human beings, in accordance with the Helsinki Declaration and subsequent declarations updating these ethical considerations' (Article 60.1); similar terms are used in Article 3.2 of the RD of 1090/2015.

273. Research with human beings excluding the one related to clinical trials with medical products and medical devices which are submitted to their specific set of legislation is regulated in Spain by Law 14/2007, of 3 July, on Biomedical Research.[379] In order to practice such research, Title II Law 14/2007 (*Researches that imply invasive procedures in Human Beings* – Articles 13–27) requires, among other conditions, the previous evaluation of the Research Project by a CEI (Article 16). The mentioned CEIs are regulated under Article 12 Law 14/2007 according to which CEIs of the centres that conduct biomedical research shall be duly accredited by the competent body of the Autonomous Community concerned or, in the case of centres run by the Central Administration, by the competent body of the same, to ensure their independence and impartiality. The functions of the CEIs are the following ones:

---

379. *See* A. Urruela Mora, 'Reflexiones en torno al marco normativo en materia de investigaciones que implican procedimientos invasivos en seres humanos', in *Estudios de Deusto*, vol. 61, núm. 1, 2013, pp. 295–348.

a. To assess the qualifications of the senior researcher and the research team and the feasibility of the project.
b. To balance the methodological, ethical and legal aspects of the research project.
c. To evaluate the balance of risks and anticipated benefits arising from the study.
d. To look after the implementation of procedures to ensure the traceability of samples of human origin, without prejudice to the legislation of protection of personal data.
e. To issue a report, upon evaluation of the research project, on all biomedical research involving human intervention or use of biological samples of human origin, without prejudice to other reports to be issued. No Research Project may be authorized or developed without the previous and mandatory favourable report of the CEI.
f. To develop codes of good practice in accordance with the principles established by the Spanish Committee on Bioethics and to manage conflicts and generate non-compliance records.
g. To coordinate its activities with similar committees of other institutions.
h. To ensure confidentiality and exercise all other functions assigned by the regulations implementing this Act.

III. The Experimental Subject: Guarantees

A. Weighing Up of Risks and Benefits

274. The weighing up of risks and benefits is fundamental in medicine and, by extension, in pure experimentation. This process of evaluation is essential because of the need for the researcher to observe a duty of care so as to avoid possible liability for negligence or liability of another type. Nevertheless, it is generally agreed that the level of acceptable risk in healthy individuals is not the same as for those suffering from diseases. This holds true only when experimentation on patients is carried out for their benefit, that is to say when experimentation is therapeutic.

Following the criteria set out in the Additional Protocol to the Convention of the Council of Europe on Human Rights and Biomedicine on Biomedical Research (Strasbourg, 25.I.2005), Law 14/2007 establishes some rules related to this aspect:

1. Research involving human subjects may only be conducted in the absence of an alternative of comparable effectiveness (Article 14.1 Law 14/2007).
2. Research shall not involve risks and burdens to the human being disproportionate to its potential benefits (Article 14.2 Law 14/2007).
3. In addition, where the research does not have the potential to produce results of direct benefit to the health of the research participant, such research may only be undertaken if the research entails no more than acceptable risk and acceptable burden for the research participant (Article 14.3 Law 14/2007).

Similar provisions are established in the field of pharmaceutical clinical trials by Legislative Royal Decree 1/2015 (Article 60.2) and Article 3 of the RD of 1090/2015.

275. Experimentation for scientific ends on *persons suffering from illnesses* is effected through the use of new substances or techniques that have no relation to the illness or that, although related to it, are not primarily for the treatment of the illness. In therapeutic experimentation, these substances or techniques can take the place of proven and recognized medical treatments; this is the case of *placebos*, be they inert or active, or of drugs or surgical procedures whose properties, efficacy and secondary effects are still not fully understood. Clearly, then, excessive and, therefore, unacceptable risk would be involved if any measures were taken that would interfere unnecessarily with the course of the illness by prolonging or aggravating it or that would result in irreversible injury unrelated to the spontaneous pathological process.[380]

276. Needless to say, with *healthy persons* there is no risk of interference with pre-existing illnesses. However, in view of the principles whereby, on the one hand, a person cannot do with his/her body exactly as he pleases and, on the other, the inviolability of the human body (which means that it shall not be violated by others), and also given that the health of such individuals will not be benefited in any way by the experimentation, the potential risks of physical injury should be weighed up very carefully; moreover, where the research does not have the potential to produce results of direct benefit to the health of the research participant, such research may only be undertaken if the research entails no more than acceptable risk and acceptable burden for the research participant. The regulations governing clinical trials with medical products and research with human beings establish special guarantees and precautions for particular groups who may incur additional risks to their health: children and incompetent persons, research on persons in emergency clinical situations, pregnant women or women who are breast-feeding (Articles 5, 6, 7 and 8 of the RD 1090/2015 in the field of clinical trials with medical products and Articles 19, 20 and 21 Law 14/2007 in the rest of researches that imply invasive procedures on human beings).

B. Consent

277. The experimental subject's informed consent (Article 13 Law 14/2007 and Article 60.4 Legislative Royal Decree 1/2015, of 24 July, which approves the refunded text of the Law on guarantees and rational use of medicines and health products) constitutes the most important element in guaranteeing that the person may freely exercise his/her will and accept any risks involved. The subject may withdraw his/her consent at any time and is not obliged to give reasons for withdrawal, which under no circumstances will give rise to liability or loss of any kind or to any form of discrimination against the person concerned, in particular regarding the right to

380. G.H. Kieffer, *Bioética* (Alhambra Universidad, Madrid 1983), p. 287.

medical care (Articles 4 and 13 Law 14/2007 and Article 4.5 of RD 1090/2015 in the field of pharmaceutical clinical trials).

The scope and efficacy of consent are conditioned by various factors – particularly relating to legal capacity to give consent – and the potential dangers to the subject's health. For this reason, it would seem appropriate to draw distinctions between the most significant groups of experimentation subjects.

278. Patients and healthy volunteers. While the consent of patients who are to undergo experimental therapies poses no major problems, or, to be more accurate, these problems are similar to those that arise in the course of normal treatment,[381] very complex issues are entailed in the case of purely scientific experimentation, especially the requirement that the subject be informed prior to the experiment (applicable to both patients and healthy adults).

In fact, the free and informed consent requirement is often difficult to fulfil as it is incompatible with the nature and methodology of research itself. At some stage of the experimental process (phase III), in a bid to avoid subjective influence, the person is not told whether the new drug or a *placebo* is being administered. In some cases, even the researcher is kept in the dark (simple blind, double-blind, crossed double-blind method).

It would appear that these factors were not taken into account in the current regulations on clinical trials, judging from the emphasis they place on the duty to inform. These regulations stipulate that for the freely given consent requirement to be satisfied (preferably written consent or, failing that, witnessed consent; it must always be written if the test has no particular therapeutic value for the experimental subject), the subject must have been informed as to 'the nature, importance, scope and risks of the trial', and that he must have understood this information (Article 60.4 Legislative Royal Decree 1/2015, of 24 July, which approves the refunded text of the Law on guarantees and rational use of medicines and health products); the RD 1090/2015 is more specific in this regard in that it requires that consent shall be given after having understood the information furnished with regard to (among other aspects) the nature, the objectives, benefits, implications, risks and inconveniences of the clinical trial (Article 4.1 which connects with Article 29 of EU Regulation No. 536/2014 of the European Parliament and of the Council of 16 April 2014 on clinical trials on medicinal products for human use, and repealing Directive 2001/20/EC); consequently, there is no mention that information should be given as to the methodology to be followed. In our view, it would be adequate to provide full information on the trial process, at least in cases where there is no therapeutic benefit to the subject, including the use of a *placebo*, but to keep the subject in ignorance as to the point at which it will be administered or whether indeed it has been administered at all.

381. Ataz López, *Los médicos y la responsabilidad civil, supra.*, pp. 57–99; Romeo Casabona, *El Médico y el Derecho Penal, I, supra.*, pp. 311–385.

279. *Minors and incompetent persons.* The problems in relation to these groups are even more complex both from the ethical[382] and legal points of view. The Legislative Royal Decree 1/2015 merely indicates that the information must be provided and that consent is the responsibility of the legal representative in the case of persons who cannot freely give consent, although the latter must express their agreement if they are able to understand the nature, importance and risks entailed in the experiment (Article 60.4). Related to research with human beings different from the above-mentioned clinical trials with medical products and medical devices, Article 20 Law 14/2007 on Biomedical Research (*Protection of persons not able to consent research*) establishes – following the criteria of Article 15 Additional Protocol to the Convention of the Council of Europe on Human Rights and Biomedicine, on Biomedical Research – that Research on a person without the capacity to consent to research may be undertaken only if all the following specific conditions are met: (a) the results of the research have the potential to produce real and direct benefit to his or her health; (b) research of comparable effectiveness cannot be carried out on individuals capable of giving consent; (c) the person undergoing research has been informed of his or her rights and the safeguards prescribed by law for his or her protection, unless this person is not in a state to receive the information; (d) the necessary authorization has been given specifically by the legal representative and after having received the information required by Article 15 Law 14/2007, taking into account the person's previously expressed wishes or objections.

Exceptionally and under the protective conditions prescribed by law, where the research has not the potential to produce results of direct benefit to the health of the person concerned, such research may be authorized subject to the conditions laid down in previous letters b, c, and d, and to the following additional conditions: (1) The research is intended to contribute, through significant improvements in the understanding of the individual's disease or condition, to a beneficial outcome for other persons of the same age or with the same disease or condition, within a reasonable time frame. (2) The research involves minimal risk and minimal burden to the individual participant. (3) The authorization of the research is brought to the attention of the Public Prosecutor's Office.

Persons in emergency clinical situations may take part in clinical trials in the field of medical products or in research that imply invasive procedures in human beings as far as existing specific legislation is respected. At this point, regulation is set in Article 7 RD 1090/2015 (*Clinical Trials in emergency situations*) and Article 21 Law 14/2007 (*Research on persons not able to consent due to their clinical situation*).

280. *Self-experimentation.* It is contended that self-experimentation is acceptable since the researcher is in the best position to know and judge at each stage of the process the risks involved in the experiment. From the legal point of view, there is in fact nothing to prevent it, even in the event of injury or damage being sustained, given that the Penal Code does not punish self-inflicted injury.[383]

---

382. *See* J. Gafo Fernández, 'Dilemas éticos de la experimentatión humana', in *Razón y Fe*, No. 1042, 1985, pp. 616 and f.
383. Muñoz Conde, *Derecho. Parte Especial*, *supra*, p. 127.

IV. Payment

281. It is currently felt that all experimental subjects should have *insurance* cover for all the risks entailed. The Legislative Royal Decree 1/2015, of 24 July, which approves the refunded text of the Law on guarantees and rational use of medicines and health products (Article 61; developed further by Articles 9 and 10 of the RD 1090/2015), establishes this as a prior condition in all cases and makes the instigator of the trial, the senior researcher and the hospital or centre where the trial is to be carried out jointly liable for any injury sustained that is not covered by insurance, even where they are not at fault (objective liability for risk);[384] the Law also establishes an assumption – although evidence to the contrary can be presented – that any injury to the health of the experimental subject occurring during the trial or up to a year later is the result of the trial.

Payment to *compensate* for expenses or loss of earnings incurred as a result of the experiment is also admissible, provided that this does not take the form of a true financial reward and is not the only reason why the person has agreed to undergo the experimental treatment. The payment of an indemnity to cover possible injury or discomfort as a result of the experiment is a different matter that comes closer to the idea of remuneration. We will now turn to this issue.

282. The issue of *remuneration* in the strict sense of the word has been hotly debated in both bioethical[385] and legal circles. There is a tendency to see it as acceptable in countries with an Anglo-Saxon legal tradition but to reject it in continental Europe. In other legal texts where the possibility of a person making his/her body available is discussed, there is an assumption that this is done without reward as an act of human solidarity.[386] Nevertheless, the RD 1090/2015, which regulates clinical trials with medicines, the Research Ethics Committees with medicines and the Spanish register of clinical trials, establishes that in special situations, CEIs with medicines may report favourably compensation to trial subjects for the inconveniences resulting from their participation in it, as long as they ensure that such compensation does not influence the subject's decision to participate in the study (Article 3.1.h). Compensation, if agreed upon beforehand, can be demanded, though needless to say, any such amount will diminish proportionally to the participation of the experimental subject if he opts out at some point.

V. Guarantees in Relation to Research

283. Research in which human subjects are implicated must adhere to the strictest precautions in order that the interests of the individuals involved can be safeguarded. Regulations governing clinical trials of pharmaceutical products also

384. *See* Ataz López, *Los Médicos y la responsabilidad civil*, *supra*, pp. 257 and ff.; Romeo Casabona, *El Médico ante el Derecho*, *supra.*, pp. 117 and ff. on objective liability in medical practice.
385. On this *see* Gafo Fernández, 'Dilemas éticos de la experimentatión humana', *supra.*, p. 616.
386. For example, the Law on the Removal and Transplant of Organs, Art. 2.

address this issue in great detail, so much that in fact they have even caused irritation among some researchers (Legislative Royal Decree 1/2015, of 24 July, which approves the refunded text of the Law on guarantees and rational use of medicines and health products and RD 1090/2015). Obviously, specific regulations also apply to experimentation on human subjects with non-pharmaceutical products (Title II Law 14/2007).

284. Among the more important guidelines that might be mentioned are the following: the need for the research team to be in possession of professional and technical *qualifications*, the availability of appropriate staff and equipment in the centre and the fact that the scientific value of the experiment itself should be assessed (among others, *see* Articles 16 and 22.2 of Law 14/2007).

285. There is also *control* on the part of the Health Administration (Spanish Agency on medicines and medical devices in the case of pharmaceutical clinical trials – Chapter V RD 1090/2015 – and competent health authority in the rest of researches with human beings), whose prior authorization is required. Monitoring and inspections ensure that the entire clinical trial process is formalized and time periods and conditions are established for the carrying out of any such trials.

286. In certain cases, the Spanish Agency of Medicines and Medical Devices may interrupt a clinical trial or insist that modifications be made to the protocol (Article 59.2 Legislative Royal Decree 1/2015, of 24 July, which approves the refunded text of the Law on guarantees and rational use of medicines and health products). This is possible in situations where the law has been broken, where the conditions under which authorization was granted are altered or where the above-mentioned ethical principles are not adhered to. The aim of such intervention is to protect trial subjects and to protect public health (Article 59.2 of the Legislative Royal Decree 1/2015). Needless to say, criminal liability may arise in serious cases involving homicide or grievous bodily harm, in addition to any liability in relation to the Administration.

§8. Gender Identity and Gender-Affirming Procedures

I. Introduction

287. Academic literature tends to assert that the phenomenon of gender incongruence or *trans identity* is closely associated with an irreversible desire to belong to the sex opposite to the one biologically assigned. This desire includes assuming the corresponding gender role and, if necessary, undergoing hormonal and surgical treatments to correct the perceived incongruence between mind and body.[387] In this

387. This definition was developed by H. Benjamin. *See* Armaza Armaza/Atienza Macías, 'El tratamiento jurídico de las intervenciones en el aparato reproductor humano: esterilización, castración química y cirugía de reasignación sexual', *supra*, p. 754.

sense, gender incongruence implies a misalignment between physical and psychological sexuality, affecting all aspects of an individual's behaviour.

In Spain, the legal regulation of gender incongruence has undergone a complex and evolving process in recent years. The first major milestone in this regard was the enactment of Law 3/2007, of 15 March, which regulated the rectification of sex designation in civil registries and was pioneering in recognizing the right to gender identity. A second key moment occurred in 2023 with the approval of Law 4/2023, of 28 February, on the real and effective equality of transgender individuals and the protection of LGTBI rights. This law, which remains in force, has sparked intense debate within Spanish society.

In addition to this national framework, various autonomous communities have enacted their own regulations, which complement the national law while also introducing notable differences. However, most of these regional provisions were adopted prior to the enactment of Law 4/2023. As a result, they may become obsolete over time, as their practical contribution to the current legal framework is limited.

II. Changing Legal Identity: The Subjects

288. The question of whether it is possible to change the sex recorded in the Civil Registry without undergoing sex reassignment surgery or, at a minimum, hormone treatment has long been a subject of debate. The 2007 law permitted such a change without requiring surgery, though it imposed certain prior conditions.

Currently, these requirements have been eliminated, allowing individuals to modify their legal gender solely based on their expressed will. Compared to the 2007 law, the 2023 legislation has not only reinforced the principle of personal autonomy in determining one's legal sex but has also introduced significant changes. Notably, the right to rectify the sex designation in the Civil Registry is no longer contingent upon the prior submission of a medical or psychological report diagnosing gender incongruence nor on any prior modifications to an individual's physical appearance or bodily functions through medical, surgical, or other procedures.

289. However, certain clarifications are necessary regarding the ability of minors to request such a change. In this regard, four distinct age groups must be considered:[388]

1. *Individuals aged 16 and over.* In Spain, 16 is the age at which a minor can autonomously provide consent in the healthcare field, with certain exceptions.

388. *See* E. Atienza Macías, 'Lección 7. Identidad sexual y sexualidad', in C.M. Romeo Casabona/P. Nicolás Jiménez/S. Romeo Malanda (Dirs), *Manual de Bioderecho* (2ª edición, Dykinson, Madrid 2025), pp. 169 ff. https://bioderecho.eu/manual-bioderecho/; S. Díaz Alabart, 'El cambio de la mención registral de sexo de los menores en la ley trans de 2023', *Revista de Derecho Privado*, Número 1, 2024.

Therefore, in principle, granting autonomous consent to individuals over 16 years old in this context aligns with the broader legal framework.

2. *Individuals aged 14 to 16.* Legally, the autonomy of minors in this age group is limited, as they remain under parental authority or guardianship. They may only act independently in cases where the law explicitly allows it. The legal framework expressly authorizes them to 'submit the application themselves, assisted in the procedure by their legal representatives'. Given the highly personal nature of this act, legal representation is not admissible; only the individual concerned may initiate the request, though they must be assisted by their legal representatives. The law has not deemed it appropriate to grant them full autonomy in this matter without at least involving their legal guardians. However, this provision underscores that while legal representatives participate in the process, the minor's will is decisive in determining the outcome. Furthermore, although not explicitly stated in the regulation, if two individuals share legal guardianship (typically in the case of parental authority), both must be present. In the event of a dispute between the legal representatives or between the minor and their guardians, a judicial guardian must be appointed.
3. *Individuals aged 12 to 14.* Despite their minor status, individuals in this age group are in puberty and have begun the process of sexual maturation. This developmental stage, defined within a specific age range, serves as the basis for their eligibility to request the correction of their registered sex. However, given their legal minority, judicial authorization is required. This authorization must follow a specific procedure expressly established and regulated in Law 15/2015, of 2 July, on Voluntary Jurisdiction, as detailed in Articles 26 bis, ter, quater, and quinquies.
4. *Individuals under 12 years old.* Law 4/2023 does not contemplate the possibility of changing the registered sex for minors under the age of 12. However, a constitutional challenge may arise if a Civil Registry judge, when faced with a request for a change from a minor under 12 years old, questions the constitutionality of the minimum age requirement. Such a challenge would be based on the legal precedent established by Judgment 99/2019 of the Spanish Constitutional Court.

III. The Procedure

290. The procedure for changing the registered sex is straightforward.[389] It begins with the submission of an application by the authorized individual at any Civil Registry office. The authority responsible for processing the request is the official in charge of the office where the application is filed.

The required documentation includes, in addition to the application itself, a literal birth certificate of the applicant (unless the Civil Registry office can obtain it directly), a valid identification document (ID card) of the applicant, and, in cases

389. M.C. Gete-Alonso Calera, 'La rectificación del sexo en la nueva legislación española: A propósito de Ley 4/2023, de 28 de febrero, para la igualdad real y efectiva de las personas trans y para la garantía de los derechos de las personas LGTBI', *Revista de Ciencias Sociales*, Número 82, 2023.

where the applicant is under 16 years old, the ID card(s) of their legal representative(s). Furthermore, unless the applicant wishes to retain their current name, the application must specify a new name that complies with the applicable registration regulations. During the initial hearing, the Civil Registry official must inform the applicant of the legal consequences of the requested rectification, the process for reversing the decision if desired, and the available support and information services related to the registration change. These services include assistance in the areas of healthcare, social welfare, employment, education, and administration, as well as measures aimed at preventing discrimination, promoting respect, and ensuring equal treatment. Additionally, the applicant must be informed about relevant associations and organizations that advocate for rights in this area should they wish to seek support.

The Civil Registry official must summon the applicant for a second appearance within a maximum period of three months from the initial request. During this second appearance, the applicant must formally ratify their decision, confirming their intent to proceed with the correction of their registered sex.

Following this confirmation, and within a maximum period of one month from the second appearance, the Civil Registry office must verify the submitted documentation and issue a resolution on the requested correction.

291. In the case of individuals over 12 but under 14 years of age, judicial authorization is required. This authorization must be obtained through a special voluntary jurisdiction procedure, as established in Articles 26 bis to 26 quinquies of Law 15/2015, of 2 July, on Voluntary Jurisdiction.

This procedure does not require the mandatory intervention of legal counsel or a legal representative and is processed before the Court of First Instance corresponding to the domicile of the individual requesting the rectification of their registered sex. If the individual does not have a fixed domicile, the procedure is conducted at the court of their place of residence. The application must be initiated by the minor themselves, assisted by their legal representatives or, in cases of disagreement, by the person legally appointed to defend them. Additionally, in situations where the applicant has a disability, the necessary support measures must be provided in accordance with Article 26 ter of Law 15/2015, of 2 July, on Voluntary Jurisdiction.

IV. Reversal of the Process

292. Article 47 of Law 4/2023 establishes that individuals who have requested the modification of their registered sex may revert to the original registration prior to the rectification, following the same procedure previously described. However, this reversion is only permitted after a minimum period of six months has elapsed since the initial modification was recorded in the Civil Registry.

If, after this reversion, the individual wishes to request a new rectification, the procedure outlined in Chapter I ter of Title II of Law 15/2015, of 2 July, on Voluntary Jurisdiction must be followed. This entails judicial intervention.

Notably, Spanish legislation presents certain contradictions in its aim to protect transgender individuals. Those who have modified their registered sex are subject to specific deadlines and procedural requirements that do not apply to individuals who have not undergone such a change. The rationale behind these restrictions likely stems from a desire to prevent potential fraudulent use of the process, although the legislators who promoted the law considered this risk to be minimal. In practice, however, concerns about legal fraud have gained significant attention in Spanish society, particularly due to suspicions arising from high-profile cases.[390] To date, there has only been one court decision in this regard. A court in Las Palmas, in the Canary Islands, denied a sex change to a man on the grounds that the reason for his request was to obtain the advantages of being a woman. For this reason, it was considered that the request was against the law.[391]

V. Consequences of the Change

293. The primary effect of a request to change one's registered sex is the modification of the sex designation recorded in the Civil Registry, which is replaced by the sex declared by the applicant. Additionally, the individual may request a change of name (Articles 48 to 51 of Law 4/2023). Once the modification has been made, the individual is legally recognized as belonging to the rectified sex (gender), with all corresponding legal implications.

294. However, to prevent potential inconsistencies, the law establishes a series of specific clarifications:

a. The law includes a safeguard to prevent its misuse as a means of circumventing the provisions of Organic Law 1/2004, of 28 December, on Comprehensive Protection Measures against Gender Violence. Specifically, the rectification of the sex designation in the Civil Registry, as well as any corresponding name change, does not alter the legal status that applied to the individual prior to the modification, particularly concerning the provisions of Organic Law 1/2004 (Article 46.3 of Law 4/2023).

   Thus, if an individual who has rectified their registered sex was subject to sanctions or legal measures under this law, the change does not render those measures ineffective. This provision is intended to prevent the fraudulent use of the sex registration rectification process as a means of evading or avoiding compliance with imposed sanctions.
b. An individual who modifies their registered sex from male to female may benefit from positive action measures specifically established in favour of women, as outlined in Article 11 of Organic Law 3/2007, of 22 March, for the Effective Equality of Women and Men. However, such measures apply only to situations arising after the registry modification has taken effect and do not extend to legal situations predating the rectification.

---

390. M.E. Serrano Chamorro, 'El género como voluntad de elección y constancia legal ¿puede suponer un fraude de ley? (a propósito de la nueva ley 4/2023 de 28 de febrero conocida como ley Trans)', *Revista de Derecho de Familia: doctrina, jurisprudencia, legislación*, Número 101, 2023.
391. Auto del Registro Civil de Las Palmas de Gran Canaria de 18 Sep. 2023.

Part III. The Physician and HealthCare System

Chapter 1. Relation with Other HealthCare Providers

295. In the field of healthcare, other professionals work alongside doctors and perform an important role in assisting and treating patients. Under the broad term, 'other health-care providers' include nurses, midwives and auxiliary nurses. Traditionally, these professionals have assisted the physician, but as medicine has become increasingly reliant on technology and more and more specialized, largely because of the advent of new and complex diagnostic and surgical techniques, it is now essential for these individuals to be highly qualified and, in most cases, have university level training.[392] They perform a series of tasks which are sometimes absolutely vital and it is often the case that the doctor cannot or does not know how to perform them.[393] Because of the increasing importance of these healthcare providers and the need for greater control over medical activity (applicable here also),[394] more rigorous regulation of these professions is crucial. That is why, in Spain, the configuration of the studies that qualify for obtaining these degrees has been considerably improved.

Other qualified personnel such as pharmacists, psychologists and opticians also participate in healthcare. When we say that healthcare teams are multidisciplinary, it is not only because they comprise participants from the various branches of medicine but also because such persons perform important functions.

296. A number of different provisions make reference to the relations among the different categories of healthcare providers. In various Statutes governing the activities of medical personnel and paramedical healthcare workers, the maintenance of good relations and cooperation among these professionals is demanded. In the particular case of physicians, Chapter XI of the Code of Medical Deontology (2022) of the Spanish OMC (Organización Médica Colegial) and the General Council of Colleges of Physicians (Consejo General de Colegios Oficiales de Médicos) is devoted to the relationship of the physicians with each other and with other healthcare providers. Indeed, its *Article 50* states that:

392. *See* C. Segura/L. Martínez-Calcerrada, 'El médico ante el Derecho Civil', in L. Martínez-Calcerrada, *Derecho Médico I* (Tecnos, Madrid 1986), p. 54.
393. Llamas Pombo, *La responsabilidad civil del médico*, *supra*, p. 335.
394. *See above.*

Article 50.1. Physicians should maintain good relations with other health professionals and take their opinions into consideration for the benefit of the patient.

Article 50.2. The doctor, when working in a team, must respect the sphere of competence of the rest of the professionals, ensuring that the healthcare work is the most correct at that moment.

§1. Pharmacists

297. Pharmacy as a profession forms part of the community healthcare system and contributes to the common cause of the other healthcare professions, namely, the preservation and recuperation of health.[395]

The specific know-how of pharmacists confer on them an important role which consists of the following functions:[396] control over the pharmaceutical products dispensed to the patient; in the case of minor ailments that do not require medical attention, dispensing medicaments for symptom relief; ensuring that medicines are used correctly and patients are warned as to any adverse effects; clinical pharmacy and vigilance in relation to pharmaceutical products in the community; the furnishing of information on medicines; the making up of prescribed medicines; the proper conservation of medicines in the pharmacy; the storage of substances that are subject to special restrictions on their use. As a healthcare professional, the pharmacist plays an active part in programmes for the promotion of health and health education in the community and any other activities for which his university education has specially prepared him, particularly those relating to food and environmental health.

298. The pharmacist cooperates with the physician in the preparation of prescriptions and the dispensing of medicines and undertakes clinical analyses which provide vital information on which diagnosis may be based.

§2. Dentists

299. *See* Part I, Chapter 1, §2, paragraph 32

§3. Nursing Profession

300. Traditionally included within the broad category of 'nursing' are a group of professionals who perform a wide range of functions that aid and complement medical practice. A number of such professions were recognized by Spanish health

395. Martínez Cañizares, 'Farmacéutico y Sociedad', in *Revista ACOFAR*, 206, 1983, p. 13, quoted in F. Rico Pérez, *La responsabilidad del farmacéutico* (Trivium, Madrid 1984).

396. E. Lluch Martín, *Política Farmacéutica del Ministerio de Sanidad y Consumo* (Servicio de Publicaciones del Ministerio de Sanidad y Consumo, Madrid, 1983), p. 21, quoted in Rico Pérez, *La responsabilidad civil del Farmacéutico*, *supra*, p. 10.

regulations as far back as 1860. In 1952, a distinction between ATS (a type of nurse) and midwife was established. In 1963, recognition was given to a further category, auxiliary nurses, the formal qualification for which is obtained in the vocational training system ('formación professional'). Auxiliary nurses assist hospital nursing staff with the care of the patient by performing tasks such as bathing, feeding, etc.

In 1977, with the establishment of Schools of Nursing, a new professional category requiring three years of university education was created.[397] The previous categories of ATS and midwife were given equal status to the new Diploma in Nursing and began to disappear as professions in their own right. At present, the figure known as ATS is now TCAE (técnico en cuidados auxiliares de enfermería), which jointly works with nurses but does not require a university degree. On the other side, midwife did not entirely disappear but became a nursing speciality.[398]

301. As of today, the organization of studies related to the nursing profession comprises four main regulations:

- Law 44/2003, of 21 November 2003, concerning the organization of health professions.
- Order CIN/2134/2008, of 3 July 2008, establishing the requirements for the verification of the official university degrees that enable the practice of the nursing profession.
- Royal Decree 450/2005, of 22 April, on Nursing Specialties.
- Royal Decree 1509/2005, of 16 December, which regulates official postgraduate university studies.

302. With regard to the regulation of the practice of the profession, there are two regulations of particular importance in Spain. First, Law 44/2003, of 21 November 2003, on the LOPS, which regulates the conditions of practice of the different health professional fields, as well as the measures that guarantee the basic, practical and clinical training of its members.

303. Secondly, Royal Decree 1231/2001, of 8 November, approving the General Statutes of the Spanish Nursing Association, of the General Council and of the Organization of Nursing Professional Activity, recognizes that the Professional Nursing Associations are public law corporations, protected by law and recognized by the State and the Autonomous Communities, within the scope of their respective competencies, with their own legal personality and full capacity for the fulfilment of their purposes. These regulations define:

- The objectives of the Professional Nursing Associations.
- The rights and obligations of the nursing members.
- The functions of the General Council of Nursing.
- The functions of the nursing professionals.
- The definition of nursing care.

---

397. *See* Segura/Martinez-Calcerrada, *Derecho Médico I*, *supra*, p. 54.
398. *See* Art.2a) of Royal Decree 450/2005, of 22 April, on Nursing Specialties.

§4. PARAMEDICAL PROFESSIONALS

304. Physiotherapists: This was originally a branch of the profession of ATS, although since 1980 and the setting up of Physiotherapy Schools training has been taken out of Nursing Schools.

Current legislation establishes the profession of physiotherapist as a regulated profession whose practice, in accordance with the provisions of Royal Decree 822/2021, of 28 September, establishing the organization of university education and the procedure for quality assurance.

Physiotherapy is aimed primarily at the rehabilitation of patients.

305. Chiropodists: This profession was established as a specialization within the broader category of ATS and is primarily concerned with the non-surgical treatment of the feet. At the present moment, chiropody is a four-year university degree where students acquire the knowledge of a branch of medical activity aimed at the prevention, diagnosis, treatment and rehabilitation of foot disorders and pathologies.

306. Optometrists: Optometry Schools have offered university training since 1974. Optometrists's work involves chiefly the grading and production of lenses. This is a group which often suffers from illegal practices.

Chapter 2. Relationship with HealthCare Institutions

§1. Hospitals

307. Hospitals are the foundation of the system of specialized medical care. Historically, they were not strictly speaking healthcare institutions but charitable hostels for the elderly, the poor, pilgrims, etc. In the nineteenth century, the functions that hospitals perform today were the province of charitable organizations.[399] A major expansion in hospital services took place at the end of the sixties as a result of improved human and material resources, though this was still not sufficient to satisfy the demands of public health due to the lack of a true hospital network. This was in part because specialized medical care was provided by the Social Security system, which still lacked the means available in other centres to attend to the needs of public patients.[400] Hospitals belonging to the Provincial Governments, 'Cabildos Insulares' (organs of government in the Balearic and Canary Islands) and city councils were able to offer such services. This meant that there was the danger of duplicating specialized healthcare services as a result of the 1944 Law establishing the basis of the National Health Service. Aside from other factors, this alone was good reason to claim that the way in which the hospitals functioned was not entirely satisfactory and the idea of a coherent network of hospitals began to emerge as a means of achieving greater efficiency in hospital care. This was attempted through a number of statutory provisions, the first of which was Law 37/1962 of 21 July, which still constitutes today the basic legislation governing hospitals.[401] This law defines hospitals as follows: 'establishments providing medical/clinical care, regardless of the names they bear, without prejudice to the fact that such establishments may provide preventive, convalescent and outpatients' treatment as appropriate'.[402] However, neither this law nor any of the subsequent legislation has succeeded in arriving at an efficient specialized healthcare organization: 'the situation of specialised care in 1982 is characterised by the disorganization resulting from the multiplicity of

399. *See* J. Ortíz Díaz, 'Hacia una reordenación de la Sanidad Pública española: el problema hospitalario', in *Revista de Administración Pública*, No. 51, 1986, pp. 153–160 on the historical origins of hospitals.

400. Because of this, Social Security Service established agreements with other private and public hospitals. These hospitals catered for public patients or provided the Social Security system with the material and human means of providing such a service.

401. Article 4 of the law refers to the setting up of a National Hospital Network. To this end, it establishes a Central Coordinating Committee for Hospital Services which, among other things, is responsible for (Art. 7) maintaining information on hospital needs and for building, adding extensions to, modifying or closing hospitals (Art. 5).

402. Article 1 includes a second paragraph that states: 'hospitals are also centres for the training of technical and health care personnel, for scientific research so long as the appropriate conditions for such purposes are satisfied in accordance with the nature and aims of each Institution. At the same time there should be adequate coordination between teaching centres'. Article 65.2 of the LGS states that 'the hospital is responsible for inpatient care as well as specialised and complementary care as required in its area'.

public administration hospital management bodies and the failure to set up a satisfactory instrument for hospital coordination'.[403]

308. The 1962 Law regulating hospitals was developed further by Decree 575/1966, of 3 March, on the classification and regionalization of hospitals. This was followed by a number of other pieces of legislation on various aspects of the hospital service, including the still operative RD 521/1987, of 15 April, on the structure, organization and functioning of hospitals managed by the INSALUD and the reform of our NHS introduced by the LGS of 1986. Article 65.1 of the LGS states that every Health Area should have at least one General Hospital, which should be involved in the promotion of health, disease prevention, research and teaching as well as attending to patients' needs. These hospitals should thus complement the primary care network.

The public hospital infrastructure is sometimes not sufficient on its own to provide healthcare services to the total population. For this reason, the LGS, while still seeking to establish a single hospital network, arrived at a system under which private hospitals participate in public healthcare in two ways, namely, through association agreements and the linking of private hospitals to the public system.

With regard to *agreements* with private healthcare institutions, the Public Administration, having previously given approval to the institutions and evaluated the optimal use that can be made of their healthcare resources, establishes the requirements and minimum conditions that are applicable to all agreements. The conditions and requirements established must include the reciprocal rights and obligations of both parties, guarantees that the service provided will be of the same quality for all clients and a prohibition against the introduction of services that are complementary to those already provided by public healthcare centres. Under similar conditions of efficiency, quality and cost, priority shall be given to institutions belonging to non-profit making organizations.[404] The Public Administration is charged with carrying out inspections of these private centres as regards healthcare services, administration and financial matters concerning each patient referred to them for admission (Article 94.2 of the LGS).

The *linking up of* private hospitals to the NHS enables them to enjoy a closer relationship with the public system.[405]

309. Access to hospitals, which is open to all those who are ill regardless of their financial or social position, including prison inmates,[406] is granted once all other avenues of diagnosis and treatment in primary services have been explored, save for

403. Elola Somoza, *Crisis y Reforma de la asistencia sanitaria pública en España*, *supra*, p. 155. The author adds 'the efforts – efforts that have not been put into practice – to rationalise hospital management can be seen in various areas: the appointment of professional managers who are not necessarily medical professionals, the widely expressed desire to make the budget the responsibility of management, the development of a system to assess the quality of care and efficiency, and finally the drawing up of a list of rights of hospital users'.

404. *See* Art. 90 of the LGS.

405. *See* Pemán Gavín, *Derecho a la salud y Administración sanitaria*, *supra*, p. 213.

406. The Art. 35 of the Prison Regulations ('Reglamento Penitenciario') brought in by RD 190/1996 of 9 February, states that: '*Article 35. Consultation or admission to non-penitentiary hospitals.*

emergency cases. Hospital care is provided on an inpatient basis, through admission to hospital and via outpatients' offices and medical leave services.

Outpatients' offices enable specialized care to be provided without the need for the patient to be admitted to hospital. The physician completes a Referral for Outpatients' offices, which the HealthCare Area Authority sends to the hospital concerned and the patient is given an appointment through the Admissions Service. There is direct access, however, to the medical leave service in very serious cases.

A number of beds for desintoxication from drugs or any other kind of addiction are often set aside in hospitals and associated private hospitals. However, this depends on the autonomous regional authorities for this purpose, as they are the ones that have the competences on these matters. Thus, for example, Law 1/2016, of 7 April, on Comprehensive Care for Addictions and Drug Addictions establishes the criteria for the allocation of hospital resources for people with addiction problems in its Title III, emphasizing the need for such access to be equitable.

310. Royal Decree 521/1987, of 15 April, passed the Regulations governing the structure, organization and functioning of hospitals managed by the INSALUD. These regulations were aimed at improving the management and quality of care provided by hospitals in accordance with the principles laid down in the LGS. In this way, hospital services and activities are grouped together under the following categories: Hospital Management Division, Medical Division, Nursing Division, Management Services and General Services.

1. The top level of hospital management is the Hospital Manager ('Director-Gerente'), who represents the hospital and is its highest authority, with responsibility for the hospital's human, physical and financial resources. This person plans, manages, controls and evaluates the performance of all the hospital divisions and takes measures to ensure the smooth running of the hospital, especially in times of crisis and emergency. The Administrator produces periodic reports on hospital activities and an annual report (Article 7). The areas of responsibility of the Administrator's Division are patient relations, management, computing services, legal affairs, admissions, reception and information, staffing policy, analysis and planning (Article 9).
2. The Medical Division, which covers the areas of Medicine, Surgery, Obstetrics and Gynaecology, Paediatrics, Central Services, Documentation and Clinical Files, Day Hospitalization, Home Hospitalization and any other activity in which medical care is involved, is headed by the Medical Director, whose most important functions are the management, supervision, coordination and evaluation of medical and other healthcare services in the hospital.

---

1. The departure of inmates for consultation or admission, as the case may be, to non-custodial hospitals shall be agreed upon by the management centre. 2. Once the transfer has been agreed upon, the Director of the establishment will request the civil Governor or, if necessary, the competent autonomous body, the public force that will carry out the transfer and will be in charge of the subsequent custody of the inmate in the non-custodial hospital centre, without prejudice to the provisions of Article 155.4. 3. In the event of an emergency, according to medical opinion, the Director shall proceed with the transfer and admission to the hospital centre, subsequently informing the management centre.'

3. The Nursing Division is concerned with coordination of the units and services under its responsibility (wards, operating theatres, special units, outpatient's department, casualty, etc.), while the Management Division and General Services Department provide the administrative support and technical assistance necessary for the running of all other hospital divisions (financial management and administration, supplies, catering and maintenance, etc.)

From 1987 to the present, this organizational and management structure of the hospitals of the NHS has basically been maintained. Law 15/1997, of 25 April 1997, on enabling new forms of management of the NHS, endorsed forms of public management other than administrative ones which, although the available information seems to show that they are more efficient, have not become widespread. Attempts to organize hospitals on the basis of 'clinical management units' have not been successful either, except in very specific centres, and the 'institutes' created by INSALUD have very limited autonomy.[407]

§2. Preventive HealthCare and Public Health Law

311. Originally, public healthcare in Spain was more preventive than treatment-oriented. During the nineteenth century and up until the middle of this century, the Administration took responsibility for public health only within the parameters of disease prevention, particularly the prevention of epidemics and other health hazards arising from poor hygiene and medical treatment provided by unqualified individuals.[408] The Administration took on this preventive role because epidemics affected a considerable sector of the population. What the Administration was in fact concerned with was protecting collective health rather than individual health, which was primarily treatment-oriented.[409] This preventive focus can be seen in the Law of 28 November 1885, the General Public Health Instructions of 12 January 1904 and the Law establishing the bases of the National Health Service (1944).[410] However, the social and political situation in Spain led to the development in the public

407. *See*: VV.AA., *El Hospital Del Futuro Un proyecto de la Sociedad Española de Medicina Interna para el Sistema Nacional de Salud* (Sociedad española de medicina interna-Instituto para la mejora de la asistencia sanitaria, 2019), at: https://www.fesemi.org/sites/default/files/documentos/quienes-somos/futuro_hospital_vision_20191030.pdf.

408. *See* L. Morell Ocaña, 'La evolución y configuración actual de la actividad administrativa sanitaria', in *Revista de Administración Pública*, No. 63, 1970, pp. 136–140.

409. *See* Pemán Gavín, *Derecho a la salud y administración sanitaria*, *supra*, p. 104, who gives more emphasis to the idea of the protection of collective health than to prevention as the basis on which the traditional healthcare administration was founded. On the other hand, the protection of individual health lacked a preventive element and was centred rather on care provided by the Welfare ('Beneficencia') that catered for the needs of the poor.

410. The Law of 1944 devotes its Fourth Foundation to the fight against infectious diseases, and to disinfection, and fumigation and established preventive measures such as an obligation for the physician to notify the existence of disease or isolation measures; in the Fifth Foundation, all matters related to External Health are dealt with, such as inspection and control of health hazards; and in the Tenth Foundations, specific measures to fight trachoma, sexually transmitted diseases and leprosy are stipulated. *See* Cobreros Mendazona, *Los tratamientos obligatorios y el derecho a la salud*, *supra*, pp. 350–359.

arena, and not just in the area of healthcare, of a greater concern with individual needs and an appreciation of the fact that the person in need of medical treatment could not, in most cases, afford to pay for treatment. As a result, the public healthcare service was made available not only to the poor and destitute but also to those with insufficient means of support. In this way, the original State practice of organizing healthcare from a preventive perspective for the population as a whole was finally abandoned in favour of an approach that took account of the dangers to individual health caused by common and frequent diseases and illnesses. The final stage in this process of evolution was the constitutional recognition of the right to health protection for all citizens resident in Spain.[411] Article 43.2 of the Constitution, apart from recognizing the right to health protection, states in its second paragraph that the organization of and responsibility for public health shall be achieved through preventive measures and the provision of the necessary services. Similarly, the LGS states explicitly that the actions of the Public Administration in the area of healthcare should involve the treatment as well as the prevention of disease and illness (Article 18.2).

312. The right to protection of health includes, therefore, not only treatment to restore good health in cases of illness but also the right to protection from possible health hazards that might affect the individual. For this reason, the LGS lists in Article 18 – in Chapter II, entitled 'public intervention in individual and collective health' – a large number of specific actions in Preventive Medicine, such as:

1. The care of high-risk groups in the population and the prevention of both congenital and acquired disabilities.
2. The promotion and improvement of sanitation, water supply, removal of liquid and solid residues, air pollution control, health inspections and the improvement of environmental health in all contexts, including the home.
3. Family planning.
4. The promotion of mental health and health in the workplace.
5. The control and prevention of food and drug-related health hazards.
6. Informing the public on epidemiology.

Intervention by the public administration can consist of requiring authorization to be sought for any activity that might imply a risk or danger to health and may, in cases of imminent and exceptional risk, involve the seizure or impounding of products, the imposition of temporary bans on activities, or the closure of businesses or facilities (Article 23 of the LGS). In short, all this means that, in contrast with the nineteenth-century approach to healthcare, the current view is that the individual, and not just the social group, should be afforded health protection (prevention and treatment) in accordance with his rights as laid down in constitutional principles governing social and economic policy which the authorities are duty-bound to observe.

411. This is expressed in Art. 1.2 of the LGS as follows: 'All Spaniards and foreign nationals resident in Spain have the right to health protection and health care.'

This has led the Legislature to confer on health the protection which it deserves and which is demanded by the Constitution, by legally regulating the manner in which certain dangerous activities should be carried out and stipulating the administrative sanctions applicable to breaches of these regulations. Moreover, actions that endanger or damage public health are treated as criminal offences.[412] However, this does not include the punishment of conducts aimed at spreading infectious and contagious diseases, which was the case prior to 1995.

313. In order to assure the effectiveness of preventive medicine, when the risk to public health is imminent, provision is made for the adoption of government measures, including the curtailment of rights and constitutional freedoms, under Organic Law 3/1986 of 18 March, on Special Preventive Health Measures. This law grants the health authorities the right to impose treatment aimed at protecting the individual or aiding his recovery. These measures may range from a simple medical examination to hospitalization and may affect the individual or groups of people or those engaged in a particular activity. Along with this first regulation, Law 33/2011, of 4 October, General Law on Public Health, is of special relevance. This law establishes the legal basis for the coordination and cooperation actions of public administrations in the field of public health in Spain.

In the area of epidemics, the Decree of 26 July 1945, approving the Regulations for the Control of Infectious Diseases, Disinfection and Pest Control, established special measures for the control of outbreaks of disease, such as the obligation of the public to inform the authorities if they have contracted certain diseases and the drawing up by the authorities of weekly statistical reports containing specific information on cases of epidemics treated. In turn, Royal Decree 2210/1995, of 28 December, created the national epidemiological surveillance network.

314. In certain fields, preventive medicine has achieved a greater degree of organization, specification and stability, thanks to the maintenance of a preventive medical service made up of permanent units and specific types of healthcare services in certain healthcare contexts. Specific programmes have been drawn up for primary healthcare, family planning, mental health and obstetric psycho-prophylaxis. We refer here to the Family Planning Centres and Units, staffed by specialists in various fields (gynaecologists, midwives, psychologists etc.), in which advice is given on sexuality and contraception. Prenatal, genetic and legal abortion counselling is also provided in these centres, as is treatment for sexually transmitted diseases. For their part, Mental Health Units are responsible for more than just treatment and they are involved in promotion, education and prevention through specific programmes related to problems such as alcoholism, drug abuse, etc. Lastly, Obstetric Psycho-prophylaxis Units are intended to provide pregnant women with information and health education to prepare them for the birth, puerperium and care of the newborn infant.[413]

---

412. The second section of Ch. III of Title XVII of the Spanish Criminal Law.

413. *See* the Order of 28 Mar. 1984 on care coverage by obstetric teams from the first trimester of gestation.

In the area of drug abuse, the Spanish administration's action is based on a tool called the Action Plan on Addictions. This contains the actions to be developed to achieve the objectives set out in the Strategy. All the bodies of the Central Administration involved also participate in its elaboration, all the Autonomous Plans on Drugs and other addictions, representatives of the Local Administration, as well as Third Sector Organizations and representatives of scientific societies. It is developed around six main lines of action: Coordination; Prevention and Social Awareness; Comprehensive Care; Knowledge Improvement; Supply Reduction; and International Cooperation. It is valid for four years.

Actions in the field of occupational health to achieve the best risk prevention in the workplace are included in the General Law on Public Health, in coherence with the provisions of Law 31/1995, of 8 November 1995, on Occupational Risk Prevention. Both norms complement each other, thus facilitating the promotion of health in the same field.

§3. Health Insurance

315. Historically, healthcare services were provided by means of private health insurance. The State did not take on responsibility for healthcare in the same way as it did for other public services. It only catered for those in the terminal stages of an illness and for the destitute, and did not concern itself with the medical profession, which was conducted entirely through private practice. For these reasons, it is hardly surprising that at the beginning of this century, there was a plethora of private health insurance companies through which physicians offered their services to individuals and families in exchange for regular payment. But this lack of interest on the State's part in community health and the medical profession has gradually become a thing of the past as a result of the fact that most citizens were not in a position to pay for their own medical treatment. This led to the State taking on the role of social protector, using its public resources in the service of community health, initially through obligatory health insurance and later with the establishment of the Social Security system. Today, both types of health services (private healthcare and Social Security) co-exist.

316. The Spanish Constitution states in Article 41 that 'the public authorities shall maintain a public Social Security system for all citizens that shall ensure a minimum level of care and service in situations of need, especially in cases of unemployment. Care and complementary services shall be free of charge'. Although the system was created to cover health risks to a specific group of people, namely wage-earning workers, it has gradually widened its scope to include a larger number and range of beneficiaries and to offer more services. 'In this way, the protective action of the Spanish Social Security system is currently based on a comprehensive and universal protection model that includes, pharmaceutical-health care, family protection, social services and, in certain cases, unemployment benefit. All citizens can access this protection, under identical terms, irrespective of whether or not they have made contributions to the Social Security system and it is completed, on the one hand, by a financial benefits system which, in a harmonious and differentiated manner, is included in the contributory level, where incomes to replace the wages earned when working are provided (with proportionality between salary-contributions and benefits) and, on the other hand, by the non-contributory level, aimed at providing compensation income for basic needs to those citizens who, finding themselves in a situation of need, are unable to access the contributory model.'[414]

317. Law 55/2003, of 16 December, of the General Statute of Statutory Personnel of the Health Services establishes the different kinds of legal-administrative relationships between physicians and Social Security. The Medical Personnel Statutes alone are applicable to Social Security physicians and leave room for the individual or collective autonomy of physicians when contracted by Social Security.[415] The statutory relationship between physicians and Social Security does not preclude private practice, as the aforementioned article indicates elsewhere.

318. The Social Security system currently covers all citizens resident in Spain, together with certain non-residents and foreigners with work and residence permits. It comprises a General Regime and various Special Regimes, which are reminiscent of the old private health insurance systems. There are also differences in terms of the services which one is entitled to according to whether one is registered under the General Regime or one of the Special ones. The latter are an open list and the Government may at any time include them within the General Regime, although it should be said that they are becoming quite similar to their general counterpart in terms of the cover provided.

I. The General Regime

319. The General Regime of the Social Security system includes:[416]

- Spanish workers employed by others in industry and services and those assimilated to them who normally exercise their activity in national territory.
- Employees and working partners of capitalist mercantile companies, even when they are members of their administrative body, if the performance of this position does not entail the performance of the functions of direction and management of the company, nor do they have control over it. As assimilated to employees, with exclusion of unemployment protection and the Wage Guarantee Fund, the directors and administrators of capitalist mercantile companies provided that they do not have control of these, when the performance of their position entails the performance of the functions of direction and management of the company, being remunerated for it or for their condition of workers of the same. In both cases, it

414. *See*: https://www.seg-social.es/wps/portal/wss/internet/PortalEducativo/Profesores/Unidad2/PESS21.
415. M. Alonso Olea/J.L Tortuero Plaza, *Instituciones de la Seguridad Social* (12ª ed. Civitas, Madrid 1990), p. 280.
416. Source: Information provided by the Ministerio de Incluisión, Seguridad Social y Migraciones at: https://www.seg-social.es/wps/portal/wss/internet/Trabajadores/Afiliacion/10548/10562/4072.

will be presumed, unless there is evidence to the contrary, that the employee has effective control of the company when any of the following circumstances apply: that at least half of the capital stock for which he/she renders his/her services is distributed among partners, with whom he/she lives and to whom he/she is related by marriage or kinship by blood, affinity or adoption, up to the second degree; that his participation in the capital of the company is equal or superior to one-third of the same; that his or her participation in the capital stock is equal to or greater than one-fourth of the same, if he or she has been attributed management functions in the company.

- Spanish workers not residing in national territory, in certain cases (civil servants or employees of international organizations, non-civil servant Spaniards hired in the service of the Spanish Administration abroad, etc.).
- Foreigners with a residence and work permit in Spain who work as employees in industry and services and exercise their activity in national territory. Community workers do not need a work permit. Personnel (civil servant or labour) of the Local Administration.
- The drivers of vehicles of tourism to the service of individuals
- The civil personnel who are not civil servants, dependent on organisms, services or entities of the State.
- Laymen or laymen who render paid services in ecclesiastical institutions.
- Persons who render paid services in entities or institutions of a social charitable nature.
- Personnel hired to the service of Notaries, Property Registries and other similar offices or centres.
- Civil servants in practices that aspire to join Corps or Scales of civil servants that are not subject to the Regime of Passive Classes and the high positions of the Public Administrations that are not civil servants, as well as the civil servants of new entrance of the Autonomous Communities.
- Civil servants transferred to the Autonomous Communities, who voluntarily join the Corps or Scales of the Autonomous Community of destination. Interim personnel in the service of the Administration of Justice.
- Workers engaged in banana handling, packaging, packing and marketing operations.
- Finally, Royal Decree 2621/1986, of 24 December 1986, trade representatives, artists and bullfighting professionals are also included in this regime:[417]

The duty to contribute commences at the onset of employment activities. The simple request for the worker's registration will, in any circumstance, yield the same outcome. The omission of submitting the application for affiliation or registration will not hinder the inception of the obligation to contribute once the criteria for inclusion in the relevant regime are satisfied. It is sustained throughout the entire duration of the worker's activity. Contributions are determined based on the total compensation to which the employee is entitled. Contracts between the employee and the employer stipulating that the employee is responsible for paying part or all

---

417. Further information can be found here: https://www.seg-social.es/wps/portal/wss/internet/Trabajadores/Afiliacion/10548/10562/32737.

of the employer's contribution are invalid.[418] Registration in the General Regime automatically confers multiple benefits: healthcare, unemployment financial aid, retirement pensions, and widow's pensions, among others.[419]

The services are accessible not only to the registered worker but also to their spouse or an individual in a comparable affective relationship, who must present the requisite official registration, as well as to descendants and individuals assimilated to them who are under 26 years of age or possess a disability of 65% or greater, provided that: (a) they maintain their legal and habitual residence in Spain, unless exempted by applicable international regulations, or they are individuals temporarily residing in Spain and are dependent on workers assigned by their company outside Spanish territory in a situation analogous to being registered in the relevant Social Security regime. (b) Must not be in any of the following circumstances: employed or self-employed, affiliated or in a status equivalent to registration, possessing pensioner status under these regimes in their contributory form, or receiving any other periodic benefit from these regimes.

Healthcare service covers common illnesses and non-work-related accidents, occupational disease and work-related accidents and maternity (pregnancy, childbirth, and postpartum). The right to healthcare arises from the moment it is certified that all conditions for access are met and medical care will be provided according to the medical criteria of the National Health Service.

Care is provided in health centres and hospitals of the National Health Service in the holder's place of residence, in outpatient, hospitalization, or home care settings. Outside the usual residence and within the national territory, medical care can be received by presenting the user identification card of the public health system or a photocopy of it, accompanied by the National Identity Document or another document that reliably certifies the person's identity. It is possible to freely choose a GP and family paediatrician of interest within the same Health Area, as long as the chosen doctor has not reached the assigned patient quota. When it comes to population centres with more than 250,000 inhabitants, the choice can be made among the GPs and paediatricians available in the entire locality. It is also possible to choose a specialist doctor in certain specialities, both at the reference hospital of their Health Area and at the speciality centres dependent on it, taking into account the number of people assigned by the corresponding Public Health Service to each specialist.[420] In accordance with the provisions of Royal Decree-Law 16/2012, of 20 April, on urgent measures to ensure the sustainability of the NHS and improve the quality and safety of its measures benefits, the contribution of citizens to pharmaceutical services is related to their classification as active or pensioner and their income level, updated annually. The citizen does not have to provide any document to prove their income level. The INSS (National Institute of Social Security) assigns the pharmaceutical contribution to each user based on their income level data (data provided

418. Further information can be found here: https://www.seg-social.es/wps/portal/wss/internet/Trabajadores/CotizacionRecaudacionTrabajadores/9896/4903.

419. Further information can be found here: https://www.seg-social.es/wps/portal/wss/internet/Trabajadores/PrestacionesPensionesTrabajadores/12778.

420. Source: Guía Laboral. Ministerio de Trabajo y Economía Social. Ministerio de Inclusión Seguridad Social y Migraciones 2024, at: https://www.mites.gob.es/es/Guia/pdfs/Guia_Laboral_2024.pdf#page=581, p. 596.

by the Tax Agency). The INSS communicates this data to the Health Services of the autonomous communities. Pharmacies can check the assigned contribution segment when presenting the health card.[421] The funding percentages corresponding to each user are described in Article 102.5 of Royal Legislative Decree 1/2015, of 24 July, which approves the consolidated text of the Law on Guarantees and Rational Use of Medicines and Health Products.

There are, however, a number of groups that can obtain the medicines they need for free, in accordance with Article 102.8 of the same regulation. These include:

- Those affected by toxic syndrome and people with disabilities in the cases contemplated in their specific regulations.
- Those receiving social integration benefits.
- Non-contributory pensioners.
- Long-term unemployed without unemployment benefits.
- Victims of workplace accidents and occupational diseases in treatment.
- Minors with certified disabilities of 33% or more.
- Beneficiaries of the minimum vital income.
- Recipients of economic benefits for children or minors in their care with permanent foster care status or guardianship for adoption purposes.
- Pensioners with an income of less than EUR 5,635 or pensioners exempt from filing (EUR 11,200 annually).

Free healthcare services are also provided for those without sufficient means of support (an income lower or equal to the minimum wage). Foreigners who are not registered or authorized as residents in Spain have the right to health protection and healthcare under the same conditions as Spanish nationals, subject to certain conditions. This right does not cover healthcare outside Spanish territory, without prejudice to the provisions of applicable international social security regulations.[422]

According to Article 1 of Order of 13 October 1967, establishing regulations for the application and development of the benefit for temporary work incapacity (temporary disability) in the General Social Security Scheme, they will be considered states or situations that determine temporary work incapacity:

a. Those due to common or occupational illness and accidents, whether or not they are work-related, as long as the worker receives healthcare assistance from Social Security and is unable to work.
b. The so-called observation periods and their assimilated or equivalent periods in cases of occupational diseases.

The financial benefit associated with this work incapacity is called the Temporary Disability benefit. A worker who is temporarily unfit for work, although he is still

421. Source: Servicios de Información de la Comunidad de Madrid, at: https://www.comunidad.madrid/servicios/salud/cuanto-tengo-pagar-mis-medicamentos.
422. Source: Information provided by the Ministerio de Inclusión, Seguridad Social y Migraciones at: https://www.seg-social.es/wps/portal/wss/internet/Trabajadores/PrestacionesPensionesTrabajadores/10938/30476.

III. Special Regimes Within the Social Security

A. *Self-employed Persons (RETA Regime)*

321. A self-employed or autonomous worker is someone 'who habitually, personally and directly performs a profit-driven economic activity, without an employment contract and may use the paid service of other people, whether or not the owner of an individual or family company'.[430] RETA is the Special Regime for Self-Employed Workers, in which self-employed or freelance workers must register. Social Security understands that those who engage 'habitually, personally, and directly in an economic activity for profit, without being subject to an employment contract, and even if they use the paid services of other people, whether or not they are the owner of an individual or family business' fall into this category.

322. Self-employment or freelance work is mainly regulated by the Statute of Self-Employment approved by Law 20/2007, of 11 July. The Self-Employed Workers' Statute determines the scope of application; the professional regime of the self-employed worker, establishing rights and duties and regulations on risk prevention; it creates the figure of the economically dependent self-employed worker, and professional interest agreements; collective rights are recognized, the representativeness of their associations, social protection is provided, and the promotion of self-employment is encouraged. In recent years, various regulations have been approved that have amended both the Statute and the General Social Security Law in order to equalize the rights of self-employed workers with those of salaried workers.

B. *Seamen*

323. This includes both self-employed persons and wage-earners and offers the same entitlements as the General Regime, save for a number of special features.[431]

C. *Coal Miners*

324. Wage-earners employed in the following fall into this category: underground coal mining, opencast mining, manufacture of coal products, research, detection and extraction of coal from slag heaps, extraction of carbon and residual carbon-bearing water and other complementary activities. There are some special features in comparison to the General Regime.[432]

---

430. Source: Ministerio de Inclusión, Seguridad Social y Migraciones, at: https://www.seg-social.es/wps/portal/wss/internet/Trabajadores/Afiliacion/10548/32825.
431. Further information can be found here: https://www.seg-social.es/wps/portal/wss/internet/Trabajadores/Afiliacion/10548/32840.
432. Further information can be found here: https://www.seg-social.es/wps/portal/wss/internet/Trabajadores/Afiliacion/10548/32836.

D. Domestic Staff

325. This includes workers over 16 who are exclusively engaged as domestic staff for one or several heads of a family, provided that the work is done in the habitual place of residence of said person and in return payment is made for his work. The category includes child-minding, gardening, driving and other similar activities. Here again, there are special features in relation to the General Regime.

Since 1 October 2022, employers have to contribute to unemployment and the Wage Guarantee Fund (FOGASA). Household employees also contribute to unemployment insurance.[433]

E. Students

326. The student insurance system is established in the Law of 17 July 1953 regarding the implementation of School Insurance in Spain. It encompasses Spaniards under 28 years old who are engaged as full-time students or are involved in secondary education, vocational training, University Orientation Courses, undergraduate studies, and postgraduate studies culminating in a doctorate. Foreign students under 28 from nations with tacit or explicit reciprocal agreements are also included when undertaking the aforementioned studies. Affiliation to the system occurs automatically upon enrolment. Medical intervention is mandatory in instances of tuberculosis, surgical procedures, neuropsychiatry, and toxicology. Access to other services is contingent upon financial circumstances.

327. Social Security also protects those who are willing and able to work but who lose their jobs temporarily or permanently or whose hours of work are reduced by at least a third, resulting in loss or reduction of earnings. Social Security provides two levels of unemployment benefits: contributory and supplementary:

1. Contributory unemployment benefit is paid to persons who are in any of the established legal situations of unemployment, have the minimum contribution period required and are not in any of the situations of incompatibility, and belong to any of the following categories: Employees included in the General Social Security System who pay contributions for the unemployment contingency; Employees included in the Special Social Security Schemes that protect this unemployment contingency (Coal Mining, Special Scheme for Sea Workers), permanent employees of the Special Agricultural Social Security System, temporary employees of the same System and employees of the Special System for Household Employees; The partners of associated work cooperatives and cooperatives of communal exploitation of the land, as well as the working partners of other cooperatives, who are included in a Social Security Scheme that protects this contingency; Those convicted persons who have been released from prison due to the completion of their sentence or parole;

433. Further information can be found here: https://www.mites.gob.es/es/Guia/texto/guia_14/contenidos/guia_14_30_6.htm.

Returning emigrant workers; Foreign workers in Spain, nationals of countries belonging to the EU or to the European Economic Area or not belonging to the EU or to the European Economic Area who are legally resident in our country and who meet the legal requirements, will be entitled to unemployment benefits at the contributory level provided that they are registered as job seekers; Civil servants and temporary staff hired under administrative law in the service of the Public Administrations; Complementary military and professional military of Troops and Marines; Members of local corporations and General Councils of the Historical Foral Territories, Canary Island Councils and Island Councils of the Balearic Islands, who hold such positions with exclusive or partial dedication and receive remuneration for the performance of the position; Representative positions of the trade unions constituted under the Organic Law 11/1985, on Trade Union Freedom, who perform trade union management functions with exclusive or partial dedication, provided that they receive remuneration; Senior officials of the Public Administrations who have exclusive dedication, are remunerated and are not civil servants and are not entitled to receive any type of compensatory benefit as a consequence of their dismissal. Benefit is paid by the Servicio Público de Empleo Estatal (SEPE), which is an autonomous agency attached to the Ministry of Labour and Social Economy. The SEPE, together with the Public Employment Services of the Autonomous Communities, make up the National Employment System, with the purpose of contributing to the development of the employment policy, managing the unemployment protection system and guaranteeing information about the labour market.

2. If a person is not entitled to contributory benefit, has exhausted it or is in any of the situations protected by unemployment benefit, he/she can still obtain any of the subsidies approved in Royal Decree-Law 2/2024, of 21 May, adopting urgent measures to simplify and improve the assistance level of unemployment protection, and to complete the transposition of Directive (EU) 2019/1158 of the European Parliament and of the Council of 20 June 2019 on the reconciliation of family and working life for parents and caregivers and repealing Council Directive 2010/18/EU. In this new legal framework, two categories of unemployment subsidies have been established: one for individuals who have exhausted their contributory benefits and another for those with insufficient contributions. In both instances, certain general prerequisites must be met to qualify for the subsidy. Persons eligible for this subsidy must belong to one of the following groups:
   - People who are unemployed and have exhausted the contributory benefit. In the case of those under 45 years of age who have no family responsibilities, the exhausted unemployment benefit must have lasted 360 days or more.
   - Unemployed persons who are legally unemployed without at least 360 days of contributions to qualify for the contributory benefit, provided that they have contributed for at least 90 days.
   - Individuals who are 52 years of age or older and meet a series of specific requirements.
   - Spanish emigrants returning from certain countries in which they have worked, provided that they are not entitled to the contributory benefit for

having paid unemployment contributions for less than 360 days in the six years prior to their departure from Spain.

– Persons who are victims of gender violence, sexual violence or violence by parents or children, if they meet the requirements.
– Temporary workers of the Special System for Agrarian Workers of the Social Security (SEASS) residing in any town in Andalusia or Extremadura.

In general, applicants must not be entitled to contributory unemployment benefits at the time of application, must not be in a situation of incompatibility, must lack personal income, or alternatively, must demonstrate family responsibilities. Additionally, applicants are required to be registered as job seekers and to have signed the activity agreement. The subsidy for the depletion of contributory benefits has been extended to individuals under the age of 45 who do not have family responsibilities, those who can demonstrate contributions of less than six months without family obligations, temporary agricultural labourers, cross-border workers from Ceuta and Melilla, as well as victims of gender-based or sexual violence.

3. In addition to all of the above, in Spain, it is possible to access a retirement pension despite not having contributed sufficiently to the system, if certain conditions are met. This issue is regulated under Royal Legislative Decree 8/2015, of 30 October 2015, approving the revised text of the General Social Security Law, Royal Decree 357/1991, of 15 March 1991, which implements Law 26/1990, of 20 December 1990, on non-contributory pensions, and Order PRE/3113/2009, of 13 November 2009. Conditions include: be 65 years of age or older; reside in Spanish territory and have done so for a period of ten years between the date of reaching the age of 16 and the date of accrual of the pension, two of which must be consecutive and immediately prior to the date of application; and lack of sufficient income. There is a lack when the income or personal income available in annual computation for 2025 is less than EUR 7,905.80 per year. The non-contributory retirement pension provides all citizens over 65 years of age and in a state of need with a financial benefit, free medical-pharmaceutical assistance and complementary social services.

328. Apart from Social Security, there exist Mutualidades libres de Previsión Social (Mutual Pension Funds), which are governed by Law 9/2000, of 30 June 2000, on Mutual Benefit Societies. These are aimed at protecting their members in case of death, old age, disability, medical treatment, and other situations where a benefit or pension might normally be paid. They exercise a voluntary insurance modality complementary to the social security system.

Any natural or legal person may set up a Mutual Pension Fund, but any such funds must not be profit-making, must have a minimum of fifty members and must be authorized by the government. Fundings come from members' contributions, which may take the form of fixed or variable premiums. The Funds are governed by Statutes, which must be approved by the Ministry of Economy and must stipulate, among other things, equal rights and obligations for all members, that the administrators shall not receive remuneration and that members' liability for debts is limited to an amount less than a third of the contributions paid in the last three financial years.

Colleges of Physicians' agreements with a number of Mutual Pension Funds mean that these benefits are available to members. Joining a social protection scheme at the minimum level of contribution is a compulsory requirement for college membership and members have a duty not to fall in arrears with their payments (Articles 36.4 and 43b of the Statues of the OMC).

Selected Bibliography

Abellán, F., *Selección genética de embriones. Entre la libertad reproductiva y la eugenesia*, 'Biblioteca de Derecho y Ciencias de la Vida', Comares, Granada, 2007.

Alastuey Dobón, C., 'Aspectos problemáticos del delito de tráfico de órganos', *Revista Penal*, núm. 32, 2013.

Andreu Martínez, B., 'Lección 8. Intimidad, confidencialidad y documentación clínica', *Manual de Bioderecho (Adaptado para la docencia en ciencias, ciencias de la salud y ciencias sociales y jurídicas)*, C.M. Romeo Casabona/P. Nicolás Jiménez/S. Romeo Malanda (Dirs), 2ª edición, Dykinson, Madrid, 2025.

Angel Yagüez, R. de, 'Problemas legales de la historia clínica en el marco hospitalario', *La Ley*, 1987.

Armaza Armaza, E.J., *El tratamiento penal del delincuente imputable peligroso*, Comares, Granada, 2013.

Arruego Rodríguez, G./Chueca Rodríguez, R., 'Tribunal Constitucional y nuevos escenarios de la biomedicina', en *Rev Der Gen H*, nº. 12, 2000.

Ataz López, J., *Los médicos y la responsabilidad civil*, Madrid, Montecorvo, 1985.

Aznar López, M., *Internamientos civiles y derechos fundamentales de los usuarios de centros sanitarios, sociales y sociosanitarios*, Comares, Granada, 2000.

Barahona Miguelañez, M./ González García, M.C., 'Capítulo 42. Error sanitario y responsabilidad jurídica por asistencia sanitaria', *Tratado de Derecho Sanitario. Volumen II*, A. Palomar Olmeda/J. Cantero Martínez (Dirs), Thomson Reuters, Aranzadi, Cizur Menor, 2013.

Bellver Capella, V., 'El Tribunal Constitucional ante la Ley sobre Técnicas de Reproducción Asistida: una valoración crítica', in *RevDerGenH*, Nr. 11, 1999.

Benítez Ortúzar, J.I., 'Delitos relativos a la reproducción asistida', en J. Vidal Martínez (Coord.), *Derechos reproductivos y técnicas de reproducción asistida*, Ed. Comares – Ministerio de Sanidad y Consumo, Granada, 1998.

Bercovitz Rodríguez Cano, R., 'La protección jurídica de la persona en relación con su internamiento involuntario en centros sanitarios o asistenciales por razones de salud', *Anuario de Derecho Civil*, 1984.

Berenguer Albaladejo, M.C., 'Los internamientos no voluntarios por razón de trastorno psíquico: especial consideración al procedimiento a seguir en los casos de urgencia médica', in *Derecho privado y Constitución*, 2014, n. 28.

Bueno Arús, F., 'El consentimiento del paciente en el tratamiento médico-quirúrgico y la Ley General de Sanidad', in *Estudios de Derecho Penal y Criminología*, UNED, Madrid 1989.

Selected Bibliography

Cabañas García, J.C., 'Internamiento involuntario urgente por razones de trastorno psíquico y tutela del derecho fundamental a la libertad personal', in *Anuario de Derecho Civil*, 2012.

Campuzano Tomé, H., 'Reflexión en torno a los derechos de la viuda para ser inseminada artificialmente', *La filiación a finales del siglo XX. Problemática planteada por los avances científicos en materia de reproducción humana.* Departamento de Derecho Privado de la Universidad del País Vasco (ed.), Editorial Trivium, Madrid, 1988.

Carrasco Gómez, J.J., *Responsabilidad médica y Psiquiatría,* 2nd ed., Colex, Madrid, 1998.

Cobreros Mendazona, E., *Los tratamientos sanitarios obligatorios y el Derecho a la salud*, Gasteiz, IVAP, 1988.

Comisión Nacional de Reproducción Humana Asistida, *Primer Informe*. Madrid, 1998.

Comisión Nacional de Reproducción Humana Asistida, *Segundo Informe. Investigación con embriones sobrantes*, Madrid, abril de 2000.

Comité Asesor de Ética en Investigación Científica y Técnica, *Informe La investigación sobre células troncales*, FECYT, Madrid, 2003.

Comité de Expertos sobre Bioética y Clonación, *Informe sobre clonación. En las fronteras de la vida*, FCS, Madrid, 1999.

De Miguel Beriain, I., 'Capítulo 26. El Derecho en el final de la vida: Rechazo al tratamiento, limitación del esfuerzo terapéutico, sedación en la agonía, auxilio al suicidio y eutanasia', *Tratado de Derecho Sanitario. Volumen I*, A. Palomar Olmeda/J. Cantero Martínez (Dirs), Thomson Reuters, Aranzadi, Cizur Menor, 2013.

De Miguel Beriain, I., *El embrión y la biotecnología. Un análisis ético-jurídico*, 'Biblioteca de Derecho y Ciencias de la Vida', Comares, Granada, 2004.

De Miguel Beriain, I., *La clonación, diez años después*, Cátedra Interuniversitaria Fundación BBVA – Diputación Foral de Bizkaia de Derecho y Genoma Humano, Universidad de Deusto y Universidad del País Vasco y Comares, Bilbao-Granada, 2008.

Elola Somoza, F.J., *Crisis y reforma de la asistencia sanitaria pública en España (1983–1990)*, Madrid, FISSS, 1991.

Emaldi Cirión, A., 'Una respuesta jurídica necesaria a un problema urgente', *Perspectivas en Derecho y Genoma Humano*, n. 25, Junio 2025, Cátedra Interuniversitaria – Diputación Foral de Bizkaia de Derecho y Genoma Humano Universidad de Deusto – Universidad del País Vasco UPV/EHU.

Emaldi Cirión, A., *El Consejo Genético y sus implicaciones jurídicas*, Cátedra Interuniversitaria Fundación BBVA – Diputación Foral de Bizkaia, de Derecho y Genoma Humano, y Comares, Bilbao – Granada, 1999.

Farre Trepat, E., 'Sobre el concepto de aborto y su delimitación de los delitos contra la vida humana independiente', *Anuario de Derecho Penal y Ciencias Penales*, 1990.

Fernández Costales, J., *El contrato de servicios médicos*, Madrid, Civitas, 1988.

Fernández Costales, J., *Responsabilidad civil médica y hospitalaria*, Madrid, Edilex, 1987.

Fernández Hierro, J.M., *Responsabilidad civil médico-sanitaria*, Pamplona, Aranzadi, 1983.

Ferrando López, A., 'El derecho a la vida en la Constitución española de 1978', *Revista General de Derecho*, 1988.

Flores Mendoza, F., 'Capítulo 11. Omisión del deber de socorro', in C.M. Romeo Casabona/E. Sola Reche/M.A. Boldova Pasamar (Coords), *Derecho Penal. Parte Especial,* Tercera Edición, Granada, Editorial Comares, 2023.

Flores Mendoza, F., 'Lección 17. Objeción de conciencia', *Manual de Bioderecho (Adaptado para la docencia en ciencias, ciencias de la salud y ciencias sociales y jurídicas),* C.M. Romeo Casabona/P. Nicolás Jiménez/S. Romeo Malanda (Dirs), 2ª edición, Dykinson, Madrid, 2025.

Gallego Riestra, S., 'Capítulo 23. Información y consentimiento informado: De la Ley General de Sanidad a la Ley 41/2002', *Tratado de Derecho Sanitario. Volumen I*, Palomar Olmeda/Cantero Martínez (Dirs), Thomson Reuters – Aranzadi, Cizur Menor, 2013.

García González, J., *Límites penales a los últimos avances de la ingeniería genética aplicada al ser humano*, Edersa, 2001.

Gascón Abellán, M./González Carrasco, M.C./Cantero Martínez, J. (Coords), *Derecho sanitario y Bioética. Cuestiones actuales*, Tirant lo blanch, Valencia, 2011.

Gómez Rivero, C., 'El delito de tráfico ilegal de órganos humanos', *Revista Penal*, n. 31, 2013.

Gómez Rivero, C., *La responsabilidad penal del médico. Doctrina y jurisprudencia*, 2ª ed., Tirant lo Blanch, Valencia, 2008.

González Morán, L., *De la Bioética al Bioderecho. Libertad, vida y muerte*, Universidad de Comillas – Dykinson, Madrid, 2006.

González Morán, L., *La responsabilidad civil del médico*, Bosch, Barcelona, 1990.

González Pernía, J./Hidalgo Carballal, A., 'Capítulo 44. Responsabilidad penal sanitaria', *Tratado de Derecho Sanitario. Volumen II*, A. Palomar Olmeda/J. Cantero Martínez (Dirs), Thomson Reuters – Aranzadi, Cizur Menor, 2013.

Jiménez De Asúa, L., *Libertad de amar y derecho a morir*, Buenos Aires, Losada, 1984.

Jorge Barreiro, A., *La imprudencia punible en la actividad médico-quirúrgica*, Tecnos, Madrid, 1990.

Junquera de Estéfani, R., 'Capítulo 6. La reproducción médicamente asistida. Su regulación jurídica en España', in A. Serrano Maíllo/J.A. Sánchez Sánchez (eds), *Una introducción criminológica a la Medicina Legal y Forense*, Dykinson, Madrid, 2020.

Lema Añón, C., 'Los problemas pendientes de la regulación jurídica española sobre reproducción asistida: la sentencia del Tribunal Constitucional y el primer Informe de la Comisión Nacional de Reproducción Asistida (Parte I y II)', *RevDerGenH*, n. 12 y 13, 2000.

Libano Beristain, A., 'Reflexiones críticas en torno al valor normativo de los Códigos deontológicos (en particular, vigentes en la esfera sanitaria) así como algunas consideraciones acerca de la competencia objetiva en este ámbito', *Justicia: revista de derecho procesal*, n. 2, 2016.

Llamas Pombo, E., *La responsabilidad civil del médico*, Madrid, Trivium, 1988.

Mansilla Izquierdo, P.P., *Reforma sanitaria. Fundamentos para un análisis*, Ministerio de Sanidad y Consumo, Madrid, 1986.

Marcos del Cano, A.M., 'Capítulo 2. La eutanasia: cuestiones ético-jurídicas', in A. Serrano Maíllo/J.A. Sánchez Sánchez (eds), *Una introducción criminológica a la Medicina Legal y Forense*, Dykinson, Madrid, 2020.

Martín Mateo, R., *Bioética y Derecho*, Ariel, Barcelona, 1987.

Martín-Retortillo Baquer, L., 'Derechos fundamentales en tensión (¿Puede el Juez ordenar una transfusión de sangre en peligro de muerte, aún en contra de la voluntad del paciente?)', *Poder Judicial*, 1984.

Mendoza Calderón, S., *Derecho Penal sanitario*, Tirant lo Blanch, Valencia, 2019.

Millán Calenti, R.A., 'Capítulo 22. Historia Clínica Electrónica: accesos compatibles', *Tratado de Derecho Sanitario. Volumen I*, A. Palomar Olmeda/J. Cantero Martínez (Dirs), Thomson Reuters – Aranzadi, Cizur Menor, 2013.

Ministerio de Sanidad y Consumo, *Análisis y benchmarking del tratamiento de las reclamaciones y sugerencias en el Sistema Nacional de Salud*, Ministerio Sanidad y Consumo, Madrid, 2008, at: https://seguridaddelpaciente.sanidad.gob.es/informacion/publicaciones/2008/docs/InformeIReclamaciones.pdf

Ministerio de Sanidad y Consumo, *Ensayos clínicos en España (1982–1990)*, Ministerio de Sanidad y Consumo, Madrid, 1990.

Moya Guillem, C., 'Consideraciones sobre el delito de tráfico de órganos', *Anuario de la Facultad de Derecho de la Universidad Autónoma de Madrid*, 18, 2014.

Nicolás Jiménez, P., *La protección jurídica de los datos genéticos de carácter personal*, Cátedra Interuniversitaria Fundación BBVA – Diputación Foral de Bizkaia de Derecho y Genoma Humano, Universidad de Deusto y Universidad del País Vasco y Comares, Bilbao – Granada, 2006.

Núñez Fernández, J., 'Capítulo 4. El consentimiento informado', in A. Serrano Maíllo/J.A. Sánchez Sánchez (eds), *Una introducción criminológica a la Medicina Legal y Forense*, Dykinson, Madrid, 2020.

Palomar Olmeda, A. /Cantero Martínez, J. (Dirs), *Tratado de Derecho Sanitario, Vol. I y II*, Aranzadi, Cizur Menor, 2013.

Panes Corbelle, L.A., 'Capítulo 43. Responsabilidad patrimonial de los servicios de salud', *Tratado de Derecho Sanitario. Volumen II*, A. Palomar Olmeda/J. Cantero Martínez (Dirs), Thomson Reuters – Aranzadi, Cizur Menor, 2013.

Pemán Gavín, J., *Derecho a la salud y Administración sanitaria*, Bolonia, Publ. Real Colegio de España, 1989.

Perin, A., 'El fenómeno de la medicina defensiva como cuestión político-criminal. ¿Cómo conjugar autonomía y responsabilidad?', in C.M. Romeo Casabona/A. Perin (eds), *Derecho y medicina defensiva: legitimidad y límites de la intervención penal*, Comares, Granada, 2020.

Puente Aba, L.M., 'La protección frente al tráfico de órganos: su reflejo en el Código penal', in *Revista Derecho y proceso penal*, núm. 26, 2011.

Queralt Jimenez, J.J., 'La eutanasia: perspectivas actuales y futuras', *Anuario de Derecho Penal y Ciencias Penales*, 1988.

Rodríguez Mourullo, G., 'Derecho a la vida y a la integridad personal y abolición de la pena de muerte', *Comentarios a la Legislación Penal I*, M. Cobo del Rosal (Dir.),/M. Bajo Fernández (Coord.), Madrid, Edersa, 1982.

Rodríguez Pastrana, J.M., *El servicio público de la sanidad: el marco constitucional*, Madrid, Civitas, 1984.
Romeo Casabona, C.M. (Dir.), *Enciclopedia de Bioderecho y Bioética, Tomos I y II,* Comares, Granada, 2011
Romeo Casabona, C.M./Perin, A., 'Capítulo 1. El homicidio y sus formas', in C.M. Romeo Casabona/E. Sola Reche/M.A. Boldova Pasamar (Coords), *Derecho Penal. Parte Especial,* 3 ed., Comares, Granada, 2023.
Romeo Casabona, C.M./Martínez-Berganza Asensio, A., 'Le Médecin et les Droits de l'Homme en Espagne', in Conseil de l'Europe (ed.), *Manuel sur le Médecin et les Droits de l'Homme*, CEDAM, Milano, 1990.
Romeo Casabona, C.M., 'El Proyecto Genoma Humano: implicaciones jurídicas', in *Etica y Biotecnología, Fundac. Humanismo y Democracia,* Fundación Konrad Adenauer, Universidad Pontificia de Comillas, Madrid, 1993.
Romeo Casabona, C.M., 'El tratamiento jurídico del enfermo mental en el Consejo de Europa y sistema de garantías en el Derecho Español', *Actualidad Penal*, 1991.
Romeo Casabona, C.M., 'Human Life as Juridictional Value Protected by Criminal Law', in *XXth Colloquy on European Law*, Council of Europe, Glasgow, 1990.
Romeo Casabona, C.M., 'La prohibición del tráfico ilegal y la exclusión de la comercialización de los órganos y tejidos', in *Revista Aranzadi Doctrinal*, n. 7, 2010.
Romeo Casabona, C.M., 'La reforma penal del aborto: Límite mínimo, figuras delictivas y sistema de las indicaciones', *Propuestas para la reforma penal*, Centro de Estudios Criminológicos, La Laguna, 1992.
Romeo Casabona, C.M., 'Límites penales de la manipulación genética', *Reunión Internacional sobre el Proyecto Genoma Humano*, Fundación BBV, Madrid-Bilbao, 1994.
Romeo Casabona, C.M., 'Responsabilidad médico-sanitaria y SIDA', *Actualidad Penal*, 1993.
Romeo Casabona, C.M., 'Some Implications of Human Genome Analysis and Research in Spanish Law', *Genome Analyse*, Coimbra, 1994.
Romeo Casabona, C.M., *Configuración sistemática de los derechos de los pacientes en el ámbito del Derecho español*, Instituto Nacional de la Salud, Madrid, 1992.
Romeo Casabona, C.M., 'El Derecho ante los trasplantes de órganos. La ordenación jurídica de los trasplantes de órganos en España: Principios rectores', in *Revista General de Derecho*, n. 582 y 584, 1993.
Romeo Casabona, C.M., *El Derecho y la Bioética ante los límites de la vida humana*, CERA, Madrid, 1994.
Romeo Casabona, C.M., *El Médico ante el Derecho (la responsabilidad penal y civil del médico)*, Ministerio de Sanidad y Consumo, Madrid, 1985 (3rd. reprint 1990).
Romeo Casabona, C.M., *El Médico y el Derecho Penal, I, La actividad curativa (licitud y responsabilidad penal)*, Bosch, Barcelona, 1981.
Romeo Casabona, C.M., *El médico y el Derecho Penal, vol. II, 1*, Rubinzal Culzoni, Santa Fe, 2011.
Romeo Casabona, C.M., *Los trasplantes de órganos. Informe y documentación para la reforma de la legislación española sobre trasplantes de órganos*, Barcelona, Bosch, 1979.

Selected Bibliography

Romeo Casabona, C.M./Nicolás Jiménez, P./Romeo Malanda, S., (Dirs), *Manual de Bioderecho (adaptado a la docencia en ciencias, ciencias de la salud y ciencias sociales y jurídicas),* 2nd ed., Dykinson, Madrid, 2025.

Romeo Casabona, C.M., 'Biodroit', in Hottois/Missa (eds), *Nouvelle encyclopédie de bioéthique*, De Boeck Université, Bruxelles, 2001.

Romeo Casabona, C.M., 'Editorial. The European Constitution, establishing a core of human rights as applied to the fields of Medicine and Biology', *RevDerGenH*, n. 21, 2004.

Romeo Casabona, C.M., (Coord.,) *Derecho biomédico y bioética*, Comares & Ministerio de Sanidad y Consumo, Granada – Madrid, 1998.

Romeo Casabona, C.M., (ed.), *El Convenio de Derechos Humanos y Biomedicina. Su entrada en vigor en el ordenamiento jurídico español*, Cátedra Interuniversitaria de Derecho y Genoma Humano, Universidad de Deusto y Universidad del País Vasco/Comares, Bilbao – Granada, 2002.

Romeo Casabona, C.M., *Genética, Biotecnología y Ciencias Penales*, Ibáñez & PUC Javeriana, Bogotá, 2009.

Romeo Casabona, C.M., *Los genes y sus leyes. El Derecho ante el genoma humano*, Cátedra Interuniversitaria de Derecho y Genoma Humano, y Comares, Bilbao – Granada, 2002.

Romeo Malanda, S., *Intervenciones genéticas sobre el ser humano y Derecho penal*, Cátedra Interuniversitaria Fundación BBVA – Diputación Foral de Bizkaia de Derecho y Genoma Humano, Universidad de Deusto y Universidad del País Vasco y Ed. Comares, Bilbao-Granada, 2006.

Ruiz Sáenz, A., 'Capítulo 64. Gestación por sustitución: Problemática jurídica de los vientres de alquiler', *Tratado de Derecho Sanitario. Volumen II*, A. Palomar Olmeda/J. Cantero Martínez (Dirs), Thomson Reuters, Aranzadi, Cizur Menor, 2013.

Ruiz Vadillo, E., 'La investigación científica y el Derecho. Especial consideración de la ingeniería genética', *Revista General de Derecho*, 1986.

Serrano Alonso, E., 'El depósito de esperma o de embriones congelados y los problemas de la fecundación *post mortem*', *La filiación a finales del siglo XX. Problemática planteada por los avances científicos en materia de reproducción humana.* Departamento de Derecho Privado de la Universidad del País Vasco (ed.), Trivium, Madrid, 1988.

Silva Sánchez, J.M., *La esterilización de disminuidos psíquicos*, PPU, Barcelona, 1988.

Silveira Gorski, H./Méndez Baigés, V. (eds), *Bioética y Derecho*, UOC, Barcelona, 2004.

Sola Reche, E./Sánchez Lázaro, F., 'Lección 19. Responsabilidad jurídica del profesional sanitario', in C.M. Romeo Casabona/P. Nicolás Jiménez/S. Romeo Malanda (Dirs), *Manual de Bioderecho (Adaptado para la docencia en ciencias, ciencias de la salud y ciencias sociales y jurídicas)*, 2nd ed., Dykinson, Madrid, 2025.

Sola Reche, E., Hernández Plasencia, J.U./Romeo Casabona, C.M., 'La responsabilidad profesional del médico en el Derecho español', *Responsabilidad penal y responsabilidad civil de los profesionales. Presente y futuro de los conceptos de negligencia y riesgo. XXII Coloquio de Derecho Europeo*, Centro de Estudios Criminológicos, La Laguna, 1993.

Torío López, A., 'Instigación y auxilio al suicidio, homicidio consentido y eutanasia como problemas legislativos', *Estudios Penales y Criminológicos, IV,* A. Fernández Albor (ed.), Santiago de Compostela, 1981.

Urruela Mora, A., 'La clonación humana ante la reforma penal y administrativa en España', in *Revista Penal*, n. 21, 2008.

Urruela Mora, A., 'Reflexiones en torno al marco normativo en materia de investigaciones que implican procedimientos invasivos en seres humanos', in *Estudios de Deusto*, vol. 61, n. 1, 2013.

Urruela Mora, A., 'Sobre el delito de aborto imprudente a la luz del anterior y del actual Código Penal', *Actualidad Penal*, n. 6, 2000.

Urruela Mora, A., *Imputabilidad penal y anomalía o alteración psíquica*, Comares, Bilbao-Granada, 2004.

Urruela Mora, A., *Las medidas de seguridad y reinserción social en la actualidad*, Comares, Granada, 2009.

Urruela Mora, A./Libano Beristain, A., 'Lección 16. La ordenación de las profesiones sanitarias. Las agresiones a los profesionales sanitarios', in C.M. Romeo Casabona/P. Nicolás Jiménez/S. Romeo Malanda (Dirs), *Manual de Bioderecho (Adaptado para la docencia en ciencias, ciencias de la salud y ciencias sociales y jurídicas)*, 2nd ed., Dykinson, Madrid, 2025.

Valle Muñiz, J.M./González González, M., 'Utilización abusiva de técnicas genéticas y Derecho Penal', *Poder Judicial*, n. 26, 1992.

Valle Muñiz, J.M., 'Relevancia Jurídico-penal de la eutanasia', *Cuadernos de Política Criminal*, n. 37, 1989.

Vega Ruiz, J.A. de, *El tratamiento jurídico del SIDA*, Madrid, Colex, 1992.

Vega Vega, C./Bañón González, R.M./Fajardo Agustín, A., 'Internamientos psiquiátricos. Aspectos medicolegales', in *Atención Primaria*, 2010, vol. 42, n. 3.

Vicente Remesal, J. de, 'El grave peligro para la salud psíquica de la madre en la nueva ley del aborto', *La Ley*, 1985.

Vidal Martínez, J., 'Comentario a la Sentencia del Tribunal Constitucional de 17 de Junio de 1999 resolviendo el Recurso de inconstitucionalidad número 376/89 contra la Ley 35/1988, de 22 de Noviembre, sobre Técnicas de Reproducción Asistida', in *RevDerGenH*, n. 12, 2000.

Vives Antón, T.S., 'Valoraciones ético-sociales y jurisprudencia constitucional: el problema del aborto consentido', *Revista Española de Derecho Constitucional*, 1985.

VV.AA, *Genética y Derecho*, Consejo General del Poder Judicial, Madrid, 2001.

VV.AA, *Información y documentación clínica. Su tratamiento jurisprudencial (1990–1999)*, Ministerio de Sanidad y Consumo, Madrid, 2000.

VV.AA., *Controles éticos de la actividad biomédica. Análisis de situación y recomendaciones*, Instituto Roche, Madrid, 2009.